Good luck from friends
and colleagues at the

Hursley Lab.

31st July 1985

TROUT FROM STILLWATERS

THE STILLWATER FLY FISHER'S QUARRY. A rainbow trout (above) and a brown (below) from Blagdon. These two fish, weighing 2¼ lb apiece, were taken by the author from North Shore on successive casts.

TROUT FROM STILLWATERS

Peter Lapsley

Adam and Charles Black · London

First published 1981
by A. & C. Black (Publishers) Ltd
35 Bedford Row, London WC1R 4JH

ISBN 0–7136–2171–0

Lapsley, Peter
  Trout from stillwaters.
  1. Trout fishing
  I. Title
  799.1'755   SH687
  ISBN 0–7136–2171–0

Filmset in Monophoto Baskerville and
printed in Great Britain by
Latimer Trend & Company Ltd, Plymouth

Contents

List of Illustrations

Foreword

I was privileged to read the manuscript of this book before it was completed as well as later, and I was immediately impressed by the breadth of the author's knowledge.

In the last decade, a number of very good books have been published about stillwater trout fishing, but each has dealt with a particular aspect of this sport; for example with fishing large reservoirs, or small man-made lakes, or with emphasis on particular methods, like lure-fishing, or nymph-fishing.

Some books have emphasised the importance of good casting; others have virtually ignored it. Peter Lapsley has missed nothing. His work is comprehensive. At a time when more than half of the anglers who fish for trout are novices, this is important, because the angler who starts his trout fishing career on, let us say, a small lake will, sooner or later, wish to test his ability on a large reservoir or an extensive loch. If his first attempts have been confined to the use of conventional wet flies, he will soon want to see what nymphs, dry-flies or lures will catch. In Peter Lapsley's book, he will find sound, succinct advice about all of it; advice based on successful practical experience.

In any branch of angling, differences of opinion between one man and another are inevitable, and there are some that can never be resolved because so much can be said, both for and against, differing points of view. What has greatly impressed me about Peter Lapsley is that when he encounters opinions that differ from his, he invariably examines them with care, never dismissing them without good reasons, and being always willing to change his own opinion if the evidence convinces him. The importance of such an attitude in producing a book whose scope is as wide as this one is immense. It has enabled Peter Lapsley to evaluate the views of other anglers in a thoroughly objective manner, by practical trial allied to logical assessment, and any advice he gives is therefore of much greater value. Nobody is always right; the author of this book will be found to be right much more often than readers of angling literature can normally expect.

Richard Walker

Introduction

Relatively few of our grandparents or great-grandparents fished for trout in lakes, lochs or reservoirs. In the 1890s and early 1900s no more than a handful of people cast their flies upon the waters of Loch Leven, Lake Vyrnwy, Ravensthorpe or Blagdon. Today, thousands of anglers throughout the length and breadth of these islands have come to look upon stillwater trouting as their primary recreational activity. In the space of no more than eighty years, increased leisure time and affluence, enormous improvements in transport and communications, a growing willingness on the part of water authorities to open their facilities to the public, and great advances in the rearing of trout for stocking purposes have all combined to transform the sport into one of the most popular in the country.

During its recent evolution, stillwater trout fishing has grown away from the more traditional and established discipline of river trouting. New minds have brought new ideas and the tackle, techniques and tactics now used on lakes and reservoirs up and down the country bear but scant resemblance to those which might serve on the Itchen, the Usk or the Eden. River fishermen coming to highland lochs or fertile lowland reservoirs would do well to understand this. From time to time a fellow angler tells me that he finds stillwaters boring, or that he regards them as a poor substitute for 'the real thing', by which he means running water. The comparison is an unsatisfactory one for the two branches of the sport have become as dissimilar as rugby and soccer. In fact, it is quite often clear that the river man's dislike for lakes lies in his lack of success on them, and that this lack of success results from a failure to recognise stillwater trout fishing as a craft in its own right, worthy of serious thought and application.

A similar lack of success must frequently lie behind the statements of those people who say that they do not mind whether they catch fish or not. Perhaps some of them mean it, but I rather suspect that it is more commonly an excuse used to conceal ineptitude. Few would deny that the peace of the countryside, opportunities for close observation of wild life, and the companionship of fellow anglers all contribute to our overall enjoyment of a day's fishing, or that these factors can (and should) be adequate compensation for occasional and inevitable blank days. But anyone who can honestly claim to set out in the morning without the express intention of bringing home a decent bag of trout must be a most unusual being.

So let us not fool ourselves; we go fishing chiefly to catch fish. Which is not to condone the activities of the 'fishmongers', those whose sole purpose it is to catch as many trout as possible in as short a time as possible without respect either for their quarry or for their fellow anglers.

A good deal has been written about sportsmanship over the years, much of it ill-considered – particularly when it has centred upon such mindless exercises as the use of light leaders or small hooks 'to give the fish a sporting chance'. But in stillwater fly fishing, as in any other field sport, there are standards to be maintained and they must be clearly understood. Essentially, they boil down to observing the rules of the fishery in spirit as well as in letter, and being careful to do nothing that might damage the pleasure of other fishermen. Some, hopefully unpompous, notes on this latter subject are included in the chapter on Waterside Ways in the hope that they may prove useful to newcomers.

Within the limitations imposed by our definition of sportsmanship, how one actually sets about catching trout is entirely a matter for personal preference.

From regular reading of the angling press it will be found that each of the half-dozen or so writers who regularly hold forth on stillwater tactics has his own favourite style or technique and spends a good deal of time extolling its particular virtues. One man favours nymph fishing, another prefers to use large, deep-sunk lures, someone else may be an exponent of the dry fly and another a member of the traditional wet fly school. Such specialisation is valuable for it means that each method is subjected to careful and detailed research. However, if the truth were to be known, we would probably find that each of these experts catches just about the same number of trout as each of the others during the course of a season. Specialist angling journalists provide a useful service; they collect and produce bright new ideas to refine or develop their chosen branches of the sport yet further, and they pass on their findings to other anglers. But we should always bear in mind that, while any angling writer is at liberty to make his views and attitudes publicly known, nobody has the right to insist that others accept them, or to criticise people who choose to ignore them.

Perhaps more important than total mastery of a particular style of fly fishing is the ability to select a suitable method to meet the given conditions at a particular time, and to employ that method effectively. The really competent all-round fisherman is he who can find the rising fish and successfully stalk them with a dry fly one day; realise that the trout are feeding twenty feet down on daphnia (creatures far too small to be imitated on a hook) and catch his share with a lure on another; notice sub-surface movement around a weed bed and tempt trout with a nymph on a third and successfully fish the shallow, windswept, lee-shore margins with a minnow imitation on a fourth. He may well alter his tactics several times during the course of a single outing to meet changes in fish behaviour and the weather. Flexibility must be the hallmark of a really proficient trout fisherman, and herein lies one of the exceptions to the old adage, 'Jack of all trades; master of none'. None of the basic techniques is difficult to acquire once the principles of casting have been mastered and a small stock of understanding has been built up. Although most people find that one style appeals to them more than others, it undoubtedly pays to spend a little time on each of them so that, whatever the conditions when you arrive at the waterside, you should be able to set out confidently, with reasonable expectation of success.

Which brings us to the content of this book, written for newcomers to the sport, for those who have so far limited themselves to one style of angling and wish to try others, and for those who may only ever have fished one type of water and hope to broaden their horizons.

As an advocate of flexibility, I have sought to consider all aspects of fly fishing for stillwater trout – from the fish themselves, their environments and their food, to the various forms of tackle, techniques and tactics used in their capture.

Any fisherman, however elementary his skill, owes much of what he knows to other people, either to other fishermen of his acquaintance or to those whose articles or books he has read. The more experienced the angler, the more he owes to others. I am no exception. The thoughts and observations contained within these pages represent a distillation of knowledge gleaned from many fellow fishermen over a number of years, from books and articles read and re-read, and from a good deal of practical trial and error.

Some critics may comment upon the fact that I make no mention of spinning or bait fishing. There are three reasons for this. Firstly, although some authorities allow the use of bread, maggots, worms or whatever, there is substantial evidence to suggest that the ground baiting which almost invariably accompanies this style of angling has an adverse effect on the feeding habits of trout, and that the practice is detrimental to the sport. Secondly, occasional trials over many years have shown fly fishing to be by far the most consistently effective method of extracting trout from stillwaters. Thirdly, because I am not personally attracted to these particular trout fishing methods, I have never employed them, and it would be foolish in the extreme to write on subjects about which one really knew very little. So, this is a book on fly fishing.

Finally, I hope that nobody will be tempted to regard this work as being, in any sense, a definitive study of stillwater trouting. One of the great pleasures of our sport is that there is always something new to be learnt. However experienced an angler, however specialised a specialist, the weather, the season and the place can always combine to produce surprises; add the vagaries of the trout themselves and you have an ever changing spectrum. I can think of no other pastime which offers such unending scope for research and experimentation. If the contents of this book can provide a sound base upon which others may build, studying the ways of trout in stillwaters and improving on existing methods of catching them, then I shall be well satisfied.

Acknowledgments

Many people have helped me most generously in the preparation of this book, and to each of them I owe a specific debt of gratitude. Individually, I wish to record my thanks:

To Fred Beckett and Fred Darlison; the former for his splendid pencil drawings which now adorn the chapter on casting, the latter for his excellent colour photographs of the flies.

To Fred Buller, Francis Lodge, David Pilleau, Michael Reay and Richard Walker for reading the book in manuscript and for their invaluable comments on it at that stage. Additionally, to G. R. Carlisle for allowing me to use his magnificent photograph of Lough Corrib, to Michael Reay for researching the figures on trout growth rates and to Richard Walker for allowing his name to be formally associated with the completed work.

To Lt.-Col. Sir John Baynes, the late Lt.-Col. J. K. B. (Jock) Crawford, Major David Fleming Jones, Jim Latimer, Mr G. R. Porter and Mr E. J. Sharpe for the background information they provided on the waters with which they are associated when I was researching the history of our sport.

To Vera Bryant of The Royal Society for the Prevention of Accidents for her advice on water safety.

To my sister, Penelope Fairrie, for providing several of the recipes for the chapter on preparing trout.

To Anne Watts and Phil Harris of A. & C. Black Ltd for their painstaking work on the manuscript, and for their patience and sympathetic help during the making of the book.

And finally to my wife, Jennifer, for furnishing the rest of the recipes and for allowing me the time both to write and to fish while the garden turned to a jungle, the house went undecorated and our two children and three dogs became increasingly impatient.

For my father, Sir John Lapsley, who took me on my first fishing trip over thirty years ago, and who has given me such enthusiastic support in all my subsequent angling ventures.

CHAPTER 1

In the Beginning

There is a noticeable tendency nowadays for people to grasp at anything new as though it were some sort of panacea for all their ills and to discard much, even most, of what has gone before. Although fly fishing is a relatively traditional pursuit, it is not exempt from this peculiar characteristic of modern life. Successive issues of angling journals contain articles on revolutionary developments in rod design, stories of ever more efficient techniques, and startling dressings for gaudy new artificial flies. Writers sing the praises of 'advanced' and 'sophisticated' fishing methods and sometimes seem to forget their predecessors' work. Many of today's stillwater fishermen would be surprised indeed to discover just how many current 'innovations' are, in fact, merely resurrections of old ideas. Perhaps the most dramatic example of this was provided by the public hullabaloo which heralded the introduction of American brook trout (*Salvelinus fontinalis*) into some lakes here during the 1970s. That the species had been tried with but indifferent success from time to time since the middle of the nineteenth century, and that its initial importation into Britain had preceded that of its infinitely more useful compatriot, the rainbow trout (*Salmo gairdneri*), were conveniently overlooked.

So it would seem sensible to consider the history of stillwater fly fishing in Britain before going on to any study of the sport as it exists today.

Although people have been fishing for trout in lakes and lochs for generations, the sport has only become widespread in this country during the past hundred years. Until the last decade or so of the nineteenth century, this particular branch of angling was almost exclusively reserved for those whose good fortune it was to live close to a natural expanse of water with a self-perpetuating population of native trout, or for those wealthy enough to be able to stock their own natural or man-made lakes. Few waters were properly managed and available to the public on a commercial basis.

The first major stillwater to be opened to paying customers was probably Loch Leven. By the middle of the last century, netting rights on the loch had been let out by the owners for two hundred years or more. Although trout fishing with rod and line had grown in popularity during the late eighteenth and early nineteenth centuries, it was said that Leven's fish rarely rose to a fly, and the loch was little used by anglers. During the 1850s things started to change and fly fishermen began to patronise it in increasing numbers. I have not been able to establish precisely when day-ticket fishing became available to the public here, but the records show that by 1872 ten trout were being taken with rod and line for every one caught by the netsmen.

Loch Leven's 3543 acres are shallow and fertile. At its maximum the loch is 83 ft deep, but mostly it is under 15 ft. It is a self-stocking water (although small numbers of fish may have been introduced into the feeder streams from time to time) and the native brown trout are as famous for their pink flesh and their table qualities as for their handsome appearance. The largest fish ever taken from the loch was a monster of $9\frac{3}{4}$ lb, but the trout average between $\frac{3}{4}$ lb and 1 lb and have done so since records were first kept there.

In spite of its fame as a fishery and its long history, Loch Leven has never really made any very dramatic contribution to the development of stillwater tackle or tactics. Indeed, the equipment and methods used there today differ little from those employed by our forebears a hundred years ago. This may be partially accounted for by Leven's relative remoteness, but the fact that bank fishing has never been allowed there may also have been a contributory factor.

Loch Leven had only just begun to acquire its reputation as a sport fishery when the most significant single incident in the whole history of British stillwater trouting occurred. Trout had been cultivated in continental Europe, particularly in France and Germany, since the 1840s, but no trout farm was established in the United Kingdom until fifteen or twenty years later. Before artificially reared fish became available, trout fishing was entirely limited to lakes and reservoirs fed by streams in which indigenous piscine populations could spawn naturally. The advent of trout farming opened the door for the owners and managers of otherwise barren waters up and down the country to stock with hand-reared fish, and to offer this new type of fishing to the public on a commercial basis.

The arrival from America of the first batch of rainbow trout ova at Sir James Maitland's hatchery at Howeiton in 1885 was another major landmark in the sport's development. Brown trout (*Salmo trutta*) are native to Britain. Long-lived and slow-growing, they are expensive to rear, and they are only really at their best as sporting fish in stillwaters from March to early June and again in September; throughout the summer they tend to retire to the deeps where they can be very difficult to tempt with a fly. In contrast, and although its life span may be only half that of the brown trout, the rainbow grows quickly and is therefore relatively economical to rear. It is often in poor condition during the spring but can provide excellent sport from June onwards.

British fishermen were initially sceptical about the rainbow trout's prospects in this country. They well remembered the expense and lack of sport which had accompanied the introduction of American brook trout into several waters here only a few years earlier. Ignoring the fact that brook trout, as a species of charr, behave entirely differently to rainbows or browns, and that they are native to the cold north-east of their home continent while rainbows come from the substantially warmer west coast, they associated the two species in their minds and were mistrustful of the newcomer. Their lack of faith was compounded by the rainbow trout's penchant for disappearing from waters into which it had been stocked. Indignant letters to *The Field* and other august country journals in the 1890s complained that rainbows put into lakes one year had completely vanished a season or two later, and attributed the losses to a migratory instinct which drew the fish towards the sea, even when the water had no apparent or reasonable escape route. Although it is probable that some rainbows did indeed leave their new abodes, it seems likely that the primary cause of our forefathers' dissatisfaction was, in fact, the fish's short lifespan. Brown trout may live for twelve years or more and, since they cheerfully reproduce in the streams feeding many British stillwaters, the demise of original stock may not be readily apparent. Rainbows rarely live for more than four or five years and only breed naturally in this country in quite a small number of places, so their heirless deaths a couple of years after being put into the water as two-year-olds quite understandably left unhappy question marks in the minds of fishery owners.

However, by the mid-1890s the rainbow seems to have been recognised as an economical and sporting fish, well suited to the stocking of British stillwaters, and more and more trout farms were rearing them.

But rainbows played no part in the early years of Lake Vyrnwy, a beautiful man-made water in north-east Wales which, having been completed and filled in 1889, opened for trout fishing two years later. During its first five years or so, it was stocked with some half a million Loch Leven strain brown trout, reared in stew ponds built

LAKE VYRNWY. The first man-made water in Britain to have been opened to the public as a trout fishery, this lovely North Wales water is more akin in character to a highland loch than to a lowland reservoir.

Photo: The author

on site for the purpose. By about 1895 or 1896, the fish were assessed as being sufficiently plentiful and well established to be self-supporting, and the trout farm fell into disuse. Vyrnwy's trout were relatively small from the outset, averaging about 1 lb each with a 2-lb specimen being considered exceptional. This average weight quickly dropped to around $\frac{3}{4}$ lb, and within fifteen years was down to the $\frac{1}{2}$-lb mark where it remained until restocking of the reservoir and the importation of trout food in the form of snails and freshwater shrimps began in the late 1920s and early 1930s. In terms of fertility as well as of character, Lake Vyrnwy bore a marked similarity to many highland lochs. Its water, both soft (infertile) and deep, offered little opportunity for the trout to grow to any great size.

Ravensthorpe reservoir in Northamptonshire, which opened as a trout fishery in 1893, was different. Records of the Northampton Corporation Water Works Department's early stocking policy seem to have disappeared, but it is clear that the fish put into this fertile midlands water grew rapidly. During the opening season, 481 fishermen caught 1013 trout averaging 2 lb 6 oz each in weight. During the following three years the average rose to a remarkable

BLAGDON. The *alma mater* of modern reservoir fishing; as lovely today as it was when it was first opened in 1904.

Photo: The author

$3\frac{1}{4}$ lb but then, quite suddenly, it dropped dramatically, steadying at about $1\frac{1}{2}$ lb in 1902. This has proved to be a recurring trend in newly filled reservoirs where the fish thrive in water enriched by decaying terrestrial vegetation for the first few seasons and then settle to a lower average weight once the chemical balance has stabilised. Considering that it was close to several large towns, surprisingly few people fished Ravensthorpe during its first ten seasons, an average of only 323 per year. Nevertheless, it seems to have been the first large, man-made, lowland, public water supply reservoir to have been opened to trout fishermen, and it showed anglers the sort of sport to be had from a shallow, hard-water lake where plentiful marginal weed growth could harbour a mass of natural trout food.

And then came Blagdon, set among the gently rolling Mendip Hills. When it was flooded in 1902 the rising waters covered fertile land and the trout, introduced as fry and fingerlings from the newly built Ubley hatchery, thrived on a banquet of earthworms, slugs, caterpillars and beetles. Blagdon, nowhere more than 42 ft deep, quickly became a veritable soup of insect life and has remained an extraordinarily rich water to this day. But it has never quite been able to match consistently the remarkable weights reached by its fish during those first few years. In a history of stillwater trouting these figures not only make dramatic reading, they are also highly significant. Never before or since have such spectacular catches been recorded. Even widely lauded Grafham lagged way behind when it opened in 1966. The average weight of the trout taken from Blagdon during the period 1904 to 1909 was 3 lb 8 oz.* Individual brown trout of 5 lb were far from uncommon, and bags of three fish for 20½ lb and three fish for 24 lb were recorded. Even as late as 1918 (fourteen years after the reservoir first opened as a fishery), H. S. Hall, a mathematics master at Clifton College, writing in *The Flyfishers' Journal*, was able to record the capture of 549 Blagdon trout weighing 11 cwt 105 lb in all, an average of more than 2 lb 4 oz per fish. This astonishing total had included three fish over 6 lb, ten over 5 lb and four fish in a day totalling 18 lb 7 oz.

Stories of the trouting to be had at Blagdon were told and retold up and down the country, and there was no need for them to grow in the telling. People were beginning to realise that increased fishing pressure would soon push the price of a rod on an English trout stream way beyond the means of the ordinary angler, and the tales kindled public interest in a hitherto largely neglected branch of the sport.

Encouraged by Blagdon's success, other water authorities in England and Wales quickly followed the Bristol Waterworks Company's example and opened their stillwaters to trout fishermen. By 1912 Ernest Phillips was able to record that some sixty public water supply reservoirs had been stocked and were available as day-ticket fisheries.

Those who had pursued Lake Vyrnwy's trout in the 1890s had found little difficulty in deciding upon suitable tackle and tactics with which to do so. The lake was, to all intents and purposes, a Scottish highland loch, and the techniques for catching brown trout from such waters were well known. 'Black Palmer's' *Scotch Loch Fishing*, published in 1882, had gathered together much of the existing knowledge on the subject and seems to have been the first book unequivocally to have advocated fly fishing as the most consistently effective means of taking trout from lakes with rod and line. Whether they had read it or not, early fishers of Vyrnwy adhered to the principles described by its author. Boat fishing was

---

* This (official) figure is at variance with that given by Ernest Phillips in his book *Trout In Lakes and Reservoirs*, published in 1912. The reason for the disparity may lie in the fact that during the reservoir's early years many fishermen imposed an unwritten rule upon themselves, returning all fish under 2 lb. Phillips may have used the statistics of fish taken away, rather than fish caught, for his calculations.

accepted practice as it enabled the angler to cover the offshore shallows so attractive to trout, and it also made possible the use of blow lines, a technique not dissimilar to dapping. Rods were long, rarely less than twelve feet, and of cane or greenheart. They were used with teams of traditional Scottish flies on gut leaders. The March Brown, Mallard and Claret and Mallard and Black were all noted as having been amongst the most popular patterns during those early years and would, indeed, work just as well today. The trout were hungry, there was little food for them in the water and they were prepared to grab at almost anything that looked even vaguely edible.

Blagdon was a different matter altogether. In its shallow, fertile waters the fish were growing fat on a vast array of food. Although they were sometimes prepared to try hitherto unseen and therefore untasted morsels – which they occasionally found to contain fish hooks – they could well afford to pick and choose what they ate. Their sheer size also presented new problems. Clearly, tackle suitable for removing $\frac{1}{2}$-lb or 1-lb trout from Scottish lochs or Irish loughs was unlikely to serve where fish of 3 lb were the norm and monsters of twice that size were not uncommon, or where long casting from the bank was as potentially profitable as short lining from a boat.

The pioneers at Blagdon tried a wide assortment of techniques— from spinners to traditional wet flies and from fly-spoons (very small, plain spoons) to dry flies. For fly fishing, long, heavy cane or greenheart rods, sometimes two-handed ones, silk lines and gut leaders of 10 lb breaking strain were standard equipment. Fifteen years after the reservoir opened, H. S. Hall recommended a small Silver Doctor, a Dusty Miller or an Alexandra as being suitable lures for use there, and Colonel J. K. B. Crawford recalled that on his first visit in July 1922 he accepted the advice he was given and bought a Jock Scott, a Thunder and Lightning and a Dunkeld from Donald Carr who managed the fishery. The obviously widespread use of such relatively large and gaudy salmon patterns in the 1920s must, to some extent at least, undermine the arguments of those who claim that lure fishing was born of the boom in stillwater trouting in the 1950s and 1960s, as, indeed, does the fact that some tandem lures like the Worm Fly can be traced back to the middle of the nineteenth century.

While many of Blagdon's anglers were plying the reservoir's waters with this heavy tackle, another school had already begun to experiment with smaller, imitative dressings. In his book, *Fly Fishing, Some New Arts and Mysteries*, published in 1915, Dr James Mottram, later well known for his research into cancer, gave his dressings for midge and sedge pupae and for mosquito larvae, and described nymph and dry fly fishing on the reservoir between 1911 and 1913. And, in *Where The Bright Waters Meet* (1924), the Irish opera singer, Harry Plunket Greene (who is reputed to have regaled the setting sun with arias from North Bank), told of successes with bushy, palmered floating patterns.

Much of our knowledge of the evolution of stillwater trouting is, inevitably, based upon the works of authors who have gone before. It is interesting, therefore, and a little sad, that one of the most famous, intelligent and inventive lake fishermen of the century appears to have written not a single article about the sport.

Dr Howard Bell, the general practitioner for Wrington and Blagdon, established his practice in 1922 and, thereafter, fished Blagdon almost every Friday and Sunday throughout each season until failing health prevented him from doing so in 1969, five years before his death. A born fisherman, Dr Bell studied the underwater life of the lake carefully and soon proved that imitative patterns could produce fish for bank anglers in daylight. Prior to this, fly fishing from the bank had generally been regarded as a late evening pastime. Dr Bell, who was not a long caster by present-day standards, fished with a double tapered silk line and rarely, if ever, used anything other than a sunk fly. His imitative dressings are used to this day although some of them have been modified. His imitation of the Silverhorns Sedge (greenish body, oval silver tinsel and a sparsely dressed turkey quill wing) was eventually superseded in his armoury by the Worm Fly, a traditional tandem lure dating from the middle of the nineteenth century. Of far greater significance were his corixa, his red and black midge pupae and the amber nymph which he used to represent a sedge pupa.

It has been suggested that Dr Bell's success was due in no small part to his tenacity. Having waded into the water at some favourite spot he would remain there, casting away, with only the shortest possible break for a picnic lunch on the bank. But this in no way detracts from his skill, or from the more important philosophical contribution which he made to the sport with his imitative approach to stillwater trouting.

Although there had been a substantial growth in the number of reservoirs available for trout fishing during the first twenty years of the century, the same could not be said for smaller stillwaters. Many lakes, both natural and man-made, had been stocked with trout either for private or for syndicate use as far back as the middle of the nineteenth century, but few, if any, had been opened to the public. Enton Lakes in Surrey, excavated from the Witley marshes in 1912 and opened for commercial membership in 1921, was one of the first of a new type of fishery. Set in attractive surroundings and markedly smaller than most public water supply reservoirs, the lakes were altogether more intimate than places like Blagdon and Ravensthorpe. The membership had to be strictly limited so that the lakes would not be over-fished, and this helped to create a club atmosphere rarely to be found at the larger expanses of stillwater. Perhaps more important than this, the long casting normally associated with reservoirs was not at a premium here, long drifts were obviously impracticable in so confined a space, and the water was generally both clearer and calmer than it was in lochs, loughs or reservoirs. A new style of fishing began to evolve to cater for these factors, and it was from these beginnings that modern nymph-fishing techniques for small stillwaters developed.

Throughout the 1920s and 1930s the sport as a whole appears to have made little progress. Dr Bell improved on his imitative patterns and designed new ones, and a few more fisheries were opened to the public, but there seem to have been no real innovations either in fishery management or in angling techniques. Indeed, if we are to judge by books like Sidney Spencer's *The Art of Lake Fishing*, published in 1934, it would seem that stillwater trouting was gradually slipping backwards at this time. Even as late as 1939 one Colonel Graham, writing in that year's Farlows' Catalogue on bank fishing at Blagdon, recommended spinning with a metal minnow through the day and reserving fly fishing for the late evening.

There were imaginative and inventive fishermen about, of course. Perhaps one of the finest books ever written on stillwater fly fishing was H. P. Henzell's *The Art and Craft of Loch Fishing*, published in 1937. But for some obscure reason this splendid work seems never to have received the recognition it deserved. Its lack of success may have lain in the title (which could be taken to imply dedication to fishing north of the border) or in the fact that it appeared only shortly before the outbreak of World War II and became lost amongst the pressing problems of the early 1940s. Whatever the cause of its premature demise, any present-day trout angler who can find a copy would do well to read it. The author's philosophy towards the sport and his broad, unbiased approach to techniques and tactics are as valid today as they were when committed to paper more than forty years ago, as are his recommended fly patterns.

The 1939–45 war and the period of austerity which followed it effectively stunned stillwater trouting for several years. The only major development in the late 1940s was the inception of Two Lakes at Romsey in Hampshire. The single-mindedness and sheer hard work that Alex Behrendt and his wife put into the building of this now legendary fishery are well documented in David Jacques' book, *The Development of Modern Stillwater Fishing*. Actually opened in 1953, Two Lakes has produced some remarkable fish and some remarkable fishermen. It was here that Commander C. F. Walker did much of the research for his most excellent book *Lake Flies and Their Imitation* and Barrie Welham developed his tactics for stalking large trout in still, clear water. But perhaps more significant than the fishery itself has been Mr Behrendt's contribution to the sport as a whole through the symposia and courses he has run each year. Few well-known fisheries would be as good as they now are had he not organised these facilities for the exchange of knowledge.

The early 1950s saw the start of a most remarkable expansion in the sport. T. C. Ivens' *Still Water Fly Fishing*, published in 1952, represented the first detailed and scientifically thought out work on the new craft of reservoir trouting. It provided thousands of newcomers to these waters with a sound base upon which to build their skills. And thousands of newcomers there were; from river fishermen dispossessed of their running water by pollution, abstraction and rising costs, through converts from the ranks of the so-called 'coarse anglers', to those who had never wielded a rod in their lives. Ivens explained his attitudes to fly selection and fishing styles in detail and with clarity. His blind spots are well known – he has little time either for the dry fly or for specifically imitative patterns – and the influence of his book has been evidenced as much by the wide acceptance of his prejudices as by the almost universal adoption of the methods he advocated.

The 1950s saw the opening of increasing numbers of reservoirs to the public as day-ticket trout fisheries. Blagdon's big (and rather less intimate) companion, Chew Valley Lake, made its debut in 1957 and, with brown and rainbow trout of 7 lb 4 oz and 6 lb 2 oz respectively during that first season, quickly established itself as being amongst the country's leading stillwaters.

By the early 1960s, with increasing affluence and mobility, the demand for stillwater trout fishing was still growing at an astonishing rate. Landowners, both public and private, recognised this and it seemed as though any piece of water that could conceivably hold trout was being stocked. Ponds, lakes, gravel pits and reservoirs acquired overnight populations of browns and rainbows and were opened to anglers on either a day-ticket or a membership basis.

Until this time, stillwater fishermen had had to make do either with river, sea trout or grilse rods. But with the new breed of reservoir anglers forming an increasing percentage of the tackle trade's overall custom, manufacturers began, somewhat belatedly, to produce specially designed equipment. Glass fibre proved to be a most efficient substitute for much heavier cane for rod making. Maintenance-free plastic-coated lines, which had gained wide acceptance during the late 1950s, became available in an ever wider range of weights and profiles as reservoir fishing developed. Nylon had finally and completely replaced gut for leaders and had proved to be a first-rate backing material for shooting heads, but, surprisingly, reels had not been subjected to much development. With one or two exceptions, those that serve today are little different from the small-spindled, narrow-spooled implements used by river fishermen since about 1850.

The opening season at Grafham Water in 1966 was like a carnival and drew more attention from the angling press than any previous similar event. Although Grafham's returns have never been as dramatic as were those from Blagdon during the early years,* this great east midlands water has still made an enormous impact on the history of stillwater trouting in Britain. Deep, vast and containing enormous quantities of trout food, Grafham was soon presenting anglers with another completely new set of problems. Whereas rainbows elsewhere gradually moved inshore to feed on the animal life which thrived in marginal or near marginal vegetation throughout the summer, Grafham's fish gorged themselves on huge concentrations of minute daphnia which were often to be found 30 ft or more beneath the surface. Conventional sinking lines could rarely reach down to such fish, whether cast from the bank or from a boat and, even when these rainbows were located, nymphs and traditional loch patterns seemed to interest them very little.

During the 1960s and early 1970s, a group of specialist reservoir fishermen in the midlands put a great deal of time and effort into evolving solutions to these difficulties. The answers they produced were controversial. They found that large feathered lures, frequently dressed on tandem hooks and up to 3 or 4 in long, would often be taken by daphnia-feeding trout, especially if they were predominantly black, white or orange and gold in colour. They also discovered that fast sinking lines, which had been introduced into this country from the Scientific Anglers company in the United States, could drag lures down to the fishes' feeding depths, but it soon became clear that powerful rods were needed to handle such heavy tackle. This group, which had been inspired by the perception of people like Ivens and Cyril Inwood, and included

---

* The average weight of Grafham trout during the 1966 season was 2 lb 13 oz as opposed to Blagdon's 1904 average of 4 lb 13 oz. Grafham's average over its first five seasons (1966–70) was almost exactly 2 lb as compared to Blagdon's 3 lb 8 oz (1904–8).

GRAFHAM WATER. The vast Midlands reservoir which catalysed the development of a new range of stillwater trout fishing techniques in the late 1960s and early 1970s.

Photo: Edwin M. Grant

such now famous names as Bob Church, Dick and Jim Shrive and Mick Nichols, invented boat fishing techniques which so revolutionised the sport that some of them were banned from use at certain reservoirs. The arguments of those opposed to the new style of lure fishing were that the tackle and the manner in which it was employed bore little resemblance to traditional fly fishing methods and represented at best a bending of the rules and at worst a substitute for spinning. In fact, the real problem lay not in the techniques themselves but in the way in which they were received by the public. Lure fishing as conceived by these midlands anglers is an imaginative and skilful means of catching trout under specific conditions. To be consistently effective it demands a detailed knowledge of fish behaviour, of the effects of wind and sunlight on water and of the geography of the particular reservoir being fished. Successive articles in the angling press presented the style as a solution to all fly fishing problems, and extolled the virtues of an ever gaudier collection of artificials. Many fishermen found that there was nothing very difficult about casting such lures 35 yards or more, stripping them back and re-casting. Fished like this, they caught modest numbers of trout. By the early 1970s, the results of a good deal of thought and hard work were at real risk of being transformed into a mindless and almost entirely unchallenging exercise, to be used on any water, at any time, with total disregard for conditions or the behaviour of the fish.

However, throughout this entire period several intelligent and observant angling entomologists had been busy, studying the natural fauna upon which trout feed and translating their findings into practical, imitative dressings. The first really authoritative work to result from these researches was J. R. Harris's, *An Angler's Entomology*, first published in 1952. Although Harris was not exclusively, or even largely, concerned with stillwater insects, his work provided lake fishermen with a precise and detailed catalogue of many of the creatures upon which their quarry lives. Commander C. F. Walker followed in 1959 with his *Lake Flies and Their Imitation*. Valuable more, perhaps, for its charm of style than for the absolute accuracy of its contents, this delightful book is now out of print and, sadly, has effectively become a collector's item. But the most important work done by any of these scientifically minded men was the distillation of John Goddard's knowledge and expertise into two books, *Trout Flies of Stillwater* and *Trout Fly Recognition*, in the mid-1960s. Goddard's keen understanding of aquatic insect life is fully matched by his abilities as a fly dresser and photographer, and both volumes represent essential works of reference for any fly fisherman who is truly interested in mastering his sport.

BARN ELMS. A Thames Water reservoir complex in the heart of London, the sixty acres of which provide stillwater trouting for more people than almost any other fishery in the country.

Photo: The author

   If Harris's, Walker's and Goddard's contributions to stillwater fly fishing literature had a faint aura of the academic about them, they were well balanced by the appearance in 1975 of Brian Clarke's *The Pursuit of Stillwater Trout.* Clarke's gift as a writer lies in his ability to enable other people to relate to his experiences. In his book he argued that, of all the trout's instincts, the feeding one was the most predictable and consistent, and that it therefore seemed sensible to calculatedly pander to it whenever possible. Stripping entomology of most of the mystique that had hitherto surrounded it, he presented a small collection of artificial patterns with which the greater part of the average trout's diet could adequately be represented and, having explained a system for establishing what the trout were feeding on, described his imitative fishing technique. The book was an immediate success and has probably done more than any other single work to halt the decline into the universal and unthinking use of stripped lures. All of which is not to suggest that lures, like dry flies or traditional patterns, should not form a part of the stillwater fisherman's armoury, or that they cannot provide precisely the right answer in the right place, at the right time.

LATIMER PARK LAKES. An attractive Home Counties put-and-take stillwater where the 'club' atmosphere is almost as important as the high quality of the fishing.

Photo: The author

Today, more people than ever before are fishing for trout in lakes, lochs, reservoirs and gravel pits throughout our islands, and the sport still seems to be growing. Visit any publicly available stillwater between April and September and, unless it is extraordinarily isolated or remote, you may be sure of finding a respectable number of stalwart souls hard at work.

What the future holds we cannot say. Several water authorities have recently found themselves unable to run their large reservoirs as trout fisheries on a cost-effective basis, and are seriously considering leasing the angling rights on them to other organisations. Whether such organisations will continue to offer the same remarkably cheap fishing that reservoir fishermen have hitherto enjoyed, whether fishermen will be prepared to pay higher prices in order that the quality of their sport may be maintained, or whether fly fishers will happily share the water with other money making aquatic sports, remains to be seen.

In terms of average catch to ticket price ratio, the small put-and-take fisheries generally offer better value for money than the large reservoirs do. In addition, many of them seek to provide a 'club'

LOCH MAREE. A typical highland loch, noted for its fine salmon and sea-trout, in which the wild brown trout rarely attain great sizes due to shortage of food.

Photo: The British Tourist Authority

atmosphere with a fishing lodge, pleasant surroundings, good car parking facilities and even, in some instances, meals. But they are relatively expensive to run and to fish and, if inflation were to push their prices beyond the reach of ordinary people, some would inevitably go to the wall.

One way of reducing the cost of tickets on such waters might be to introduce the sort of catch-and-return policy that has been widely and successfully observed in the United States for some time. There are various ways of implementing this. An angler can be allowed to catch and return as many fish as he likes, retaining only a pre-ordained number, or he can be charged initially just for permission to fish, paying subsequently for those trout he chooses to kill at so much per pound. In either event, fishermen must be given clear instructions as to how fish should be returned to the water in order to avoid damaging them, and the exclusive use of barbless hooks must be compulsory.

The financial security of small fisheries could be further increased if their seasons could be extended. At present, they open from (roughly) April until September in deference to the breeding habits

LOUGH CORRIB. An Irish limestone lough. Such fertile waters produce fine wild brown trout, but they can be both difficult and dangerous to fish.

Photo: G. R. Carlisle

of Britain's idigenous brown trout. But where brown trout are not stocked it is both practicable and legal for such waters to remain open for much longer, even throughout the year, as rainbows, American brook trout and hybrid tiger and cheetah trout are exotic species and are therefore not subject to a statutory closed season. It now seems certain that the techniques for producing all-female rainbows will soon be perfected. As it is the cock fish, rather than the hen, that presents the angler with so unattractive a catch during the spring, this too would seem to offer opportunities for extension of the season or, rather, for beginning it earlier. However, it should be said that both waters and fishermen require a rest period of some sort during the year and that to allow fishing from January to December would almost certainly prove to be folly.

Although the lochs and loughs of Scotland and Ireland have outwardly changed little during the past hundred years, they have not been entirely untouched by the recent upsurge of public interest in stillwater trouting. More and more fishermen are searching for peaceful and uncrowded waters. Hitherto self-perpetuating populations of wild brown trout now require the protection afforded by 'limit bags' and restrictions on fishing methods in some places, and some need supplementing with artificially reared fish. Several organisations are actively engaged in the maintenance and management of these waters, but more thought and effort must go into the protection and preservation of our natural stillwaters if irreparable damage is to be avoided. All major landowners, particularly the public ones, must recognise the leisure value of the water they control and take active steps to safeguard it. If the example set by the National Trust were to be followed by other large institutions, the future of natural stillwater trouting would be assured.

In terms of tackle, there will undoubtedly be further refinements. The last hundred years have seen a progression from greenheart through split cane to fibreglass and carbon fibre for rod making. Even steel was tried at one stage during the late 1930s and early 1940s. Unless something with carbon fibre's basic properties, but very much cheaper and very much stronger, can be found, there would seem to be little merit in searching for any new material. In lightness, power and slimness of profile, we would appear to have gone as far as could ever be considered either necessary or desirable.

Lines, reels and leaders are a different matter altogether and there is room for much progress here. No doubt somebody will produce a slender, high floating, friction-free, flash-free, crack-proof fly line one day, but how far away that moment may be we cannot say. However, we must hope that the advent of a really worthwhile range of purpose-built stillwater fly reels – light, strong, reasonably quiet, with large enough drums, truly adjustable checks and rim control – may not be too far off, and that properly tapered, knotless leaders, both with and without droppers, may become available in an assortment of lengths quite soon.

CHAPTER 2

The Trout

Some people fish for trout knowing little more about them than that they have speckled skins and live on insects. Indeed, by sheer perseverance and reasonably careful imitation of the techniques of others, it is quite possible to be modestly successful with but the minimum understanding of the fish's characteristics and behaviour. However, there can be no doubt that a little study can be well repaid, both in numbers of trout caught and in the pleasure derived from being able to stack the odds in our favour by reinforcing luck with logic.

So, in this chapter, and in the two following, we will consider the fish themselves, the food upon which they depend for survival and the environments in which they live. Armed with this basic background information, we should be able to approach virtually any water, at any stage in the season, with a shrewd idea as to where the trout are likely to be, what they can be expected to be doing, and why.

The word 'trout' has come to be used by many anglers as a generic term to cover a wide range of fish within the sub-order Salmonoidei. The most obvious of several definitive identifying features of species within this group is a small second dorsal, or adipose, fin situated immediately behind the true dorsal fin on the fish's back.

Six Salmonid species are native to British waters; the Atlantic salmon (*Salmo salar*), the brown trout (*Salmo trutta*), the Arctic char (*Salvelinus alpinus*), the grayling (*Thymallus thymallus*), the houting (*Coregonus lavaretus*) and the vendace (*Coregonus albula*). Of these, the Atlantic salmon is anadromous, breeding in freshwater and migrating to the sea to feed; the char, a cold water fish, is confined to deep lakes in Scotland, Ireland, Wales and the English Lake District, and provides but very limited sport for the conventional fly fisherman; the grayling shows a marked preference for running water and is, therefore, of little interest to the stillwater angler; and the white-

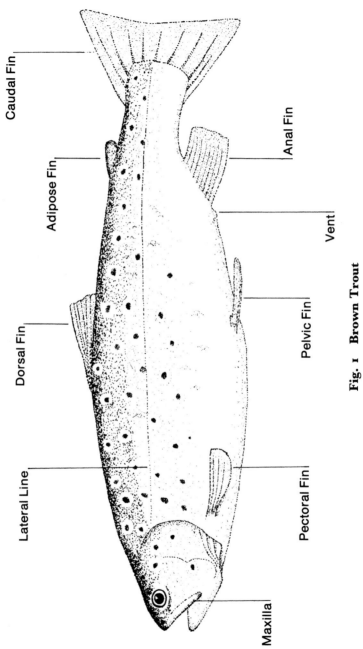

Caudal Fin

Adipose Fin

Anal Fin

Vent

Dorsal Fin

Pelvic Fin

Lateral Line

Pectoral Fin

Maxilla

Fig. 1 Brown Trout

fishes – the houtings and vendaces – are so limited in their distribution as to have little, if any, significance for most of us. Which leaves the brown trout as being by far the most important of our indigenous species from the stillwater fly fisherman's point of view, and we shall discuss him in some detail shortly.

Two Salmonid species have been imported into Britain from America during the past hundred or so years, the rainbow trout (*Salmo gairdneri*) and the American brook trout (*Salvelinus fontinalis*). Both were originally introduced specifically for their sporting value (although the rainbow is now widely farmed for the table market) and, again, we shall be considering their characteristics and habits in due course.

Finally, rainbow trout and brown trout have both been successfully crossed with American brook trout to produce hybrid 'cheetah' and 'tiger' trout.

For simplicity, the unqualified word 'trout' used henceforth in this book may be taken to refer to brown, rainbow and American brook trout, and their hybrid species.

Physiology

Apart from the basic identifying characteristics of the sub-order, all of these species have certain features in common. Trout are bony fish, streamlined in shape, with scaly bodies which they cover with a secreted layer of protective, insulating and lubricating slime. They have eight fins each, and propel themselves with undulating, side-to-side movements of their bodies, transmitting muscular power in backward moving waves to their spatulate tails. The powerful propulsion muscles down either side of their bodies are the parts we eat, and constitute almost two-thirds of the creatures' overall body weights. Compared with many other species, trout are particularly agile fish. They have remarkable acceleration and manoeuvrability, and can reach speeds of between ten and fifteen miles an hour over short distances.

While they rely on their fins for propulsion, braking and stability, trout, like almost all other fish, are equipped with an air bladder situated high in the body cavity. This enables them to adjust their specific gravities and helps them to maintain any level in the water without undue energy loss. They are able to make coarse adjustments to the pressure within the bladder by taking in air through their mouths, and fine ones by diffusing oxygen into it from the blood stream. It is worth noting that a fish hooked 20, 25 or more feet down is unlikely to survive if returned to the water as its air bladder is almost certain to have been ruptured or otherwise damaged during a rapid ascent to the surface. Also of interest is the fact that trout transferred from stock ponds to fisheries often roll on the surface shortly after having been moved. They are almost certainly gulping air, adjusting the pressure in their air bladders.

Life Cycle

Although breeding seasons and growth rates vary from species to species, the life cycles of all trout are sufficiently similar for us to outline them here, reserving any significant points of difference for our discussion on the individual species later in this chapter.

Trout require a clean gravel bed washed by smoothly flowing, well oxygenated water on which to spawn. While hen fish may deposit eggs in the shallow margins of stillwaters, very rarely will successful fertilisation or hatching take place there. So, it is axiomatic that any lake with a naturally self-perpetuating population of trout must be fed by an accessible, unpolluted and continuously flowing stream.

It seems clear that, while the instinct to migrate up on to the redds (as the breeding grounds are generally called) is triggered by a combination of an increase in the water level and a reduction in the length of daylight, the actual spawning process coincides with a specific and reasonably predictable drop in water temperature.

On her arrival at a suitable site, generally a pebble hump or ridge through which the current can percolate, the hen fish scoops out a hollow among the stones by washing away the silt, sediment and pebbles with her tail. When satisfied with the hollow's depth, she discharges a proportion of her ova into the nest while the cock fish, hovering close beside her, simultaneously fertilises it with his milt. The whole process having been completed once, the hen fish moves a foot or so upstream and repeats it, incidentally covering the ova in the first nest with pebbles from the second.

The length of time taken for the ova to hatch is greatly influenced by temperature and may vary from a month in water at a constant $10°C$ ($50°F$) to as much as five months if the water remains cold. During this time the ova provide potentially attractive meals for an assortment of aquatic predators, as do the newly hatched baby fish – the alevins. However, the ova are generally reasonably well protected in the gravel and the alevins, when they hatch, instinctively hide amongst it. Here they remain until they have almost consumed the pendulous yolk sacks with which nature provided them at birth. When their built-in food supplies are almost exhausted and the young fish emerge from their gravelly homes to start feeding in earnest, their mortality rate rises dramatically; it has been estimated that as many as 75 percent of them may be eaten by predators or die of other causes at this stage.

The growth rates of trout vary from species to species and from water to water. The figures in the following table seem to be fairly typical for fish reared artificially in stews, and account in part for the preference shown by many fishery owners for the use of rainbows for stocking purposes.

Age	*Brown Trout* *Weight*	*Rainbow Trout* *Weight*
6 months	80 to the lb	100 to the lb
1 year	8–10 oz	10 oz–1 lb
2 years	$1\frac{1}{2}$–$2\frac{1}{2}$ lb	$2\frac{1}{2}$–$3\frac{1}{2}$ lb
3 years	$3\frac{1}{2}$–5 lb	6–10 lb

In rivers or lakes, growth rates are dependent upon the availability of suitable food and, although rainbows and brook trout may grow proportionately faster than browns, in general, the maximum size of the majority of fish in a particular water will be dictated by the water's fertility – a subject which we shall be considering in some detail in Chapter 4.

Those wild trout whose parents migrated from a stillwater into a river or stream to spawn may remain in running water for one, two, three or more years. Indeed, some of them may never move into the lake. But as their appetites grow with their bodies, and the food supply becomes insufficient to support their numbers, many of them will drop back downstream to live and feed in the lake or reservoir. Not only is sub-aqueous animal and insect life likely to be much more plentiful here, but the trout will no longer be confronted with the need to expend energy constantly breasting the current; instead, they can cruise in search of food when they wish to and idle when they do not.

Most trout mature at about two years old, or shortly thereafter, and then run up the feeder streams in the autumn or winter to spawn and perpetuate the cycle. It is clear that they have strong, instinctive memories, for they almost invariably return to the streams of their births, just as salmon and sea trout nearly always migrate to their own birth places to reproduce.

Feeding

Trout are carnivorous predators, living on plankton, crustacea, insects, other small fish and so on. The diets of the various species are dictated by the environments in which they live. Where certain difficult to digest food forms are present in large numbers, the fish sometimes seem to have modified their digestive systems to cater for this. Examples are to be found in waters containing large numbers of snails. The trout in such places frequently appear to have enlarged muscular stomachs, but whether this is an hereditary characteristic, or whether the tissue simply builds up in response to a constant intake of hard, sharp food items is not clear.

Much nonsense has been talked about the feeding habits of trout, most of it as a result of fishermen crediting them with almost human moral standards. The contempt with which some people speak of 'cannibal' fish is well matched by the apparently common belief that brown trout in southern English chalk streams live exclusively on a gentile diet of Pale wateries and Iron blue duns.* Trout need food to provide energy, to repair living tissue and to sustain and increase their body weights, and they do not much care how they obtain it. The collection of food involves the expenditure of energy and, being instinctively logical, fish will rarely expend more energy on the acquisition of a particular item of food than that item is worth to them. They therefore concentrate their attention on those food forms that are easy to catch, which frequently means those that are available in substantial numbers. Although it is dangerous to generalise, it is probably true to say that sub-aqueous creatures make up 90 percent of the diets of most stillwater trout, and that floating insects do not often constitute more than about 10 percent of their total annual food intake. In some waters trout rarely, if ever, feed on the surface at all.

Trout do not normally feed on rotting animal matter, but they are extremely catholic in their diets, will try anything that looks edible, and regard a small, crippled insect or fish as easy prey.

In addition to the insects and crustacea which abound in the majority of stillwaters, fry and small fish feature in the diets of practically all trout of more than a few inches in length. For those trout that live long enough, there may come a time when they stop chasing relatively small food items but continue to take more substantial ones (including all species of suitable size). The transition may be a fairly slow one, or it may follow one of the periods of intensive fry feeding in which many trout indulge in the late summer, building up food reserves for spawning and the colder weather. The often unattractive physical appearance of such

---

* The following entry in the *Chronicles of the Houghton Fishing Club* nicely illustrates the fallacy behind this belief:

'29th July 1859 – A very large trout was known to have taken its station in the narrow channel which leads to the mill at Bossington. Many attempts were made to capture it, without success. At length, James Faithful succeeded, the bait being the intestines of a moorhen on a gorge hook. The fish proved to be a female weighing 5½ lb, in not very good condition. It was sent to the Treasurer in London.'

cannibal fish is due not to their diets but to old age and diminished hunting ability.

The minds of even the most skilful fishermen are sometimes taxed by selectivity amongst feeding trout. The phenomenon can be both intriguing and frustrating and is rarely either predictable or easily accounted for. It is certainly more common where there is a profusion of insect life and the water is particularly clear than where the water is stained or food is in short supply. And certain insects – the adult Caenis or Broadwing, for example – are clearly regarded by trout either as delicacies or as easy pickings. But the way in which fish can select individual types of food, present at the same time and in far smaller numbers than other insects or crustacea, defies explanation. Selectivity encompasses not only specific types of insect but also, amongst sub-aqueous creatures, those at very precise levels in the water. Perhaps the most frequent example of this is to be found amongst midge pupae where those hanging trapped in the surface film may be taken with great determination while their brethren an inch or so below the surface are completely ignored.

The times of day at which trout will feed at various stages of the season are governed by the types of food available and by the temperature of the water. Early in the year both water and air are cold, relatively few of the creatures upon which trout feed are much in evidence, and many of the fish are hungrily trying to regain condition after the rigours of the winter. At such times they may feed steadily all day but will usually remain close to the bottom where such insects as may be moving are likely to be found. As the water temperature rises and more food becomes available, their appetites increase and they start to move into shallower water. By mid-May they should be at their most voracious. But as the summer sun continues to heat the water, particularly the shallows where many minute creatures lurk amongst the weed, the fish confine their feeding more and more to early morning and late evening. As the weather cools down again in September and October, they will again feed through the day, sometimes with apparent urgency, in preparation for the hard times to come. It is worth remembering this and planning fishing trips accordingly. There is little to be said for reaching the water at 10 a.m. and leaving again at 6 p.m. in July or August when the rise will probably be over by the time you arrive and may not start again until the evening.

Temperature and Oxygen

Trout are particularly sensitive to changes in water temperature. The actual temperature ranges they will tolerate vary from species to species, but above and below certain maxima and minima they become torpid and stop feeding. The ranges within which they will breed naturally are narrower still, and this partially accounts for the fact that the imported species – rainbows and brook trout – rarely reproduce in the wild in Britain.

Trout also need well oxygenated water for survival. Cold, shallow, fast-flowing water absorbs oxygen more readily than warm, relatively deep, static water does. We shall be considering the oxygen content of various types of stillwater in the chapter on the trout's environment.

These two factors of temperature and oxygen content dictate the behaviour patterns of the fish to a great extent, and an understanding of them can be a most useful aid to fish location. For example, the brown trout is suited to a lower temperature range than is the rainbow so, as the surface water of a lake warms up in summer, the brown trout may be tempted to move into cooler, deeper water while the rainbow continues to feed in the shallows. And in lakes which are shallow all over, the fish will often seek out those areas in which there is most dissolved oxygen when the water warms up, for instance, around inlet valves in reservoirs or the mouths of feeder streams in lakes and lochs.

Eyesight

Trout hunt for their food by sight, rather than by any other sensory means, and a basic understanding of the fish's eyesight is of fundamental importance to the fly fisherman.

A fish's eye is not greatly dissimilar to that of a human being. Essentially, it consists of a hole (the iris) in front of a lens through which light passes to form an image on the inside of the back of the eyeball (the retina). The light falling on the retina is picked up by light sensitive cells and passed to the brain for interpretation. Whereas our eyes are protected by eyelids, the fish has none and, while humans control the amount of light reaching their retinas by dilating or contracting the iris, a fish's eye has a fixed iris and caters for alterations in light level by adjusting the relative positions of the retina's cells. This is a fairly slow process and fish can be effectively blinded for a while by a sudden increase in the intensity of the light. As is the case with most other creatures, a trout's eyes are at their most efficient when contrasts are sharp.

There is no doubt at all that fish can distinguish colour; their retinas consist of highly sensitive rods (cells which register only black, white and shades of grey) and relatively insensitive cones (colour sensitive cells), just as ours do. Whether fish perceive precisely the same colour range as ourselves is not clear. What is certain is that, water being a highly efficient light filter, the colours reaching a fish's eye at any substantial depth are markedly different to those at the surface. Broadly speaking, the warm colours – reds and oranges – are removed from the spectrum first and the colder colours – the blues and greens – penetrate furthest. This is of importance to fishermen and fly dressers alike as it should influence the choice of lures intended to be fished deep down, or which the fish may be expected to see from some distance away.

Trouts' eyes are located on either side of their heads and only provide binocular (three dimensional) vision over a fairly small arc. This three dimensional capability is important for judgment of distance which is, in turn, essential to efficient hunting.

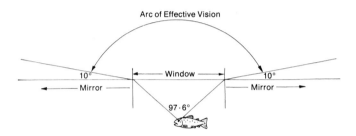

Fig. 2 The Fish's Window

One of the most significant but misunderstood aspects of piscine vision is that phenomenon known as 'the fish's window'. Only that light striking an imaginary disc on the water's surface immediately above the fish, at an angle of 10° or more, does so sufficiently directly to pass through and convey images from the outside world to the fish beneath the water. Objects near the centre of the window appear larger to the fish than do similarly sized objects towards its edge, and objects below an angle of 10° from the edge of the disc are effectively invisible to them. This window effect is vital to fishermen if they are to conceal themselves from their quarry.

Outside the window the fish sees the underside of the surface as a mirror from which, if it is calm enough, will be reflected images of his aquatic world. The mirror is just as important both to the fish and to the fisherman as the window is; perhaps more so. Insects floating on the surface above it go largely unseen by the trout but are identified by the indentations they make in it. Objects hanging from the surface in the mirror area, or positioned beneath it, including the myriad sub-aqueous creatures that trout eat, are visible in the mirror, providing the fish with two images – one directly seen, the other reflected. But perhaps the most significant feature of the mirror is the startling form in which lines and leaders cast on to it can appear to the fish below. A light-coloured fly line or leader, while possibly quite unobtrusive in the window, is likely to show in the mirror as a streak of white light, and may well scare far more fish than we realise.

It should never be forgotten that trout are shy creatures. They are easily frightened by the appearance of a man on the bank above them, the more so if he is dressed in clothing which contrasts sharply with his background and wields a gleaming rod and fly line over them.

Trout in streams and rivers have to face into the current to maintain station and to avoid drowning. The river fisherman can thus move upstream, fairly sure that he will generally be in that small blind spot immediately behind his quarry. Stillwater anglers are less fortunate. Trout in lakes and reservoirs cruise in their search for food and may face in any direction. There being no certain means of approaching them from the rear, stealth and caution become vital to success. Far too few people recognise this or realise how greatly their catches could be improved if only they would take care to conceal themselves. Indeed, I would go so far as to say that many of those who currently flail away trying to cast 35 or 40 yards could often halve their casting ranges and substantially increase their catches if only they would keep off the skyline, wear inconspicuous clothing, avoid using shiny equipment and squat or kneel down while they were fishing.

The same applies to the boat angler. There can be few more futile exercises than standing up in a boat to cast, presenting oneself to the fish as a black silhouette against a pale sky, when by sitting down fish may be caught within a rod's length.

Sensitivity to Sound and Vibration

Of course, trout can be disturbed by stimuli other than visual ones. Water is an excellent conductor of sound waves and fish have well developed sensory systems to make use of this fact. Although not externally visible, their ears, located where you would expect to find them, in either side of the head, are highly efficient. In addition, each fish has a series of vibration-sensitive cells running centrally along its flanks from head to tail and known as the lateral line. The lateral line's location can be clearly seen on trout as a dotted line on the skin. Using these two systems together fish are able to detect sounds 15 or 20 yards away and to estimate with some accuracy the direction from which the sound has come at up to about 10 yards' range. Their acute hearing serves both to attract their attention and to warn them of danger, and a heavy footfall on the bank will send them scurrying for cover whether its source is visible or not.

Fish are just as sensitive to poor boat handling as they are to clumsiness on the bank, perhaps more so. Stamping about, the thumping of anchors, oars and other equipment, and heavy rocking (usually induced by the angler who stands up to cast) are all likely to scare off any fish in the immediate vicinity.

Taste and Smell

Trout have highly developed senses of smell and are able to identify very low concentrations of noxious chemicals in the water. In contrast, their sense of taste is relatively inefficient. Although most of the creatures trout eat give off little smell, and there is therefore scant evidence to suggest that the fish use this facility in their search for food, some odours clearly attract them and they probably find others repellent. So, it is worth remembering to rinse our hands from time to time, especially when we have been fiddling with an outboard motor, smoking or whatever.

So much for the general characteristics of trout. Now let us turn our attention to the individual species.

THE BROWN TROUT (*Salmo trutta*)

In origin, the brown trout is primarily a European species and may be found in the wild from Finland in the north to Morocco and Tunisia in the south, and from Ireland eastwards to the area around the Caspian Sea. It is versatile and adaptable and has been further introduced into parts of North and South America, South and East Africa, the Indian sub-continent, Australia and New Zealand. In all of these places it has thrived and prospered, reproducing naturally wherever clean, well oxygenated water runs over a gravel bed at a steady temperature of between 5° and 13°C (41–55°F).

Brown trout are to be found in rivers and lakes throughout the British Isles. They are most prolific where the water is clean and well oxygenated and where the bottom is of rock or gravel rather than of mud. For this reason, they tend to inhabit the upper and middle reaches of rivers, rather than the slower running, more heavily silted lower ones. Where stillwaters are concerned, they are highly adaptable and do well almost everywhere except in parti-cularly shallow, muddy lakes. While they may abound in highland lochs and tarns, large trout are seldom found in such waters which are generally soft and relatively infertile. In harder lowland lakes, where prolific weed growth can support a wealth of insect life, these fish may easily grow to 6, 8, or even 10 lb in weight. Because they require running water in which to breed, brown trout can only become established in lakes and reservoirs which have suitable feeder streams.

Brown trout vary enormously in appearance and habitat, so much so that for many years biologists and anglers believed that there were many sub-species. Only fairly recently have they accepted that, for all the variations on the theme, there is no physiological difference between the silvery Loch Leven trout, the Irish gillaroo and dollaghan, Ferox – the lake trout, or even the migratory sea trout (under any of its colloquial names – sewin, peal, finnock and so on).*

Like most fish, brown trout have light underbellies and dark upper surfaces, but beyond this, it is not easy to generalise about their coloration which is highly dependent upon the backgrounds against which they live and the food they habitually eat. The base colour of a brown trout's flank may be anything from silver through assorted shades of cream, gold and bronze to a deep, rich brown. Superimposed upon this, he may have dark spots or blotches in a wide range of sizes and intensities. These marks are generally, but not always, limited to the upper two-thirds of the fish's abdomen, may or may not extend to the gill covers and often have light-coloured haloes around them. In addition to these black or dark grey markings, many brown trout have additional orange or red spots on their flanks.

The brown trout's scales are relatively small when compared with those of (for instance) the vendace or powan, but they are not so small as to give the fish the leathery appearance of the American brook trout. The brown is notable for his solid, almost straight edged tail, and for the fact that his camouflage markings do not extend to his fins. As a juvenile, the adipose fin frequently has a distinctive reddish tinge which may disappear as the fish matures.

Early in the season, in March or April, brown trout tend to lurk in the deep water, just as rainbows and American brook trout do. Hatches of surface flies are spasmodic and infrequent at this time, there is little in the way of weed growth – so such insect life as may be available is likely to be found near the bottom, and the water temperature is low, making the fish disinclined to feed seriously.

By May, the water has started to warm up, the weed has begun to grow in the shallows and the small creatures upon which trout feed

* Although there is, indeed, no identifiable biological difference between brown trout and sea trout, so distinctive is the latter's behaviour that many authorities still very reasonably prefer to give it a separate classification.

are noticeably more accessible to the fish. May and June are almost invariably the best months for brown trout fishing, regardless of the whereabouts of the lake or reservoir.

But brown trout are primarily cold water fish and, as the summer sun warms the upper layers of the lake, they tend to sink back into the cooler, deeper water. They may be very difficult to locate at such times, particularly on large stillwaters, and even when found they may not readily take a fly. Indeed, not until September do these trout present a consistently practical proposition for the conventional fly fisherman once again.

From the middle of the season onwards, stillwater brown trout often engage in ferocious bouts of fry and minnow feeding amongst the weed beds in the shallows. The angler who knows what to expect and what to look for at this time of year may reasonably anticipate a challenging and exciting day's sport.

Brown trout are generally solitary creatures but, at the approach of autumn, they may congregate around the inflows of feeder streams in preparation for their spawning runs. Here, too, the thinking angler may turn the fish's habits to his own advantage.

The brown trout holds a rather special position in the hearts of most British trout fishermen. It is native to these islands. In appearance and behaviour it has a dignified modesty unmatched by its perhaps more spectacular trans-Atlantic cousins. Unlike the rainbow, which having inspected an artificial fly and rejected it once will often ignore it entirely thereafter,* a brown trout may accept the fisherman's offering on the first, the tenth or even the hundredth presentation. And when he does so, his deep, powerful, head-shaking fight has an unmistakable bulldog quality.

THE RAINBOW TROUT (*Salmo gairdneri*)

In some respects, the rainbow trout is a more colourful creature than the brown. Native to the Pacific coastal region of North America, it is to be found from southern Alaska to California.

Unlike the brown trout, the rainbow has several distinct and separate sub-species, although they are all very similar in appearance. The overall scientific name, *Salmo gairdneri*, includes both exclusively freshwater varieties and the migratory strains, often referred to as 'steelheads'. Most, if not all, of the rainbows introduced into Britain prior to 1890 were probably *Salmo shasta*, a race originating in the McCloud River area near Mount Shasta in the Sierra Nevada. Like our own brown trout, Shasta rainbows

---

* While this is a fair generalisation, it is worth noting that a rainbow can sometimes be teased into taking a fly.

breed in the autumn or early winter, and they have a less pronounced migratory instinct than do most other varieties. Subsequent crossing of Shasta rainbows with spring spawning ones has produced an assortment of mixed strains which have become so confused that it is probably now impossible to find any single pure strain in Britain. This is unfortunate as the breeding seasons of the original sub-species varied from October or November through to March or April, and cross-bred fish from trout farms here have become highly unpredictable in their spawning habits. The sad consequence of all this is that fishermen have had to learn to live with the fact that out of condition rainbows may come to the net at any time during the first half of the trout season.

At its best the rainbow trout is a most handsome fish, but at its worst it can be a very sorry looking creature. In the late summer, when at the peak of condition, a rainbow is bright and silvery. A phosphorescent magenta stripe runs along each flank from head to tail, and the upper two-thirds of its body is liberally flecked with small black spots. The spots extend on to the fish's head, its dorsal and adipose fins and its tail, where their presence may be taken as a definitive feature of the species. The corners of the tail are generally somewhat rounded, and the vertical trailing edge has a marked indentation at its centre.

Rainbows can tolerate, and indeed prefer, higher water temperatures than do brown trout, and this may partially account for the fact that they will only breed naturally in a very small number of British streams and rivers. However, they are hardy, adaptable fish and, growing markedly faster than browns, attaining weights of up to about 3 lb in two years, are well suited to artificial breeding and rearing both for stocking fisheries and for the table.

The fact that they rarely reproduce in British waters does not prevent rainbows from undergoing the biological changes associated with spawning. Immediately prior to, during and after spawning, they darken very noticeably in colour. A cock fish can turn almost black at this time and, when caught, will often discharge a stream of white milt.

Like their brown cousins, rainbows generally remain in the deeper water early in the season but, as the temperature rises and the weed grows, providing partial sanctuary for the creatures upon which trout live, they start to feed nearer the surface and in the inshore shallows. Being markedly more tolerant of high water temperatures than browns, rainbows often remain within the angler's reach throughout the rest of the season. They may move into deeper water to feed on animal plankton from time to time, but rarely skulk on the bottom as brown trout will.

Rainbows, particularly young ones, tend to shoal, and this characteristic has two important implications for the fisherman. Whereas the capture of a brown trout provides no substantial evidence that there are more in the area, the landing of a rainbow may well indicate that others are about. But while catching a rainbow may bolster the angler's optimism, there is some circumstantial evidence to suggest that these fish have a limited ability to communicate amongst themselves. It is certainly not uncommon for a shoal to ignore an artificial fly completely once one of its number has been pricked, or hooked and lost, even when two or three fish may already have been cleanly taken on that pattern without disturbing the others.

When hooked, the rainbow frequently fights on or near the surface. But, although he may be more acrobatic and spectacular than the brown trout, he seems to lack the latter's stamina and determination, sometimes surrendering after one or two fast, powerful runs and a relatively short tug-of-war.

THE AMERICAN BROOK TROUT (*Salvelinus fontinalis*)
While rainbows and American brook trout both come from the same continent, they have little else in common. Whereas rainbows are native to America's western seaboard, brook trout – also known colloquially as speckled, mountain, native and squaretail trout – originate from the cooler, eastern coastal belt. They are to be found in the wild from Labrador and Newfoundland in the north to Georgia in the south, but they have also been planted in many other parts of Canada and the United States.

The brook trout is a species of char and, like its European cousin, the Arctic char (*Salvelinus alpinus*), shows a marked preference for cold, clear, running water, or for deep mountain lakes and tarns. It is extremely intolerant of pollution in any form but, unlike the brown trout or the rainbow, will occasionally breed in stillwater.

Brook trout were first imported into Britain in the mid-nineteenth century, and further batches have been introduced from time to time since then. Those who sought to stock British waters with them may have drawn encouragement from the fact that self-perpetuating colonies of the fish had established themselves in one or two places here, notably in the Welsh mountains and some Lake District tarns. But, in general terms, the importers' efforts have been ill-rewarded, primarily because of the brook trout's inability to survive in temperatures above about $15°C$ ($59°F$), its requirement for absolutely pure water and its particular susceptibility to several of the Salmonid diseases.

Nevertheless, the brook trout is a sporting and attractive fish, as well as an excellent table one, and continuing efforts to rear it in this country on a commercial basis qualify it for more than passing reference in a book of this sort.

In appearance, the brook trout is distinctive for the minute, deep-set scales which give its skin an almost leathery texture, and for the dark green marbling on a yellowish green background which covers the top of its body, its dorsal fin and its tail. Its flanks are generally a yellowish olive, flecked with bright vermilion spots, fading into a delicate pink beneath its belly. Its lower fins (pectoral, ventral and anal), and its tail, have sharply defined black and white stripes on their leading edges. At spawning time, the fish's whole body takes on a deep reddish tinge.

Like our native brown trout, the brook trout spawns in October or November, which fact makes it compatible with our existing closed season regulations. It regains condition rapidly throughout the late winter and can provide good sport early in the season, long before most rainbows have come back into their own. But it abhors warm water even more than the brown does, and tends to retire to the depths early in the summer, rarely to be seen again before the autumn.

The brook trout has something of a reputation for gullibility and will sometimes slash at an angler's fly time after time, until eventually hooked. I must confess to having caught few of these fish, but have found their fight to be rather unspectacular. As a table fish it has few equals; its flesh is firm and, provided that its diet has included a high proportion of carotene-rich food, it may be noticeably pinker than that of most rainbows or brown trout.

HYBRIDS

Many Salmonid species may be induced to cross-breed. Efforts have been made from time to time to produce new strains which will grow significantly faster than either parent species. While fish farmers engaged in such experiments have chiefly been concerned with the improvement of marketable table fish, the research is also of some potential interest to the angler. All the hybrids are sterile and therefore have no need to don the livery of mature, breeding fish. If it were practicable to stock a stillwater exclusively with trout of this type, there would seem to be no logical reason for the imposition of a closed season, but whether such liberalism would really benefit the trout, the fisherman or the water is a question to which serious thought should be given.

Perhaps more important than the chance of being able to extend the fishing season is the opportunity offered by hybrid trout for improvement in the general appearance of stocked fish. Stumpy tails and twisted or missing fins, caused by fighting, particularly during the breeding season, have become the grotesque hallmark of many rainbows from relatively small stewponds. Immature fish, up to two years old, are far less quarrelsome than adults, and it may be that sterile, crossed trout will be less aggressive throughout their lives than fully grown rainbows. Certainly, they seem to put on weight every bit as rapidly as any of their pure-strain parents, so there should be no commercial objection to continuing to breed them.

The 'tiger trout' (a brown trout/American brook trout cross) and the 'cheetah trout' (a rainbow/American brook trout cross) have both received publicity in the angling press. Perhaps more physically attractive than either of these is an apparently nameless rainbow trout/Arctic char hybrid which has been reared successfully by at least one British fish farmer. Although some of these strains have been used for occasional stocking of one or two small stillwaters in southern England, little objective information on their behaviour, fighting characteristics or table qualities seems to be available.

CHAPTER 3

The Trout's Diet

The fisherman who has a working knowledge of the seasons and behaviour of the creatures upon which trout feed enjoys a double advantage over his less well informed colleagues. Hungry trout tend to congregate where the food is; so, if the whereabouts of the food can be determined, as it often can, then the trout should be easier to locate. And if the shape, colour, size and movement of a particular piscine delicacy are known, then an imitation of the natural creature can be selected from the fly box and moved through or over the water realistically, pandering to the fish's most consistent and predictable instinct, the feeding one.

Trout have remarkably catholic diets. They will try almost anything provided that it is small enough to be taken into their mouths, particularly if it moves. Autopsies produce an amazingly varied assortment of strange items, from cigarette ends to buttons and from swans' feathers to pebbles, but such oddities must surely be the results of over-indulged curiosity. By nature, trout are carnivorous predators and their prey provides them with the carbohydrates, proteins and fats necessary for growth, tissue replenishment and energy. The list of the creatures trout eat is a long one and includes the larvae, nymphs, pupae and adults of a vast range of flying insect species as well as animal plankton, shrimps, snails, small fish, water boatmen (corixae), beetles, worms and so on.

Fortunately, trout tend to concentrate most of their attention on the creatures which are easiest to catch and which are available in the largest numbers. Equally fortunately, these same creatures are reasonably evenly and widely distributed throughout the British Isles, and the diets of trout in Scotland and Ireland are much the same as those of their cousins in England and Wales. Certainly, there are regional differences – some insects prefer peaty, acidic water, others favour more fertile, alkaline habitats – but, with a certain amount of justifiable generalisation, it is quite possible to draw up a reasonably concise list of those animal minutiae that most trout eat most often, and to be confident that any food item omitted from it will be taken by trout only occasionally or exceptionally rather than frequently and regularly.

MIDGES (*Chironomidae*)

The chironomids, colloquially known as midges or buzzers, are by far the most important of all the creatures upon which trout live in Britain. Widely spread throughout our islands, present in phenomenal numbers wherever they occur, and with one or more of the almost 400 identified species hatching at every stage of the season, they are bread and butter to the fish.

Midges go through four stages during their lives. Eggs laid on the water's surface hatch after three or four days and the emerging larvae sink to the bottom. These larvae, which may grow to as much as 1 in in length, are worm-like in shape. They vary in colour from a pale, translucent, watery grey through various shades of yellow and brown to green and red, depending on the species. Green and red are the commonest hues, the latter being known for obvious reasons as 'blood-worms'.

Some midge larvae build protective cases for themselves, but the majority are free swimming and move through the water with a characteristic, figure-of-eight lashing motion. They live close to the bottom and amongst the mud and weed, feeding on vegetable matter. As the day of their transformation to adulthood approaches, they pupate.

The pupal phase of the midge's life generally lasts for no more than a few days. The pupae are comma-shaped and range from less than $\frac{1}{4}$ in to over 1 in in length. They have small heads, dark, bulbous thoraces and clearly segmented, tapered abdomens tipped with short, feathery 'tails'. The larger, bushier filaments which protrude from the fronts of the creatures' thoraces are used for breathing. Midge pupae are to be found in a wide assortment of colours with black, green, orange-silver and brown being the commonest.

The pupae lurk amongst the weed near the bottom until almost ready to hatch, and then wriggle up to the water's surface. Here they have to penetrate the surface film before the winged adults can emerge. This may take some time, particularly on still days when the film has a high degree of elasticity.

When a pupa eventually succeeds in breaking through, its skin splits from the front of the thorax backwards and the winged adult struggles free, often flying off almost immediately.

Adult midges are all similar in shape but vary widely in size and colour. They have clearly segmented bodies and translucent, heavily veined wings which they hold flat along the tops of their abdomens when at rest. They mate on the wing and often form dense clouds where buildings, high trees or shrubbery provide shelter from the evening breeze. After mating, a female returns to the water to lay her eggs, her body assuming a markedly hooked shape.

Although trout eat midge larvae in substantial quantities, pupae rising to hatch present even easier pickings. Particularly in the early morning and late evening, when the air is still and the surface tension of the water is high, the fish can become engrossed with the struggling pupae, and may feed on them to the exclusion of all other food forms. They eat the adults too, but as these winged flies generally take off almost immediately after hatching, at a time when there are plenty of pupae about, they tend to be of less interest to the fish. Females returning to the water to lay their eggs and lying 'spent' on the surface afterwards can stimulate trout into surface feeding.

SEDGES (*Trichoptera*)

After midges, sedges are probably the commonest component of most trouts' diets from the beginning of June onwards. There are about 200 species in the British Isles and they vary widely in size and colour. Here again, three stages in the insects' lives are of concern to fish and fisherman alike.

Sedge larvae, or 'caddis grubs' as they are often called, range from $\frac{1}{4}$ in to over 1 in in length. Their abdomens, segmented and rather leathery in texture, taper quite steeply, and are generally brown or buff in colour. They are bottom dwellers. Most of them build protective, tubular cases for themselves from sand, grit, shells or vegetation and, with only their heads, legs and the fronts of their bodies showing, crawl about the lake bed dragging their homes.

When ready to pupate, the larvae withdraw into their cases and seal off the ends. After a period of days or weeks, the pupae chew themselves free.

Sedge pupae, which vary in colour from dull, creamy yellow through amber to brown or green, depending on the species, have small heads and thoraces and plump, segmented bodies, pointed at the tails. While the adults' antennae and legs are generally visible, fully formed, beneath the pupal skin, and the wings are encased outside it, one pair of legs, heavily fringed with hairs, is free to be used for propulsion.

Sedge pupae do not generally remain near the bottom for long but paddle erratically up to the surface, or climb up emergent vegetation to hatch.

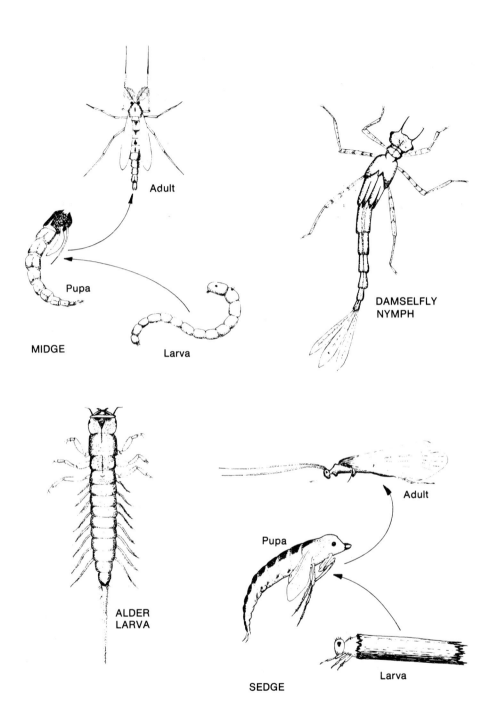

Adult

Pupa

MIDGE

Larva

DAMSELFLY
NYMPH

ALDER
LARVA

Pupa

Adult

Larva

SEDGE

Fig. 3

Adult sedge flies, which range in colour from cream to assorted shades of mottled brown and grey, are readily identifiable by the roof-like manner in which they carry their wings over their backs when at rest. Some are as little as $\frac{1}{4}$ in long while others are as much as 1 in from head to tail.

Sedges are eaten by trout in all three stages of their lives. As larvae, they provide easy bottom feeding throughout the year. The pupae, weaving their tortuous ways to the surface are particularly vulnerable and, at dusk, the newly hatched adults, fluttering and scuttering in their frantic attempts to get airborne, can cause great excitement amongst the fish which often slash at them with wild enthusiasm.

UP-WINGED FLIES (*Ephemeroptera*)

Of all the creatures trout eat, the up-winged or day-flies are probably the best known to most fishermen, mainly because of their prominent position in fishes' diets in rivers, lochs and loughs and the well established practice of using artificials tied to represent them. While stillwater trout in man-made waters do feed on up-winged flies, they do not normally seem to place the same importance on them as they do on midges and sedges. Nevertheless, some half-dozen ephemerid species are of significance to trout in British lakes, and we can realistically group them into four categories, olives, sepia and claret duns, Mayflies and caenis.

All these insects have similar life cycles. The nymphs live underwater, either crawling on the bottom or swimming amongst and around weed beds. When ready to hatch, a gaseous layer builds up beneath their skins and, aided by its buoyancy, they swim to the surface where their nymphal cases split and the duns – winged adults – emerge. After drying their wings for a short while, the duns fly off to the waterside vegetation where they undergo a further metamorphosis, their skins splitting again and the second stage adults – the spinners – emerging. Spinners tend to be markedly brighter, shinier and slightly smaller than duns. After mating, the female spinners return to the water to lay their eggs, dying soon afterwards to lie spreadeagled, or 'spent', in the surface film. Although the nymphs of most up-winged flies spend about a year growing beneath the water's surface, the adult insects are unable to feed, and the whole remarkable sequence of transitions, from nymph to dun, from dun to spinner and, thereafter, to death, rarely takes more than a day or so.

Up-winged flies are eaten by trout as nymphs, duns and spinners.

Olives (Clöeon Spp) : There are two common species of stillwater olives in Britain, the Lake olive (*Clöeon simile*) and the Pond olive (*Clöeon dipterum*). As their colloquial names imply, the former thrives in larger lakes and reservoirs while the latter prefers smaller, more sheltered waters. Both do better in hard, alkaline lakes than in soft or acidic ones.

Olive nymphs grow to about $\frac{1}{2}$ in length. Their body colours vary widely, from light yellow ochre flecked with brown, to a much darker, almost sepia hue. The gill plates which cover their thoraces are almost black and each insect has three tails, banded with brown. Olive nymphs are very agile swimmers and can dart from weed frond to weed frond with remarkable rapidity.

Pond olive duns may hatch at any time from late May to September, but the Lake olive's appearance is normally limited to the early summer. The duns each have two dusky, blue-grey wings and two tails. Their bodies may be any shade between light olive-grey and a fairly deep chestnut colour, and they are generally just under $\frac{1}{2}$ in in length.

Olive spinners are very slightly smaller than the duns, and have bodies ranging in colour from glistening apricot (hence the Pond olive spinner's colloquial name – Apricot Spinner) to quite a dark mauvish brown. Like the duns, each has two tails and two wings, the latter being clear and translucent, sometimes faintly tinged with orange or brown.

Claret and Sepia Duns (Leptophlebia Spp): Although the Claret dun (*Leptophlebia vespertina*) and the Sepia dun (*Leptophlebia marginata*) are as similar to each other in appearance and behaviour as are the Lake and Pond olive, their seasons differ much more widely. The Sepia dun is an early season fly, appearing in April, while the Claret dun hatches between May and July.

Both species seem to prefer peaty, slightly acid water to anything more fertile, and their nymphs are poor swimmers, spending their lives crawling about amongst the vegetation on the lake bed. These creatures, about $\frac{1}{2}$ in long and dark or reddish-brown in colour, have almost black wing cases, and their three tails are widely spread. As the time for their transformation to adulthood approaches, the layer of gas building up beneath their skins gives them a noticeably silvery glint.

The duns, when they hatch, have dark, chestnut brown bodies and each has three tails. The Claret dun is just over $\frac{1}{4}$ in long with large, dusky grey forewings and very much smaller, fawn-coloured rear ones. The Sepia dun is a little larger and all four of its wings are a watery yellowish-brown with heavy, dark brown veining.

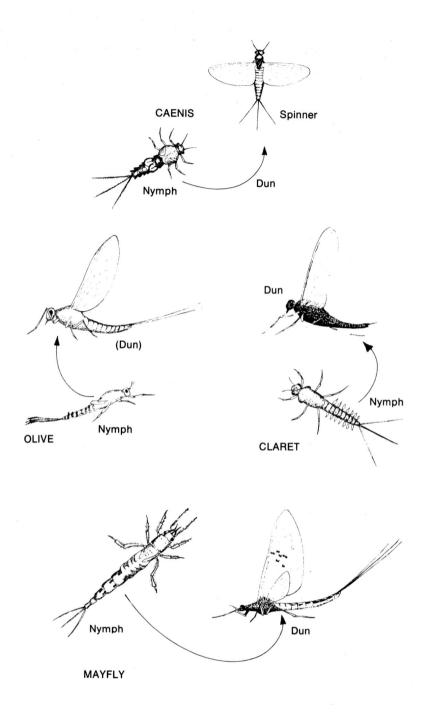

CAENIS

Spinner

Nymph

Dun

Dun

(Dun)

Nymph

OLIVE

Nymph

CLARET

Nymph

Dun

MAYFLY

Fig. 4

The spinners of both species are similar in size to the duns. Their wings are bright and clear with faint light brown veining. The Claret spinner's body is very dark, almost black, with a slight reddish tinge to it, while the Sepia spinner is a lighter shade of brown.

Although both species are eaten by trout in all three stages of their lives, the nymphs rising to the surface to hatch probably provide the easiest pickings.

Mayflies (Ephemera Spp): Mayflies hatch in considerable numbers on only a few British stillwaters, but they are more common on some of the great Irish limestone loughs. Wherever they appear in quantity, they can cause great excitement amongst trout and trout fishermen.

Three separate species of Mayfly are native to the United Kingdom – *Ephemera danica, E. vulgata* and *E. lineata*. Fortunately for fishermen, only the first two are widespread and, as they are very similar in appearance, we may reasonably treat them as a single species.

The Mayfly, our biggest up-winged fly, is unmistakable in all three stages of its life. The nymph, which grows to be about 1 in in length, is a singularly unappealing creature. Its body is a pale fawn colour, sometimes with a slight brownish tinge to it, and by the time it is fully developed the wing cases, which cover much of its thorax, are a dull brown colour. Prominent feathery gills project laterally from all but the last three segments of its abdomen and curve up over its back. The Mayfly nymph, a poor swimmer, spends most of its life burrowing in the mud and silt of the lake bed and only emerges a week or so before hatching. In late May or during the first half of June it swims to the surface where the nymphal case splits and the dun emerges.

The Mayfly dun is a full $\frac{3}{4}$ in long in the body and its three grey tails are at least twice as long again. While the insect's head and thorax are almost black, its abdomen is a pale creamy-grey colour with dark brown or grey markings on top. Its large, sail-like wings are a lustreless, dusty, pale grey, heavily veined in brown with several dark brown patches on them.

The Mayfly spinner, when it appears, looks not unlike the dun in terms of size and general colour, but is altogether more brilliant. Its thorax and abdomen gleam and its glossy, translucent wings, lightly veined, generally have only a few small, dark patches on them.

Where Mayfly hatches are sparse trout are often very wary of such outsized winged adults, but may well take the ascending nymphs with confidence. Indeed, on some waters, the Mayfly nymph is the one insect which seems to attract the larger trout which otherwise spend most of their lives grubbing about near the bottom, feeding on snails and small fish. Where Mayfly hatches are prolific and the fish become accustomed to them, both duns and spinners provide gourmet temptation to the trout, the former as they sit drying their wings on the surface, the latter when they return to the water to lay their eggs and die.

Caenis: It is difficult to conceive of a more dramatic contrast than that between the large and spectacular Mayfly and the tiny, inconspicuous caenis. Not without cause are these minute creatures known as 'the Angler's Curse'. Trout feeding on them on a summer's evening can become very selective and difficult to tempt.

Of the five species of caenis to be found in Britain only two, the Dusky and Yellow broadwings, are of any real concern to the stillwater fly fisherman, and they are so similar in general appearance that we may realistically treat them as one.

Caenis nymphs, no more than $\frac{1}{4}$ in long, somewhat rotund, and coloured dark brown with black gill plates covering their thoraces, are bottom dwellers, spending their lives crawling about amongst the gravel and pebbles on the lake bed. They hatch during the evenings from early June until August.

Caenis duns and spinners are, for all practical purposes, similar in appearance. With an overall body length of less than $\frac{1}{4}$ in, their thoraces are a dirty brown colour and their abdomens a pale, creamy yellow. Their wings, wide for their height – which provides the insect's alternative colloquial name, 'Broadwing' – are a very pale, translucent grey.

Trout occasionally feed on the nymphs both near the lake bed and as the insects rise up through the water to hatch, but they can become infuriatingly preoccupied when taking egg-laying or spent adult females from the surface. The emergent dun is of relatively little interest to the fish as it hatches quickly and flies off almost at once.

ZOOPLANKTON

Although trout do not generally make zooplankton their sole food source, they often feed intensively on these tiny creatures for short periods and, in certain reservoirs, rainbows may actually make plankton their staple diets for several months during the summer.

Zooplankton is the generic name given to a vast range of minute, even microscopic, aquatic animals. Amongst them, and of particular interest to fish (and therefore to fishermen), are some fifty species of minute crustacea including daphnia (the water fleas), rotifers (*Brachionus*), cyclops and a single insect, the Phantom larva

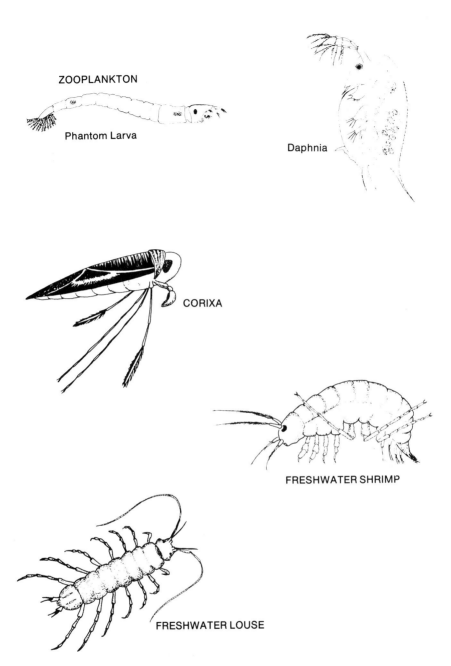

ZOOPLANKTON

Phantom Larva

Daphnia

CORIXA

FRESHWATER SHRIMP

FRESHWATER LOUSE

Fig. 5

(*Chaoborus*). Most of these animals are vegetarian, living on phytoplankton (minute aquatic plants), but a few feed on other, smaller animals. This fact is significant to the angler because the density of plankton is directly related to the availability of the plankton's food. When the water is cold in the winter there is little sunlight for photosynthesis, phytoplankton is sparse and, with virtually nothing to feed on, so is animal plankton. As the water warms up and the hours of daylight lengthen, phytoplankton reproduces rapidly (often causing a misty 'bloom' in the water) and shortly afterwards the zooplankton follows suit.

Also of importance to fishermen is the daily downward migration in which planktonic animals indulge and which seems to be a direct reaction to sunlight. During the night, clouds of zooplankton may be found at or near the water's surface but, as the sun climbs in the sky, the tiny creatures sink steadily. By 6 o'clock in the morning they can be as much as 30 ft or more down, and they may have retreated to a depth of over 70 ft by midday. Gradually rising through the afternoon and evening, they reach the surface again at about midnight, only to start the whole cycle once more. The fisherman who wishes to present his fly to trout feeding on plankton must first discover the depth at which the creatures themselves are to be found and, thereafter, make allowances for alterations in the levels at which they are concentrated.

Confirmation that trout have been feeding on zooplankton may be provided by autopsy which will reveal a tightly packed, grey, somewhat gelatinous mass in the fish's stomach.

SMALL FISH

Most stillwaters have their own populations of minnows, sticklebacks and coarse fish fry. These small fish tend to congregate in shoals in the shallows, around weed beds and close to the cover provided by wooden pilings, valve towers, landing stages and so on. Most trout will feed on them occasionally or even steadily throughout the season but, in the late summer and early autumn, quite large numbers of both browns and rainbows will often indulge in prolonged bouts of fry feeding in preparation for the more spartan months ahead and for spawning.

Although their whereabouts may not always be apparent, it is sometimes quite easy to locate fry-feeding fish. If flocks of sea birds are present they will often wheel and stoop where trout are attacking fry, picking up crippled or injured stragglers from the surface. And, at closer range, the small fish may sometimes be seen leaping in panic as a marauding trout attacks the shoal.

CORIXAE

The Lesser Water Boatman is one of those rare creatures more generally referred to by its scientific name, corixa, than by its colloquial one. Although some thirty or more species have been identified in Britain, they all look much alike apart from some variations of size and colour.

Up to $\frac{1}{2}$ in or so in length, egg-shaped in plan view and slightly flattened when seen from the side, the corixa is readily identifiable by the mottled yellow, olive or brown wing cases which cover the whole of its back, and by the two powerful paddles which stick out horizontally from either side of its thorax. Unable to extract oxygen from the water, it has to make periodic trips to the surface where it collects a bubble of air on the short hairs of its abdomen before swimming back down to its weedy, shallow-water habitat. This it does by rowing itself jerkily upwards, and its return journey, buoyed up by the newly acquired air bubble, can be a noticeably laborious affair.

Corixae can, in fact, fly and frequently do so in mid- to late-summer, covering substantial distances at remarkably high speeds. They are available in the water throughout the year. In some places – Blagdon and Eye Brook are both examples – trout feed on them voraciously; in others, the fish largely seem to ignore them, even though they may be present in considerable numbers.

FRESHWATER SHRIMPS (*Gammarus Spp*)

Freshwater shrimps are prolific in many British stillwaters but dislike stagnant, acid or peaty ones. Nine separate species have been identified, the commonest being *Gammarus pulex*, but as they are all broadly similar in appearance – apart from some variations of size – we may reasonably treat them as one.

The freshwater shrimp is a crustacean which lives among the weeds or close to the gravel on the lake bed. Requiring well oxygenated water for survival, it is often to be found near the inflows of feeder streams. Its body, ranging in length from about $\frac{1}{4}$ in to almost 1 in, is noticeably hump-backed when at rest, but straightens out as the creature moves off. Throughout most of the season, it is a watery, translucent fawn or yellow ochre colour but, as the midsummer mating season approaches, it takes on a brownish hue, sometimes tinged with blotches of red.

Freshwater shrimps generally swim on their sides and propel themselves through the water quickly and smoothly with rapid movements of their swimming legs.

Unlike their cousins in some chalk streams, stillwater trout do not generally eat large numbers of freshwater shrimps. Nevertheless, the shrimp does constitute an appreciable proportion of the diets of fish in some lakes and reservoirs, and has the merit of being available throughout the year.

DAMSELFLIES AND DRAGONFLIES (Order: *Odonata*)

Damselflies and dragonflies are commonly found around many stillwaters, especially smaller ones with plenty of marginal reeds and rushes. In their adult forms, the two groups are easily distinguished from each other by the fact that the damselfly folds its wings over its back when at rest while the dragonfly's are carried outstretched.

Damselfly and dragonfly nymphs are aquatic, living amongst the weed in shallow water.

Damselfly nymphs are elegant creatures. Their slender, brown, olive or pale green bodies grow from about $\frac{3}{4}$ in long early in the season to $1\frac{1}{2}$ in or more in midsummer. They blend in well with the leafy fronds upon which they spend much of the time crawling about in search of the other insects upon which they live. When they swim, they do so with a rapid sinuous, snake-like, wriggling motion.

Dragonfly nymphs, which may grow to be 2 in or more in length, are much stockier insects with somewhat bulbous abdomens. Their colour range is not dissimilar to that of the damselfly nymphs, but fawns and browns seem to predominate. Although they are primarily crawlers, dragonfly nymphs have a system of jet propulsion which enables them to put on remarkable turns of speed over short distances when disturbed. They are ferocious predators, living on other large aquatic insects and the fry of all fishes.

When ready to hatch, the nymphs either climb up emergent vegetation or crawl ashore. Once out of the water, their skins split and the adults emerge.

The winged insects are a familiar and colourful sight above and around many stillwaters. In their myriad, gleaming hues, they hover in the air, occasionally darting this way and that, or drifting gently on the breeze. After mating, the females return to the water, either dipping their tails to the surface film or, in some instances, actually crawling back beneath it to deposit their eggs.

Trout take the nymphs freely from early summer onwards, particularly when the insects venture into the open prior to hatching. They will take the egg-laying adults, too, slashing at them with an enthusiasm more generally reserved for struggling sedges.

SNAILS

Some fourteen species of snails are commonly found in British stillwaters, and they may reasonably be divided into two groups – the ramshorns and the bladder snails.

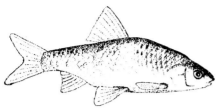

ROACH FRY

STICKLEBACK

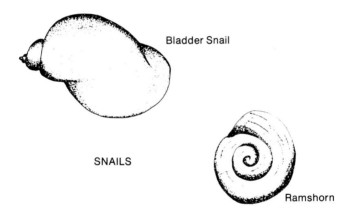

Bladder Snail

SNAILS

Ramshorn

Fig. 6

The ramshorns have flattish, disc-like shells which are actually coiled, tapered tubes, narrow at their centres and widening as they spiral outwards to their apertures. They range from less than $\frac{1}{8}$ in to over 1 in in diameter, and from a chalky, greyish-white through olive and brown to black in colour.

Bladder snails are very much more rotund and many of them resemble garden snails in appearance. They may be anything from $\frac{1}{8}$ in to $\frac{3}{4}$ in across and are most frequently mid- to dark-brown in colour.

Snails are normally fairly sedentary creatures, spending their lives trundling about on weed stems, stones, submerged timbers and amongst the silt of the lake bed. But during July, August and early September they sometimes indulge in mass upward migrations to hang in the surface film by their feet, their shells suspended below them. Although they are to be found in autopsies performed on trout throughout the season, the fish tend to concentrate on them during this late summer migration.

THE ALDER LARVA (*Sialis lutaria*)

The Alder fly is a familiar creature on many stillwaters from late April until early June. With its mottled mid- and dark-brown wings held roof-like over its back when at rest, it looks not unlike a sedge, although it is, in fact, a member of an entirely separate order, the Megaloptera. Surprisingly, stillwater trout rarely seem to take much interest in the adult insect but will sometimes eat the larvae in substantial numbers.

The Alder larva is a remarkably unattractive creature. Growing to over 1 in in length, it has a buff-coloured head and thorax, and a long, chestnut brown abdomen. Seven fibrous, yellowish tracheal gills emanate from either side of its abdomen, and it has a single, spikey tail. Its sturdy legs identify it as a crawling insect. It spends a good deal of its life buried in the mud of the lake bed, only emerging to feed at night. The Alder larva is a predator and lives on the other small creatures which abound in the silt. When disturbed, it will rear up menacingly, lifting its thorax and the front half of its abdomen into a near vertical position.

In March or early April, the larvae start to sally forth in daylight, and a month or so later they crawl ashore to pupate and hatch. It is mainly during this shoreward migration that the Alder larva falls prey to bottom feeding trout.

FRESHWATER LICE (*Asellus*)

Freshwater lice, which are to be found in teeming millions in many British stillwaters, seem to turn up only occasionally in autopsies on trout. About ½ in long when fully grown, and with brown, segmented and somewhat flattened, shell-backed bodies, they look not unlike their familiar terrestrial cousins, the wood-lice. They spend their lives crawling slowly about on water weed or amongst rotting vegetation on the lake bed and are available to the fish throughout the year.

TERRESTRIAL INSECTS

Although most of the insects and crustaceans upon which trout feed are aquatic, a few terrestrial species find their ways on to the water sufficiently often, and are eaten by fish in sufficient quantities to warrant some consideration by the angler.

One such visitor to the trout's larder is the Hawthorn fly. About the size of the common house fly, black and with a distinctive pair of long, trailing legs, it is remarkable for the fact that it is just about the only flying insect which sinks when blown on to the water. Where shrubs or trees line the windward side of a lake or reservoir, Hawthorn flies may fall on the surface in substantial numbers during the early spring, and trout are rarely slow to take advantage of their arrival.

During the late spring and the summer, several species of beetles may be blown on to the water and attract the fish. The Cockchafer and the Coch-y-bonddu are, perhaps, the best known amongst them. Beetles vary widely in appearance and the angler who wishes to take advantage of their appearance should seek local advice or personally examine specimens upon which he finds trout feeding.

Crane flies, or Daddy-long-legs, are notoriously bad fliers and are often carried on to the water by the wind during July, August and September. Although there are several hundred species of crane fly, the bodies of the commonest are about $\frac{3}{4}$ in long and dull buff or brown in colour. Each insect has six long, gangling legs. When it finally force-lands on the surface, it generally lies there with its wings buckled and its legs spread out behind it, providing a tempting target for trout. Crane flies are at their most prolific in warm weather, just after a shower.

Several varieties of moth make their homes among marginal vegetation at the waterside. Here again, there are so many species of differing shapes, sizes and colours that it would be quite impracticable to list them all in a book of this type. When carried on to the water, frequently in the late evening, they are often taken by trout feeding close inshore.

Ants have most complicated life histories and are not, day-by-day, of any great interest to fish. But, by some extraordinary quirk of nature, they may suddenly sprout wings in the summer, especially during hot, thundery weather, and a coincidence of flying ants, favourable wind and trout-inhabited water can produce spectacular fishing for the angler who is prepared for it.

Finally, where trees or bushes overhang the water, a wide range of creeping and crawling insects may fall like manna from heaven to fish waiting below. Caterpillars, grasshoppers, spiders, ants, beetles, woodlice and centipedes all make occasional mistakes and, particularly in hot weather when the foliage provides a bonus in the form of shade from the sun, it is quite usual to find one or more good-sized trout in residence, seizing feeding opportunities as they occur.

CHAPTER 4

The Trout's Surroundings

Water, the element in which our quarry lives, differs in many ways from the terrestrial environment with which we are more familiar, and exerts a powerful influence on the trout's growth and habits. An understanding of the basic physical, chemical and biological properties of stillwaters can be of great assistance when we are trying to calculate whether a lake with which we are unfamiliar will produce worthwhile trout or not, and to hazard a reasonable guess as to where they may be and what they may be feeding on.

Where locating fish is concerned, the river angler is fortunate. The flow of the current, the positions of overhanging trees, of rocks, boulders and weed beds, the angles of bends and the way in which the stream undercuts the banks are all visible aids which help him to read the water and predict where the trout are likely to be. And, because rivers are often relatively shallow and clear, it is generally quite easy to establish what the fish are eating. The stillwater fisherman has few such obvious signs to help him and must learn to rely instead on more conscious and calculated reasoning.

Trout seem to be wholly lacking in intelligence or in powers of reasoned thought, but are programmed by nature to respond to an assortment of natural stimuli – hunger and the availability of food, temperature, wind direction and wave action, and the need for shade and cover. If we can acquire a working knowledge of these factors, and of the ways in which they influence the fish's behaviour, we should be able to predict where the trout will be concentrated in a particular water at a particular time of year with reasonable accuracy and consistency.

But the study of water is a science in its own right and discourses on it tend to be punctuated with long words and unmemorable technical terms. So, in this chapter we shall examine the principles involved in water's behaviour and its effects on the fish in some detail while, at the same time, sweeping aside as much of the jargon and mystique as possible.

Having already considered the trout and their food, it will be apparent by now that, far from being independent and self-sufficient creatures, these fish must always form part of a natural pyramid of life. At the base of this pyramid are the simplest aquatic plants, at the apex the large predators – pike, herons, otters and, not least of all, men. At various levels between these extremes come all the other crustaceans, insects, snails, fish and so on.

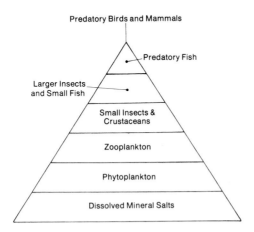

Fig. 7   The Pyramid of Life

The pyramid's structure is complex and an individual creature's size is not necessarily indicative of its position in the order of things. A classic, if somewhat extraordinary, example of this is to be found in salt water where certain whales live exclusively on plankton. But, in general terms, myriad tiny creatures are eaten by hundreds of thousands of small ones and the small ones are, in turn, preyed upon by relatively few larger ones. The foundations upon which the pyramid is built in any stillwater are the simple plant forms upon which the smallest insects and crustacea feed. Without this basic herbage, zooplankton and other minute animals would be unable to survive, the larger insects would perish, the fish would starve and we would have nothing to catch.

So, elementary plant life is essential to the maintenance of life in water, and plants themselves have certain fundamental requirements for growth. They need food, sunlight and reasonably well aerated water.

Phytoplankton and other non-rooting plants draw their food directly from the water in the form of dissolved mineral salts. Rooting water plants obtain sustenance both from the water and from the lake bed which must also provide adequate anchorages for them.

Rainwater has virtually nothing dissolved in it and the fertility of the water in a lake, measured in terms of its dissolved mineral content, is almost entirely dependent upon the geological nature of the rocks over or through which it has flowed. If that rock is soft, like chalk or limestone, the water will have been able to absorb substantial quantities of mineral substances from it and will be 'hard'. If the rock is hard, like granite, the water flowing over it will have absorbed very little and will be 'soft'.

We are all familiar with 'hard' and 'soft' water. The former, a rich mineral solution, washes soap away with ease; the latter, chemically barren, or almost so, removes soap only with difficulty. Hard water, especially that rich in calcium carbonates, is potentially fertile. Provided that it is sufficiently well aerated, that sunlight is available and that it is not polluted, it should be able to support teeming masses of plant and insect life. All aquatic animals require calcium for growth. The shells of snails are composed almost entirely of a form of chalk, as are the exoskeletons of shrimps and other crustacea and insects. With calcium, potash and phosphorous salts encourage algal and weed growth, and aquatic vegetation provides both food and shelter for the creatures upon which trout live. Very soft water is relatively infertile and cannot sustain the phytoplankton upon which the pyramid of life is built.

We should not, of course, think only in terms of black and white – there are bound to be many shades of grey in between. Few waters are very hard indeed and few contain no mineral salts, but the degree of hardness or softness will dictate the quantities of living matter that a particular lake or reservoir can support, and will exert a strong influence on the types of species available there as trout food. For example, Pond and Lake olives show marked preferences for fairly hard waters, while Claret and Sepia duns are most commonly found where the water is on the soft side.

Fish themselves need calcium for the formation of their bones and scales. The correlation between the hardness of water and the sizes of naturally fed trout, of considerable importance to fishermen, is well illustrated by the following table:*

* From an article 'Notes on the Water Conditioning of a Small Reservoir with Lime and Chalk', by D. M. G. Pilleau, published in *The Salmon and Trout Magazine*, No. 209, March 1977.

			Trout at end of 3rd year
Soft waters:	0–49 ppm	Devon rivers, Scottish lochs	15 cm (6 in)
Average water:	50–149 ppm	Lake District	20 cm (8 in)
Hard water:	150–249 ppm	Hampshire rivers	25 cm (10 in)
Very hard water:	Up to 350 ppm	Blagdon Lake	30 cm (12 in)

(ppm = parts per million)

From time to time we come across references to a water's pH value. This is a measurement of its acidity or alkalinity. The scale runs from 1 to 14 with pH7 representing the neutral value, everything below pH7 being acid and everything above it being alkaline. Generally speaking, trout can survive within the range pH4·5 to pH9·5 providing that they are acclimatised. Stock trout reared in alkaline water of, say, pH7·5 would not tolerate a sudden transfer to acid water of, say, pH6.

The pH value of a stillwater will vary throughout the season and even during the course of a single day. Carbon dioxide, introduced into lakes and reservoirs both by rain and by the respiratory action of aquatic plants and animals, combines with the water to form carbonic acid. Weeds and algae take in carbon dioxide in sunlight and emit it in the dark, causing a trend towards alkalinity in the daytime and towards acidity at night. An immense proliferation of algae in the spring, with its associated drastic reduction in the carbon dioxide (and, thus, the carbonic acid) content of the water, can raise the pH value dramatically in a short space of time, causing deaths amongst newly stocked trout.

Incompletely decomposed vegetable matter carried in suspension can markedly increase the acidity of water. Particularly where feeder streams run beneath lengthy expanses of trees or over peaty moorland, they often take on a brownish tinge, the colour of milkless tea. As the particles causing this staining have neutral or near neutral buoyancy, they do not readily precipitate out when the current slows on entering stillwater, so the lake itself is likely to be coloured.

Where a lake or reservoir lies amongst arable farmland, man's own attempts to increase the land's productivity may dramatically alter the water's character. Nitrate fertilisers spread on surrounding fields can be washed down into the valleys by rainwater, or they may seep through the underlying rock into the water table itself. In either event, the fertility of the water will be increased. On the face of it, this might appear to be beneficial, but in reality it is often disastrous. The balance of nature is a very delicate one. Algae and water plants have evolved to grow normally within only a fairly narrow range of dissolved mineral levels. When the mineral levels are artificially raised, the plants frequently grow at breakneck speeds, quickly filling and choking the water. Although the insect life may thrive in stillwaters where this has happened, larger creatures rarely do so, and the fisherman, unable even to cast a line, must give up in despair.

So much for the chemical composition of water. The next requirement for plant growth is sunlight.

Plants need sunlight for photosynthesis – the process by which they convert mineral salts into food. When discussing the fish's eyesight we noted that water was a highly efficient light filter. Even in the cleanest, clearest water all the colours of the spectrum apart from blue and, perhaps, green have disappeared by a depth of about 45 ft, and absolutely clear water is very rare indeed. Most frequently, suspended silt, particles of dead vegetation, or living algae and phytoplankton significantly reduce light's penetration of the water. It is impossible to say at what depth there will still be sufficient light for photosynthesis because the amount of suspended matter varies from place to place, and throughout the year as plant life flourishes and fades. But there are few lakes or reservoirs in which many plants can survive for long at more than about 30 or 35 ft, and most aquatic vegetation is generally found within 20 ft or so of the surface.

In addition to a plant's light requirement for photosynthesis, almost all living matter, both animal and vegetable, needs a degree of warmth for growth. Just as light is absorbed by the water, so is the heat from the sun's rays, and only the upper layers of any stillwater ever warm up sufficiently for algae, rooting plants, insects, crustacea and so on to flourish and reproduce. In fact, the whole business is rather more complicated than might at first be apparent.

Water is at its densest at 4°C (39°F). Above or below this temperature it is less dense and rises, which accounts for the fact that ice, at 0°C (32°F) floats on the surface. During the winter the water in most British stillwaters has an even temperature of 4°C from top to bottom, and is mixed by wave action and by the currents from feeder streams. As the sun rises higher in the sky during the spring and summer, the upper layers are warmed. Gales in April or May may re-mix the water, raising its overall temperature. But, by midsummer, a warm layer will be floating on the remainder and will have so increased in temperature that separation between itself and the cold mass below will be complete. The dividing line between the warm surface water and that beneath it can be very sharp; moving downwards, the temperature may drop by 10°C (18°F) or more in a matter of inches. The depth at which this dividing line occurs will depend on the clarity of the water, the amount and intensity of the sunshine to which it is subjected during a particular summer, the frequency and strength of winds in the spring and, to some extent, the temperature and volume of water flowing into the lake. A calm spring followed by a hot summer will produce a deep, warm, upper layer in a clear-water lake. A blustery spring followed by a cool summer will produce a thinner, cooler one in a lake made misty by algae and suspended matter.

While all this may sound a little complicated, it is of fundamental importance to fishermen. The vast majority of any stillwater's flora and fauna will be found in the upper, warm water layer, and trout in the open, particularly rainbows, often show a marked tendency to feed right on the dividing line between the warm and cold layers. It follows, too, that rooting plants which harbour many of the creatures upon which trout live will mainly be found where the water is less than about 20 ft deep, and that in lakes with steep sides this food-rich area will be confined to quite a narrow band around the margins and to such shoals as may project upwards from the lake bed.

Although the warm upper water remains clearly separated from that below it throughout the summer, its depth at any particular point can be altered by wind action. A persistent moderate breeze can move the warm water across a lake, piling it up against the downwind shore, and may even so denude the upwind side that the cooler mass below actually reaches the surface. Like the creatures they eat, fish show a marked preference for warmer water and actively avoid cold areas when feeding. So, when fishing a lake over which a steady breeze has been blowing for some days, it will often

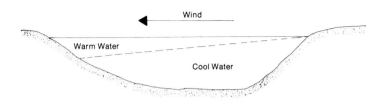

Fig. 8   The Wind Wedge

pay to make for the downwind shore where feeding fish are likely to have congregated.

The two layers having remained separate throughout the summer, the warm, upper one starts to lose heat to the atmosphere as soon as the air temperature drops below its own in the autumn. As the temperature gap between the two water layers closes, their ability to mix increases, and a few days of high winds early in the winter are generally enough to complete the blending process.

The third and final major requirement for life in lakes is that the water should be reasonably well aerated. All animals require constant access to oxygen in order to survive. Water carries dissolved oxygen and most aquatic creatures are equipped with gills of one sort or another in order to make use of this fact. Although plants give off oxygen by day, the vast majority of the water's dissolved supply comes from surface contact with the air. Cool water absorbs oxygen more readily than warmer water, and rough water has a greater surface area – and, therefore, a greater ability to absorb oxygen – than calm water. It follows that large, shallow lakes are likely to be better oxygenated than deep ones with small surface areas; that stillwaters frequently exposed to strong winds and, perhaps, fed by rippled or tumbling streams will contain more dissolved oxygen than sheltered, spring-fed ones, and that lakes or reservoirs in which even the upper layers remain reasonably cool through the summer will generally hold their oxygen better than those which become warmer.

We have already seen that the need for sunlight for photosynthesis and for warmth point to the likelihood that the majority of aquatic life will be found in the upper strata of most stillwaters; the requirement for well aerated water does nothing to contradict or alter this. While surface water can replenish its stock of dissolved oxygen through contact with the air, such gases as there may be in the cooler, deep water early in the year are liable to be exhausted quite quickly by the few creatures and plants which exist there, with little opportunity for replacement. In the summer, the deeper water is effectively cut off from the outside world and can become almost completely devoid of dissolved gases. Obviously, trout food (and feeding trout) are more likely to be found in well oxygenated areas than in ones which have become deoxygenated.

In addition to the prerequisites for life in stillwaters two more factors can exert considerable influences on the behaviour and whereabouts of our quarry.

Trout tend to congregate around underwater features – ridges, hillocks, hollows and weed beds. Aquatic landmarks are more common in artificial stillwaters than in natural ones. Where man has left his mark on land which has then been flooded, ditches, hedgerows, spinneys, paths and even buildings will still be evident after many years, and fish seem to be attracted to them. The managements of most major reservoirs sell charts of their waters and these can be of great assistance. In their pristine state they show underwater contours, deep areas and shallow ones, and the rapidity with which depths change. With a little careful study, the angler can add to this information by extending hedgerows, tracks and ditches into the flooded areas and, with experience supplemented by tactful questioning of knowledgeable locals, it should be possible to plot the positions of other features. Apart from the very considerable benefit to one's fishing success that such exercises can produce, this sort of incidental research can provide a good deal of pleasure and satisfaction in its own right.

It should be apparent by now that the wind has an important effect on the behaviour of water in lakes and on the creatures which inhabit them, and that the greater the surface area of the water, the greater the effect of the wind will be. In fact, interpretation of the influence of wind on fish confronts us with something of a dilemma. Trout generally face into the wind in stillwaters, just as they face upstream in rivers. As they feed, they tend to move upwind and it would seem reasonable to expect that in a fair and consistent breeze, they would all eventually end up with their noses pressed firmly against the upwind shore. In practice, this rarely seems to happen. The situation is further complicated by the fact that trout often feed busily in areas where wave action stirs up silt and, with it, a feast of nymphs, larvae, shrimps and so on. Such areas are invariably found on downwind shorelines and, perhaps more significantly, where waves roll obliquely on to the shore. With only personal experience rather than calculating logic to support the contention, I would suggest that the boat fisherman should take advantage of the trout's propensity for upwind travel, and that the bank angler should generally seek an area in which the wind blows diagonally towards him.

A breeze will often produce 'wind lanes' or 'food lanes' across the surface of a lake – long streaks of relatively flat water, frequently bordered by thin lines of scum or foam amongst the more general turbulence. They result from a complicated spiralling movement of the surface water. The scum is usually a concentration of phytoplankton carried up from below and the calmness in the middle of the lanes is probably caused by thin films of phytoplankton having an 'oiling' effect on the surface. Since trout habitually follow the plankton up, fishing the wind lanes, particularly along their edges, can pay substantial dividends. Wind lanes appear on small waters as well as on large ones and may be fished from the shore just as they may from a boat. Only in infertile waters, with little algal growth, are wind lanes uncommon or unknown.

If all this seems a little academic, perhaps we can bring it to life and illustrate its significance for trout fishermen by relating the theory to various types of stillwaters to be found in the British Isles.

Contours evident above the water tend to be reflected beneath it and highland lochs, generally set amongst steep-sided mountains, are often deep, shelving down quickly from their shores. Except where streams have built up underwater banks or shoals by carrying silt and pebbles down from the hills, or where a particularly hard outcrop projects upwards from the bottom, their areas of shallow water are confined to narrow bands around the margins. The hills which surround them are usually of hard rock and water flowing off them in streams and small spate rivers is predictably soft – poor in dissolved mineral salts. It may also be peat-stained or coloured with partly decayed vegetation, reducing the ability of sunlight to penetrate into it.

Such lochs are, inevitably, relatively infertile. The trout in them may be prolific if there are reasonable numbers of feeder streams with plentiful redds, but they will mostly be small and those that grow to any great size will probably do so by adopting cannibalistic diets. With little food in the water, these diminutive wild brown trout are likely to be free rising, especially in the spring, the early summer and the autumn, and they can provide exhilarating sport if reasonably light tackle is used. They will most often be found in the shallow, marginal areas, particularly where overhanging trees or well vegetated banks are likely to provide them with supplies of terrestrial insects. They can also be expected to frequent offshore shoals and the areas around the mouths of feeder streams where they may expect food to be washed down to them.

Characteristics of this sort are not reserved exclusively for natural lochs. Any stillwater with similar physical and geological attributes is likely to produce small trout which behave in this way. Lake Vyrnwy in Wales is a good example of an artificial reservoir where the fishing closely resembles that on a highland loch.

The lowland lochs and loughs of Scotland and Ireland contrast sharply with their highland counterparts. Set amongst weathered and undulating chalk, limestone or sandstone hills, they tend to be shallow with gently sloping sides. The very fact that the countryside in which they are set is low-lying and rounded is evidence that it is relatively easily eroded and that water draining off or through it is likely to be hard and fertile.

Because large areas of their beds are exposed to sunlight and their water is rich in dissolved mineral salts, lowland lakes are able to support a wealth of algae, rooting plants, animal minutiae and fish. The trout in them will generally be fat and well fed, but may not be as prolific as their cousins in highland lochs because feeder streams with suitable redds are less commonly found here than they are among the mountains. With a wide variety of food forms continuously and readily accessible to them in great quantities, lowland fish may well be selective and difficult to tempt with an artificial fly. And with their food available over so great an area of the lake, their whereabouts and movements will often be more difficult to calculate and predict than will those of trout in highland lochs. Here we must apply our knowledge of the seasons, the whereabouts and the behaviour of those creatures that trout eat, and learn to interpret the day-to-day influence of the weather on the fishes' behaviour, if we are to give ourselves a reasonable chance of locating them consistently.

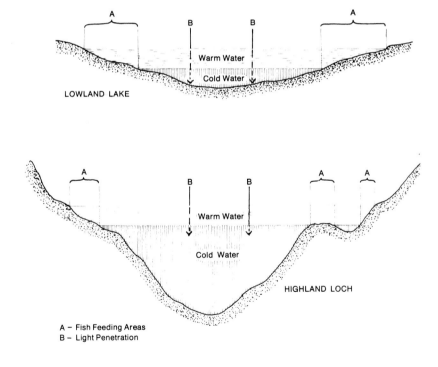

Fig. 9   Stillwaters in Section

Artificial counterparts of natural lowland stillwaters are to be found in reservoirs like Blagdon, Eye Brook and Bewl Bridge, but there is a complicating factor. A reservoir exists to provide a service to the public and, throughout each summer, water will be drawn off, lowering the levels quite considerably. The effect in these impoundments, with their often gently sloping banks, is that the marginal shallows are left high and dry for part of the year, killing weed, algae and insects which might otherwise have thrived there. Where the margins are of silt or earth, the damage caused by such exposure may be partly compensated for by the appearance of earthworms, beetles and so on, terrestrial creatures which can provide substantial if somewhat transitory feeding for hungry fish, and by the fleeting appearance of terrestrial vegetation which rots and fertilises the water when re-submerged. But where the bottom is of stone, gravel or grit, it is at risk of becoming an aquatic desert.

Small stillwaters take many forms. Some are natural, some have been left behind by quarrymen and some have been created as fisheries or ornamental lakes, either when gardens or estates were laid out or by latter-day landowners as commercial propositions. All of them tend to reflect in miniature the overall characteristics of their larger counterparts. Small highland hill lochs or lochans may not be as deep as more imposing lochs in the valleys, but they usually draw their water from similarly barren or acidic sources and their trout are very often free rising but diminutive.

Lowland areas are generally more heavily populated than highland ones, and most of their lakes are heavily fished. Few, if any, such stillwaters in Britain could now sustain entirely wild trout populations without resorting to a rigid catch-and-return policy, so stocking with farm-reared fish has become standard practice. Today's stillwater fishermen seem to expect their trout from such waters to average 2 lb or so in weight, and owners therefore feel obliged to stock with fish of about this size, with a few larger ones and, perhaps, a few smaller ones to add interest and variety.

Since these trout are introduced with a view to their being caught within weeks or even days, the nature of their environments will have little effect on their growth, although they may start to lose weight if the stocking density is too great. But certain factors will still influence their whereabouts, food, temperature, oxygenation and shade being the four most important.

While shallow lakes of about 30 acres or less in extent may not normally be subject to temperature layering in the true sense, their fish still congregate in the depths early in the season and brown trout tend to withdraw back into them again through July and August. In a long, hot summer, water coming in from spring-served feeder streams may be markedly cooler and better aerated than that already in the lake and the trout frequently seek it out, or lurk in the shade provided by overhanging trees. It is also noticeable that, on small, hard-fished stillwaters, the fish tend to gravitate towards the more lightly fished banks as the season progresses and that, by the mid to late summer, there can be quite substantial crowds in parts of the fishery inaccessible to anglers.

So far we have considered stillwaters only in general terms. Most of those in the British Isles fall into one of our three categories – highland lochs, lowland lakes and small fisheries of up to about 30 acres. Of those that do not, the vast majority come so close to one or another of the types that a little thoughtful interpolation should enable the average angler to read them intelligently. But there is one glaring exception, so different from all other stillwaters that it demands special mention.

Grafham Water in Cambridgeshire is a unique and extraordinary artefact. It is also one of Britain's most popular and productive reservoirs. 1670 acres in extent and 70 ft from surface to bed at its deepest point, it lies amongst fertile countryside. The water supplying it, fertile and rich in dissolved mineral salts, supports massive crops of phytoplankton and a consequent wealth of zooplankton upon which the fish thrive, putting on weight with startling rapidity. Many of the rainbows here live almost exclusively on plankton throughout much of the summer and have acquired a well-earned reputation for their handsome appearance and their flavour as a result.

Although the bank fishing at Grafham can be excellent, particularly late in the season when large trout move into the shallows to harry shoals of coarse fish fry and sticklebacks, the availability of such enormous quantities of plankton across the whole of this vast man-made lake can make fish location difficult and often gives the boat angler a distinct advantage over his shore-bound or wading colleague. Those who understand the significance of temperature variations in the water and can predict the vertical migrations of plankton clouds tend to do markedly better than those who rely heavily on luck or intuition.

Finally, a few words about the weather. Many non-anglers seem to believe that fishermen are only happy when it is raining. My own experience suggests that, while ideal fishing weather is hard to define, climatic extremes usually reduce sport. Rain, sleet, snow, a heavy mist lying on the surface, bright sunshine, excessive heat and winds blowing from between north and east all seem to discourage fish from feeding at or near the surface. In contrast, a mild day with broken cloud and a light southerly or westerly breeze may well produce a memorable catch. But let us not blame the weather when we fail to catch trout. Rare indeed are days when the fish are truly uncatchable, and there can be a good deal more satisfaction in the capture of a single fish under difficult conditions than of a quick limit when the piscine population of a lake is in suicidal mood.

CHAPTER 5

The Tools for the Job

Since choice of tackle is a subject upon which all experienced fishermen – and many inexperienced ones, too – have strongly held ideas, what follows must inevitably reflect my own personal views and preferences to a large extent. If some pundits disagree with my recommendations, then I would only remind them that this is the one subject upon which no two anglers are ever really likely to be in total accord.

Compared with his coarse or sea fishing counterparts, the trout fisherman travels lightly laden. Essential to his purpose are a rod, a reel, a line, an artificial trout fly and some nylon with which to connect the fly to the line. Beyond this basic equipment there is a mass of ancillary paraphernalia – landing net, priest, fly boxes, scissors, hook hone, floatant, sinkant and so on – some or all of which most fishermen will acquire and carry with them, but none of which is vital.

While a fly rod acts as a shock absorber during the striking and playing of a fish, and may be used to keep trout clear of potentially hazardous bankside vegetation and other obstructions, its primary function is to act as a spring with which the fly line, the nylon leader and the fly or flies are projected out over the water. In order to work in this way it must be loaded with a weight and, as flies and leaders weigh almost nothing, the weight is built into the fly line.

On the face of it, it might seem logical to choose a rod first and then to build up the rest of one's tackle around it. In fact, it is not. The type of tackle chosen should be dictated, firstly, by the natures of the lakes, lochs or reservoirs the angler expects to fish most often and, secondly, by the fishing technique which holds the greatest appeal for him. These two factors, combined, will provide guidance as to the types and weights of lines that will be needed, and only when the line or lines have been chosen should a matching rod be selected.

Lines

Fly lines – generally consisting of a Dacron core contained within a pliable plastic coating – are available in an extraordinary variety of profiles and weights, and may be designed to float or to sink at an assortment of speeds. In some – known as 'sink tips' – the major part of the line remains on the surface while the first 10 ft or so sink.

For some years now, a fly line's particular characteristics have been described by the use of a series of letters and numbers – the Association of Fishing Tackle Manufacturers' code – which clearly summarise the line's profile, the weight in grains of the first 10 yds and whether the line is designed to float or to sink; for example, a line might be described by the code DT6F.

The first letter (or letters) indicates whether the line is level (L), double tapered (DT), weight forward (WF) or a shooting head (ST) – all of which expressions we will discuss anon. The number which follows indicates the weight, and the last letter (or letters) indicates whether the line is a floater (F), a sink tip (F/S) or a sinker (S). There has recently been some talk of adding to the final letter for sinking lines to indicate their relative densities. This would be a useful advance as, at present, all sinking lines, from slow sinkers to high density ones, are described with the single letter 'S'.

So, our DT6F is a double tapered floating line, the first 10 yds of which weigh 6 grains; and a WF8 F/S is a weight forward line, the first 10 yds of which weigh 8 grains, the main body of which floats while the first 10 ft or so sink. If the weights mean little to the newcomer, it may reasonably be said that lines numbered 5 and below are generally regarded as being on the light side for stillwater fishing, that 6s and 7s are in the middle of the range and that 8s and above are heavy.

Level lines are cheaper than tapered ones but have few other virtues to commend them to the stillwater fisherman. They are a little difficult to cast with, particularly in a wind, they do not 'shoot' through the rod rings as, for example, a weight forward or the backing of a shooting head will, and they quite often arrive on the surface with something of a splash. Nowadays, they are only available in a limited number of weights, and few serious fishermen use them on lakes or reservoirs.

A double tapered line is easy to cast with and can present a fly delicately but, being relatively large in diameter for much of its length and therefore building up considerable friction against the rod rings, it cannot be cast as far as can a shooting head or a weight forward. Nevertheless, many experienced anglers will select a double tapered line in preference to all others, especially for boat fishing or for casting on small lakes where distance is not the main objective.

There is a myth, perpetuated by some people in the tackle trade, that when one end of a double tapered line has become worn, the whole thing can be reversed on the reel, exposing the unused end and effectively doubling the line's useful life. In fact, modern fly lines, exposed to the air, lose plasticiser whether they are actually being flailed out over the water or not. If a line is used very frequently indeed, wear and tear, rather than loss of plasticiser, may render the working end unusable. But with normal usage, by the time the line needs turning, the back end is already likely to be deteriorating to the point at which the whole thing will need replacement. Ten or twelve yards cut from one end of a double tapered line for use as a shooting head can be used just like a double taper, can be cast further when necessary and will offer less drag to a running fish. As a bonus, the remainder can be tightly sealed in a plastic bag and stored almost indefinitely in the dark, at an even temperature, for similar use at some future date.

As its name implies, the bulk of a weight forward (or 'forward tapered') line is concentrated in the front half, the rear half being, in effect, a lightweight level line. A weight forward's great virtue from the stillwater fisherman's point of view is that, once the main belly of the line has been aerialised, the slender rear half will shoot easily through the rings, allowing the angler to cast markedly further than

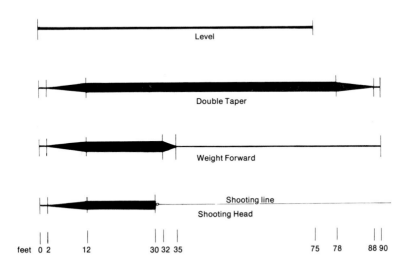

Fig. 10   Typical Fly Line Profiles

he would be able to with a double tapered line. Some people suggest that a weight forward lacks some of the finesse available from a double taper but, in my own experience, if this is so, the difference is marginal.

'Long-bellied' lines are, to all intents, weight forward lines with their main bulk concentrated over a greater length. They are claimed to combine the distance-casting qualities of a weight forward with the accuracy and delicacy of a double taper. I have never fished with one, but they do not seem to be particularly widely used, and I suspect that they may have turned out to be something of a compromise, incorporating the less desirable features of the other lines, rather than the more desirable ones.

At its simplest, a shooting head consists of 10 yds of double tapered line spliced to a flattened nylon monofilament backing line. In order to cast it, the line is extended by false casting until the splice is a foot or so beyond the tip ring of the rod and, when the final forward cast is made, the backing or shooting line runs out freely with a minimum of friction. Shooting heads are available ready-made or they may be made up by the angler in a variety of lengths and profiles from full-length fly lines. They enable the reservoir fisherman to cast for phenomenal distances – 35 yds is by no means exceptional – and they have the less obvious advantage of providing much less drag than a full-length fly line does when towed through the water by a heavy fish. Many of the leader breakages that occur on large stillwaters result from the strain imposed on the nylon by a full-length fly line, particularly when that line picks up weed. Slender backing line not only offers less resistance to the water but it may also cut through aquatic vegetation rather than collect it. A further advantage of a shooting head is that it allows a smaller and lighter reel to be used, which is important with a very light rod.

The angler who has been used to using a full-length double tapered or weight forward fly line will find that casting with a shooting head requires a little practice. In all but the most expert hands there is a tendency for the head to arrive on the water less delicately than a full-length line does and, unless it is carefully handled, the shooting line can become tangled quite easily. But there can be no doubt that for those who do most of their trouting with lures or traditional patterns on large reservoirs, a shooting head will be more generally useful than any other type of line.

It is, perhaps, worth nothing that, because of their higher densities – and, therefore, their relative thinness – sinking lines create less friction within the rod rings than floating ones, cut through the air better and can consequently be cast further.

As we have already seen, an angler's choice of line should largely be governed by the type and size of water he expects to fish most often, and by his preferred style of fishing.

For small stillwaters, up to about 30 acres, floating and medium sinking lines (either double tapered or weight forward) in the range AFTM 6 to 8 should suffice for the beginner whether he plans to fish imitative patterns, traditional ones or lures (we shall be discussing the various types of fly at a later stage in this chapter). He may wish to add a sink tip once he has gained experience, but many people find them awkward to cast with and they offer few advantages over a floating line used with a long leader, except perhaps in a strong wind.

Anglers who plan to use imitative patterns from the banks of larger expanses of water, reservoirs and lochs, should find that similar lines to those suggested for use on smaller lakes will suffice. Nymph fishing requires that the taking of the fly by a trout should be seen, rather than felt, and there is therefore little point in casting so far that the leader cannot be clearly seen on the water's surface; indeed, there may be much to be lost by so doing. However, for those who would fish with lures or with traditional or attractor patterns, the ability to cover large areas by long-distance casting may offer considerable advantages. Shooting heads, both floating and sinking, in the AFTM 7 to 10 range will help to achieve this.

The reservoir boat fisherman may use his boat as an anchored casting platform, or he may allow it to drift with the wind. In either event, but particularly in the former, he may need to be able to cover the same casting distances as those sought by his colleague on the bank, and will require similar lines, perhaps with the addition of a fast-sinking shooting head to reach down into the depths.

A note of warning should be sounded here. The advent of some very deep 'concrete bowl' storage reservoirs like the Queen Mother Reservoir at Datchet, and the discovery that large brown trout can be taken from the depths at places like Grafham and Rutland Water, have produced an upsurge in the use of level, lead-cored trolling line made up into shooting heads. Without entering into a discourse on the rights or wrongs of the practice, it should be said that such equipment is virtually impossible to cast with and that the line, heavy and thin, can be extremely dangerous in inexpert hands. No novice should contemplate including such a line amongst his initial fly fishing tackle, and even experienced anglers should fully appraise themselves of this kind of line's capabilities and limitations before trying to use one.

The traditional style of loch fishing from a drifting boat involves casting a short line downwind or slightly across the wind, retrieving it and recasting. As distance casting offers little if any advantage here, the lines chosen may be relatively light, in the AFTM 5 to 7 range, and double tapered. Although a floater is likely to be most generally useful, the armoury could be supplemented to advantage with a slow sinker or a sink tip.

Finally, and to save those who expect to fish a variety of waters with an assortment of techniques from having to permutate a single set of general purpose lines from all the information given above, a collection of AFTM 7 lines, including a double tapered or weight forward floater, a floating shooting head and a weight forward medium sinker would probably cater adequately for all but the most extreme conditions.

Having decided upon the range of lines he plans to use, the angler is now in a position to choose a rod.

Rods

Lancewood, greenheart and steel alloys having been buried in history, cane, fibreglass and carbon fibre are the materials in most general use for rod making today. Each has its advantages and disadvantages, and good, bad and indifferent rods are available in all three materials.

Cane rods, built from carefully cut and bonded triangular sectioned lengths of Tonkin bamboo, still have a large following amongst experienced and traditionally minded fishermen. Although they are heavier, length for length, than their fibreglass or carbon fibre counterparts, they often feel gentle in the hand and can deliver a fly accurately and with delicacy, particularly over short distances. It is their weight that militates against them from the point of view of the stillwater angler who is likely to have to cast further and more often than his colleague on a river. They also tend to be expensive, and I rather suspect that those who still use them for lake fishing do so out of custom and, perhaps, a little sentiment, rather than for more practical reasons.

Fibreglass rods are less expensive than either cane or carbon fibre and are probably more widely used – although carbon fibre is rapidly gaining ground now. They are reasonably light, but are almost twice as thick in section as the other two, which makes casting in a wind rather more difficult.

When carbon fibre was introduced for rod making in the mid-1970s it was claimed by some to have almost magical properties, particularly in terms of casting distance. In fact, many of the early carbon fibre rods were abominable creations, just as some of the original fibreglass ones had been, but the initial teething troubles now seem to have been resolved. The new material, although still more expensive than fibreglass and equivalent cane, is gradually coming down in price and, today, its sales constitute a substantial part of the overall rod market. Its four great qualities are that it is very light – which makes for effortless use over long periods; that rods made from it are slender and therefore cut into the wind efficiently; that the tip of a carbon fibre rod stops dead at the end of a forward cast, instead of bouncing up and down, which helps the skilful angler to throw a straighter line than he might otherwise have been able to; and that many carbon fibre rods will handle a markedly wider range of line weights than their cane or fibreglass counterparts.

Regardless of what a rod is made of, three other factors should influence our choice – line rating, length and action.

Nowadays, every worthwhile rod is marked just above the handle with the weight of line or the range of line weights to which it is best suited (thus, #6 or #6/8). This rating assumes that 30 ft of the recommended line will be aerialised. For every 6 ft more or less aerialised in actual fishing, the line needs to be one size heavier or lighter to load the rod correctly. That is to say, where only 24 ft of line are to be aerialised with a #7 rod, a #8 line should be used, and where 36 ft will be the most consistent length in use, a #6 line will be required.

If a heavier line than necessary is used, the rod will feel increasingly 'soggier' as line is extended until it has little or no effective spring to it, and is at risk of breaking. If too light a line is used, it will be impossible to realise the rod's full potential without extending a great deal of line which will, of itself, prove to be unmanageable in the air. Some rods are rated for use with only one weight of line; others, especially those made of carbon fibre, may accept quite a wide range.

If you happen to acquire an old rod which does not have the AFTM rating marked on it, the advice of an established and experienced tackle dealer should be sought.

It is generally agreed that the optimum rod length for most stillwater bank fishing is between 9 ft and 9 ft 6 in. Fly rods of this length are usually powerful and reasonably light, most of them are well suited to casting lines in the general stillwater range of AFTM 6 to 8, and they are long enough to keep a hooked fish well clear of all but the thickest and tallest of waterside vegetation. However, those who expect to fish only small lakes may well wish to use a shorter rod of (say) 8 ft 6 in with the AFTM 6 lines they will have chosen, and those who will do most of their fishing from a boat on a loch may well prefer a longer one of 10 ft or more, also designed to handle a relatively light line.

A rod's action is described in terms of the area along its length in which it bends most freely. Logically, a rod which is stiff throughout most of its length and only starts to flex easily towards its tip is said to be 'tip actioned', one that bends near the butt is described as being 'butt actioned', and one which flexes progressively from butt to tip is said to have an 'all through' action. Regardless of whereabouts a rod flexes along its length, the amount that it will bend under a given load is described in terms of stiffness or softness.

Tip-actioned rods demand a fairly rapid casting action and the loop of the line as it turns over at the ends of the forward and back casts tends to be fairly narrow, which makes for good casting into a wind. The nearer the action gets to the butt, the slower the casting rate and the wider the loop. A slow- or butt-actioned rod will present a fly more delicately than a fast- or tip-actioned one, but will not cut through a breeze as efficiently. Most stillwater fishermen find that a moderately stiff all through action will meet most of their needs.

When offered a choice between a two-piece or a three-piece rod, the former should always be selected except when shortness is of primary importance for travelling purposes. However carefully or well they are made, joints tend to interfere with a rod's action, so the fewer the better.

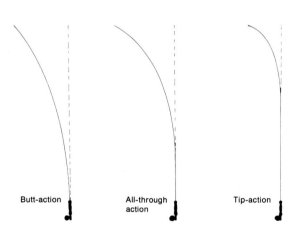

Butt-action   All-through   Tip-action
                     action

Fig. 11   Typical Rod Actions

It is not easy to pick out a small selection of rods which would suit everybody from amongst the vast range available. But for those who seek precise guidance, a brief catalogue of my own quite modest collection may help. The four rods in it have been carefully chosen and represent the product of many years of trial and occasional error. I have no cane rods. I used a 9 ft 3 in Sharpes Scottie for a long time and loved it until sentiment gave way to reason and it was ousted by fibreglass. On very small stillwaters I use the same 8 ft 6 in, #6-rated rod that I use for river fishing. It has no discernible vices although, being small and light, it has seen some anxious moments when unexpectedly heavy fish have been hooked. For almost all the rest of my bank fishing I use two very similar 9 ft 3 in rods. One is rated for lines between AFTM 6 and 8. It is light ($4\frac{1}{2}$ oz), powerful and a great pleasure to use. When I wish to carry two rods at once, one with a floating line and the other with a sinker or a sink tip, I match this rod with the slightly stiffer #7/8-rated one. Made for me some time ago, it is slightly stiffer than its partner, seems a little more powerful and has a pleasantly positive feel to it. Finally, for boat work and for bank fishing where substantial periods of long casting may be expected, or where heavy waterside vegetation is likely to hamper the playing and landing of a fish, I have recently acquired a 10 ft, #6/7-rated carbon fibre rod. It is a delight to use, especially in a wind, and can throw a remarkably long, straight, accurate line when necessary.

Reels

A great deal of nonsense has been talked in the past about choosing reels. For many years, successive generations of fishing writers perpetuated a myth about using the reel to 'balance' the rod; which presumably means, to lower the rod's centre of gravity – normally about a third of the way up from the handle – to the hand grip. This is, in fact, a counter-productive exercise. Casting is markedly easier if the point of balance is a reasonable distance beyond the hand, giving the rod a certain amount of inherent impetus. The ideal fly reel will be the lightest available for the task in hand, and its seating on the rod should position it as close to the hand as possible.

The main requirements for a stillwater reel are that it should comfortably accommodate the fly line and plenty of backing line (75 yds for small stillwaters, 100 yds for larger lakes and reservoirs), that it should have a drum sufficiently large in diameter to prevent the line from forming itself into stiff coils and to allow a fairly rapid recovery of the line, and that it should be reliable. If it has an exposed rim to the spool, allowing running fish to be controlled by finger pressure, then that will be an additional point in its favour.

Personally, I do not like multiplying fly reels (which are prone to mechanical failure) or automatic ones (which are rather heavy).

Most reels currently on the market were initially designed for river fishing. Some of them are perfectly acceptable for use on small stillwaters, but few are really big and light enough to entirely satisfy the reservoir fisherman; amongst those that do meet the requirements are, at one end of the price scale, the Intrepid Rimfly and, at the other, the Hardy Marquis 8/9.

Leaders

The next essential is a length of nylon with which to join the fly to the fly line – a 'leader' – and this is a subject which demands more attention than might be immediately apparent.

The leader's task is fourfold. It must be sufficiently long and inconspicuous to put a good distance between the fly and the potentially fish-frightening fly line; it must act in concert with the fly line, allowing the angler to cast delicately and with accuracy; it must allow the artificial fly to behave as naturally as possible in or on the water; and it should be strong and elastic enough to absorb some of the shock imposed upon it by a particularly heavy or energetic fish.

Fishermen use an extraordinary diversity of leaders, from simple, level lengths of monofilament to remarkably complex creations built up from numbers of pieces of nylon knotted together. Perhaps most widely used are the commercially available knotless, tapered leaders which are produced in an assortment of lengths and a wide range of breaking strains.

Knots weaken nylon and tend to pick up weed and scum as they are drawn through the water, so they should be avoided whenever possible. Having said this, different fishing styles and conditions require different leader lengths, and a factory-made leader will not always prove ideal for the task in hand without some modification.

For sunk line fishing, for boat fishing on either reservoir or loch and for dry fly fishing, a leader of between 3–4 yds in length should serve. A leader of similar length but with droppers will be needed for fishing a team of flies. For nymph fishing, or for fishing any weighted fly deep down with a floating line, a much longer leader may be called for – perhaps as much as 6 yds or more in length.

Any leader should be thick at its butt – certainly no less than a third of the thickness of the point of the fly line – and taper progressively towards its point. Although some manufacturers advertise them, there is no advantage whatever in using a double tapered leader; one which is fine at its butt, becomes thicker, and then tapers away towards the point. Ideally, the rearmost two-thirds should be level, or almost so, and the front third should taper quite steeply. Only thus will good turnover be attained, even in a breeze.

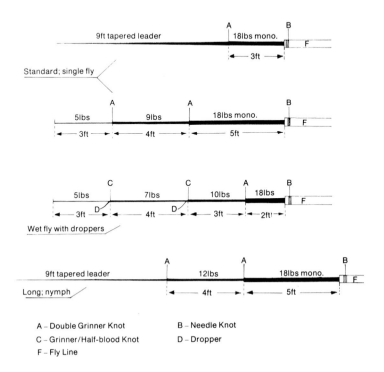

A – Double Grinner Knot   B – Needle Knot
C – Grinner/Half-blood Knot   D – Dropper
F – Fly Line

Fig. 12 Typical Stillwater Leaders

Choice of the correct point thickness for a leader is of fundamental importance to success and should largely be dictated by the size and weight of the fly being used. A small, light fly will behave unnaturally on too heavy a leader. A large, weighted pattern is liable to break the nylon by setting up the equivalent of metal fatigue during casting. As a very approximate guide, flies tied on hooks of size 8 or larger are well suited to leader points 0·24 mm or 0·22 mm in diameter (1X and 2X), patterns dressed on hooks in the 9 to 12 range are matched by 0·20 mm or 0·18 mm points (3X and 4X), and dressings on size 13 hooks or smaller perform best when used with 0·16 mm or 0·14 mm (5X or 6X) nylon. However, this is one of the areas in which the rules should be well leavened with common sense. To fish with a 5X or 6X point in a lake in which the trout average 2 lb or more, and in which 5- or 6-pounders are not uncommon, would be the height of irresponsibility. Nobody wants to let a fish swim off with a hook in its mouth and a length of nylon trailing behind it, and we should all regard being broken by a trout as a considerable disgrace. Obviously, the breaking strain of the point must be matched to the weight of the sort of fish we may expect from a particular water, as well as to the size of fly being used.

No leader of any length should ever be knotted directly to the fly line. Instead, a length of heavy (say, 0·45 mm) level monofilament should be needle knotted to the line and the butt of the leader should be attached to this 'butt length' with a double grinner knot. This arrangement is strong and neat, and allows the various joins to pass through the rod rings with a minimum of hindrance. The methods for tying the knots are described in Chapter 6.

In order to attain the lengths sometimes required of leaders for nymph fishing, the butt length may need to be as much as 6 ft long, and it may be necessary to put an additional length of slightly lighter nylon (say 0·40 mm) between the butt length and the tapered leader.

Heavy nylon, however limp, tends to form 'memory coils' when kept wound on a spool or round a reel. These can be removed by pulling it through a folded piece of rubber sheeting; an off-cut from an old inner tube is ideal.

Some fishermen like to use a fine, level nylon point in order to avoid having to cut away an inch or so of the relatively expensive knotless tapered leader each time they change a fly. Personally, I regard this as a false economy as it introduces a knot at what is already the weakest point of the overall leader, and the cost of replacing a complete leader is no more than that of a couple of shop-bought flies. However, if you wish to use it, you should ensure that the extra nylon is of a lower breaking strain than the leader itself, that it is attached with a double grinner knot rather than a much weaker and less reliable blood knot, and that it is kept short – if it is more than about 6 in long it will adversely affect the leader's performance.

Flies

Last amongst our list of truly essential equipment is a small collection of artificial flies. We shall be considering specific patterns in subsequent chapters, but this would seem to be an appropriate juncture at which to describe briefly the various types and their uses.

Several angling writers have sought to categorise trout flies into clearly defined groups, generally according to the presumed motives of the fish when taking them. For example, some have argued that flashy lures, dressed on long shanked hooks, are seen as sticklebacks or fry by the fish; that smaller, traditional Scottish loch patterns like the Peter Ross or the Mallard and Claret are taken for hatching nymphs, and that other dressings, for which no possible counterparts can be found in nature, are attacked for territorially defensive reasons, or from some other less clearly defined but still aggressive motive. Other authors have suggested that trout, being provably inquisitive, take flies into their mouths to test them, just as we might pick up and feel an unfamiliar object with our hands.

The truth, of course, is that we shall never know for certain why a particular fish took a particular fly. If swarms of midges are hatching, a trout takes an artificial midge pupa and a subsequent autopsy shows it to have been feeding heavily on natural midge pupae, similar in size and colour to the artificial, it would seem reasonable to suppose that the fish has mistaken our artificial for the real thing – but we cannot be absolutely sure.

So, I prefer to group trout flies under three very broad headings based partly on their general shapes and partly on the ways in which they are most often fished successfully.

Under the general heading of 'Traditional Patterns' I include those that have been handed down to us after generations of use on lakes, lochs, loughs or rivers; the Mallard and Claret, the Butcher, the Coachman, the Dunkeld and the Greenwell's Glory are all typical of this group. I would add to these such modern dressings as meet the basic design criteria and are not specifically intended to represent any particular insect or to be suggestive of food. In order to qualify for inclusion in this group, a pattern must be dressed on a single, ordinary shanked hook. Most traditional patterns, but not all, consist of a body, a tail of feather fibre, a pair of quill fibre wings and a hackle tied in beneath the throat. A few, like the Zulu and the Grenadier, are hackled for their entire lengths (or 'palmered'); others, generally evolved from north country river flies, are dressed as 'spiders', with fairly sparse bodies, even sparser hackles taken right around their necks, and no wings.

Traditional patterns are most often used fairly close to the surface with a floating or a sink tip line, and are frequently fished in teams of two or three.

The modern range of 'Lures' owes much to those who have fished the lowland reservoirs of England during the past thirty years. Patterns included under this heading are dressed on long shanked or tandem hooks, and are not intended to represent any natural

creature. Typical examples are the Sweeney Todd and the Whiskey
Fly. Lures may be fished at any depth or speed, although some are
noticeably more effective when retrieved close to the bottom (for
instance) or slowly. They are almost always used singly rather than
in teams.

The final, and probably the largest, group is the 'Imitative and
General Food Suggesting' one. It includes all those artificials which
have either been designed to represent specific insects, small fish,
snails, shrimps or whatever, or those which may reasonably be
assumed to trigger a feeding response in the trout and are therefore
fished in a particular way to this end. Examples of the former type
include artificial midge pupae, sedge pupae, shrimps, fry and so on
while the latter includes, for example, the Black and Peacock Spider
fished slowly just below the surface film when the snails are up and
the Worm Fly fished close to the bottom when trout are feeding on
caddis larvae. The overall group includes floating flies as well as
sinking ones.

Before we leave the subject of trout flies, a brief plea to those who
do not already tie their own – learn to do so as soon as maybe. There
are very few valid excuses for not doing so. Anybody who can read a
book and tie his shoe laces can tie flies that will catch fish. And the
satisfaction of taking trout on a pattern of one's own tying, perhaps
even of one's own design, is well matched by the quality and the
saving in cost over the shop-bought article.

Accessories

Some fishermen may assert that a landing net is an essential part of
the stillwater trout fisherman's equipment. It is not. It makes life
easier and is very useful, but it is not essential. I am one of those self-
confessed (and unashamed) philistines who carries what many
experts would call a 'tea strainer'. Worse still, it is of the folding type
which, those same experts aver, is so likely to get caught up in itself
just when it is most wanted. I have used my 'tea strainer' to land fish
of up to 10 lb in weight without difficulty, and I cannot recall
having experienced any serious anxiety when opening it. It hangs
from a ring sewn high on the left shoulder at the back of my fishing
jacket, causes absolutely no inconvenience when not in use and is
instantly available when I need it. By all means buy the biggest,
longest handled net you can find, and sling it across your back with
any contrivance that you or the experts can devise. But do not let it
become an encumbrance, or panic if you find you have left it at
home. Provided that a trout of whatever size has been fully played
out, it can be lifted from the water by gripping it firmly across its
back immediately behind the gill covers.

A landing net can be improved by fastening a small lead weight to the bottom of the mesh, thus preventing the dry netting from floating untidily while you are trying to draw a fish over the rim.

The rest of a stillwater fly fisherman's equipment is simple and can (and should) be storable in the pockets of a fishing jacket. I see no merit in carrying a bag of cumbersome and unnecessary bits and pieces around when one of the great attractions of our sport is that we travel lightly laden and remain mobile.

A pair of scissors should be fastened to a ring sewn into the jacket with a long loop of string. The best available have slightly serrated cutting edges which prevent nylon monofilament from slipping while being cut, and a small, blunt area at the nose with which firmly lodged hooks may be gripped tightly.

Although a suitably lined tin may be used to accommodate artificial flies, most of us prefer to use a purpose-built article. Many designs are available but the best are made of plastic and contain water resistant ethafoam strips into which the points of the flies are stuck. They also fit into a reasonable-sized pocket, which is important. Most stillwater trout fishermen collect flies with a squirrel-like avidity, and nobody would deny them the undoubted pleasure to be had from doing so. But far more flies than could possibly be needed for a day's fishing can easily be fitted into a pocket-sized box, and those who currently store thousands of flies in immaculately lined suitcases or massive wooden display cabinets would do well to declutter themselves by decanting those patterns they may reasonably expect to use during a day – and possibly just a few others for luck – into a smaller receptacle.

I could, perhaps, have included a priest amongst the essential items. A small club, home-made or otherwise and kept ready to hand, is the only acceptable piece of equipment for ensuring the prompt and humane dispatch of a trout. To wander off in search of a suitable stone or piece of wood while the fish flaps away its life, or to misuse such inadequate tools as a landing net handle or the top of a gate post, shows an unhealthy lack of respect both for one's quarry and for the sport. The priest, too, should be secured to the jacket.

Three types of floatant are likely to be needed; tins of mucilin and Permagrease for nylon and fly lines respectively and a liquid or semi-liquid fly floatant. Two kinds of mucilin are available; the one in the red tin is not petroleum based and will not, therefore, damage the plastic coating of a fly line; that in the green tin is and will. A small quantity of sinkant will also prove useful. It can be made by mixing fuller's earth to a putty-like consistency with equal amounts of glycerine and liquid detergent, and should be stored in an airtight container to prevent it from drying out.

Those who take their fishing seriously will wish to carry a marrow scoop with which to conduct autopsies on captured trout. The process is a simple one and is neither as messy nor as unpleasant as it may sound. Decanted into a small, shallow bowl with a little water, the fish's stomach contents can readily be examined, and if the exercise is conducted as a matter of routine it can show a good deal more than merely what a single fish has been eating recently; it is a useful way to establish the trends in trouts' diets throughout the season and to become familiar with the creatures they most commonly feed upon.

A small whetstone with which to sharpen hooks, a pair of polarised sunglasses to cut out glare from the water's surface, a couple of spare tapered leaders and a bass to carry his fish in should complete the angler's inventory.

Clothing

Clothing for stillwater trouting must meet five basic requirements. It must be warm in cold weather, cool in hot, waterproof, of drab colour, and the jacket must have a good number of large pockets. Sartorial elegance is not generally compatible with comfort and efficiency when fishing. My personal preference is for an army surplus parachute jacket which is camouflaged and has six big pockets. Its only limitation is that, being made of heavy cotton, it is not waterproof. This I overcome when necessary by carrying a large, thin, olive-coloured nylon anorak which folds to pocket size and can be worn over the jacket.

A hat is a very personal thing but, to be any use for fishing, it should have a broad enough peak or brim to shade the eyes at any time of the day. There is nothing to commend the widespread practice of smothering a hat with flies; their removal is likely to damage their dressings and certain to ruin the hat.

Waders should be tough enough to withstand occasional brushes with barbed-wire and other angling hazards and, ideally, they should be studded, although this is not as important on stillwaters as it is on rocky rivers where a secure grip is essential.

Finally, it is worth remembering that, however warm the weather may seem, large expanses of stillwater offer little shelter from often cold winds. Particularly when going afloat, it is always better to take too much clothing and discard some than to spend the day shivering miserably, dreaming of log fires and mugs of steaming cocoa. And nothing dampens angling ardour more surely than cold water trickling steadily down one's neck towards an already soggy rump.

CHAPTER 6

Knots

The trout fisherman must use knots for an assortment of purposes –
for joining the backing line to his reel, the fly line to the backing, the
leader to the fly line, nylon to nylon, the fly to the leader, for
mooring boats, and for attaching drogues and so on to strong points
within boats. Each of these instances presents the angler with a
different set of requirements, either because of the nature of the
materials being joined or because of the function the knot is
expected to fulfil, and a different knot is required to meet each of the
requirements.

In some instances – most notably when joining lengths of nylon
monofilament – knots seriously weaken the materials being used.
They should always be regarded as the weak links in the chain
between fish and fisherman and, in order to minimise the risks of
slippage or breakage, they should always be tied carefully. With
nylon, the strands should be moistened and the coils carefully
snugged down before pulling tight. It pays, too, to practise the knots
you will use most often in peace, comfort and good light at home,
rather than while wading thigh deep in a reservoir during the only
rise of the day, or in a pitching boat in an icy gale and horizontally
driven rain.

Before considering the knots themselves, perhaps we should learn
how to make a simple whipping. The process is remarkably
straightforward and is used for securing rod rings to rods, for
streamlining knots and for a host of other fishing purposes.

A knot for attaching a line to a reel must pull up tight against the
reel's drum and grip on the generally smooth, metallic surface so
that line can be wound on to the reel without slippage however light
or heavy the pressure on the line. It must also be strong enough to be
proof against sudden shock, for we may be sure that any fish that
puts it to the test will be a large one, the last that we would ever wish
to lose. Just imagine the anguish as, heart in mouth after a
succession of reel stripping runs by some leviathan of the deep, you

see the tail of your backing line disappear through the rod rings and into the water! The slip knot illustrated is both simple to tie and safe.

All sorts of weird and wonderful systems have been developed for securing fly lines to backing and monofilament butt lengths to the forward ends of fly lines. The two simple ones given here have been thoroughly tested by countless competent fishermen over many years and provide the most satisfactory solutions currently available.

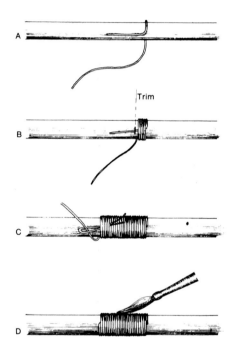

Fig. 13   Making a Whipping

A & B. Take four or five turns of silk around the object to be whipped, trapping the short end beneath them. Trim away waste.

C. Continue in tight, touching turns. About five turns from the end of the whipping, trap in a loop of silk. When the whipping is completed, use the loop to pull the loose end back through the last few turns.

D. Trim the waste end off close to the whipping. Varnish the turns of silk.

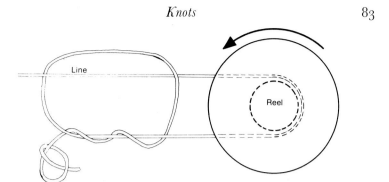

Fig. 14   Slip Knot

Tighten both knots and moisten the slip knot before drawing it firmly onto the reel drum by pulling on the line itself.

The nail knot should be used either when the fly line is not so constructed as to allow a needle to be inserted into its end or when the backing line is of a braided material and cannot, therefore, be threaded through a needle hole in a fly line. It can be improved (in terms of streamlining rather than of strength) by making a whipping over it and then varnishing it.

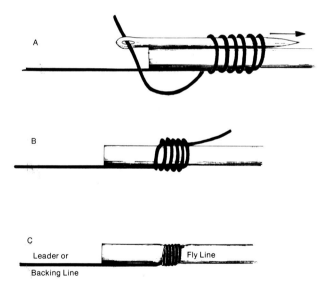

Fig. 15   Nail Knot

Various knots have been used – and, indeed, still are used – for securing nylon monofilament to fly lines. Most of them are lumpy and some can be insecure. It is particularly important that the joint between fly line and leader should be as smooth and slender as possible so that it will pass freely through the rod rings both when working line out and when playing a fish. By far the most effective knot for this purpose is the needle knot. Although it is quite easy to tie, two of the processes involved can be a bit fiddly and the job

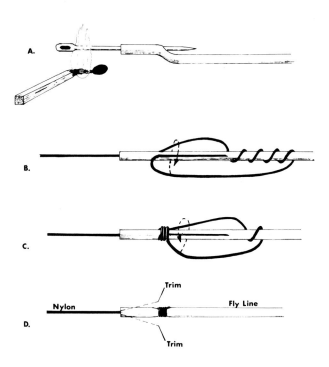

Fig. 16   Needle Knot

A. Insert needle $\frac{1}{4}$ in into core of fly line and out through side. Heat needle briefly and remove.
B. Insert nylon through needle hole, take four or five turns around fly line, bring loose end of nylon back and lay along fly line.
C. Reverse the turns to lap over the fly line and both parts of the nylon.
D. Snug turns down and pull tight. Cut away the loose end of the nylon and carefully trim the end of the fly line to a point.

should, therefore, be done in good light and comfortable surroundings. A butt length of a yard or more of 0·45 mm monofilament thus
joined to the line should last throughout the average angler's season,
despite the erosion of its forward end by the replacement of leaders.
If the point of the fly line is carefully bevelled with a razor blade and
a fine whipping is made over the join and then varnished, the end
product will be markedly smoother and more streamlined.

For many years few fishermen have used anything other than a
treacherous four-turn blood knot for joining nylon to nylon. The
blood knot's fallibility, still unrecognised by many people, is caused
by the fact that each short waste end is trapped by only a single turn
of nylon, and by the knot's propensity for slipping, particularly
when the two lengths of nylon it is used to join are of greatly
differing thicknesses. Richard Walker, who has contributed so
much to angling knowledge over the past fifty years or so, has
evolved and publicised a knot which he calls the 'double grinner'.
In addition to overcoming the blood knot's two main failings, the
double grinner weakens nylon noticeably less than a blood knot
does, and it is certainly no more difficult to tie. Its only drawbacks
seem to be that rather more nylon is used in its tying than in a blood
knot's (a small sacrifice in the interests of confidence and security)
and that, since the loose ends emerge from the top and bottom of the
knot, it tends to pull out of shape if they are used as droppers.

Fig. 17   Double Grinner Knot

For those who wish to incorporate droppers into their leaders, Mr
Walker has 'arranged a marriage' between the double grinner and
the blood knot. The important point to remember when tying this
particular variation is that the half blood knot should always be
made in the heavier nylon and that its waste end, rather than the
grinner's, should be used as the dropper.

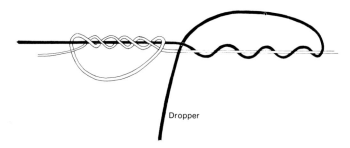

Fig. 18   Grinner Half-blood Knot

Two neat and secure knots are available for tying eyed trout flies to nylon. The first, a single 'grinner' made through the eye of the hook, is entirely satisfactory when a hinged joint between fly and leader is needed. However, if the angler wishes the hook shank and the leader to form a single, continuous axis, the turle knot will serve his purpose better.

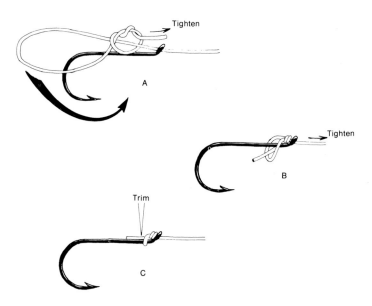

Fig. 19   Turle Knot

These half-dozen or so knots should meet all the angler's needs in the preparation of his tackle. Each is wholly reliable and easy to tie. But every fisherman should also know how to tie three more simple knots which, while having particular relevance to boating, also have a wide range of other applications. They are all well known but, for those who were not in the scouts or guides, or who do not sail, I shall rehearse them here. Re-publication of the first two may prevent some boat somewhere from being moored with a granny knot and found washed up on a distant, rocky shore the following morning. The third is a life saver.

The round turn and two half hitches is the most reliable means of tying a boat up to a buoy, a ring or a horizontal railing. It is also

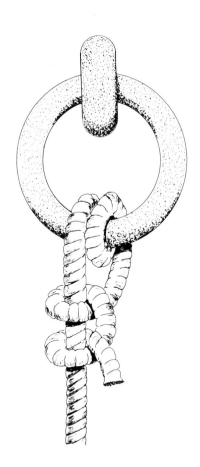

Fig. 20   Round Turn and Two Half Hitches

ideal for securing drogues and anchor ropes to strong points, and for tying the assorted impedimenta – priest, marrow spoon, scissors and so on – to rings sewn into a fishing jacket or waistcoat.

The chief advantages of a clove hitch are the speed and simplicity of its tying. Insecure as it may look, it is perfectly safe for mooring a boat to an upright post.

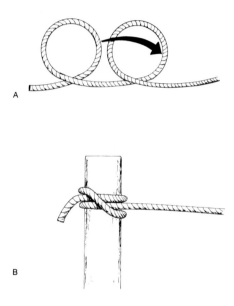

Fig. 21   Clove Hitch

Finally, every angler, whether he fishes from the bank or from a boat, should know how to tie a bowline. It is an easy knot and, forming a non-slip loop, is the most satisfactory one for use with a rope thrown to a drowning man or to anyone stuck in deep mud. Obviously, the knot should be tied (and the butt end of the rope securely trapped!) before the coils are thrown, and the loop formed should be large enough to pass easily over the victim's head and shoulders.

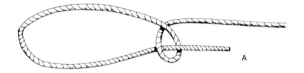

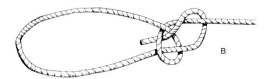

Fig. 22   Bowline

CHAPTER 7

Casting

There are four ways of learning to cast – from a qualified instructor, from a more or less competent friend, from a book, or by trial and error through one's own unaided endeavours. Of these, either of the last two should be regarded as thoroughly unsatisfactory substitutes for either of the first two. The small outlay involved in spending a few hours at a casting school will always be well repaid, and the aspirant fly fisherman would be wise to seek the assistance of a professional if at all possible. Even quite experienced fishermen can benefit substantially from formal tuition.

However, accepting the relative scarcity of casting schools and that some people may not know anybody able to teach them, we shall use this chapter to consider the basic techniques involved. Before doing so, we should understand two things clearly. The first is that casting is only a means to an end and not an end in itself. Provided that we can place our fly where we want it with reasonable delicacy and without strain, the technique and style used to do so are not of great consequence. Nevertheless, certain principles have been evolved through trial and error over many years, and to entirely ignore them is to risk reducing your casting potential or tiring yourself unnecessarily. Secondly, long casting is rarely a prerequisite for catching trout in stillwaters. While some modern writers set great store by the ability to throw a line 30 yds or more, it is often apparent that their ability to do so is really being used to compensate for lack of stealth, concealment and delicacy. A long line repeatedly snaking out over the water cannot but drive fish further from the bank (and from the angler). Since a leader or the tip of a fly line is rarely visible at 30 yds range or more, the further the fisherman casts, the more he has to rely on feeling takes rather than seeing them. And the elasticity of line and leader, and the resistance of the water, make striking at such distances a dangerously uncertain business. I would not deny that long casting can be an asset under certain circumstances, or that it is essential for particular types of fishing – when using a quick sinking line from an anchored boat, for instance – but I have no doubt that the careful, thoughtful angler who limits himself to fishing his flies within a 20–25 yds arc will do consistently better than he who thumps about on the bank, strides mightily into the water and habitually heaves his fly as far towards the distant horizon as possible.

There is much to be said for learning to cast somewhere other than on trout-stocked water. If there is a chance of catching fish, the student is more likely to be preoccupied with this possibility than with acquiring the ability to throw a reasonable line, and retrieval of the fly between each cast will considerably reduce the time actually spent in wielding the rod. As with all skills, the key to success lies in practice, and a great deal of frustration can be avoided by putting this practice in before starting to fish, rather than trying to learn 'on the job'.

Casting on to water is easier than casting on to grass. The drag of the water on the fly line helps to bend the rod and, therefore, to get the line flying quickly through the air. Under no circumstances should casting practice be conducted on hard or abrasive surfaces like concrete or gravel; nothing is more certain to ruin a fly line.

When practice casting over water, a floating line should be used rather than a sinker or a sink-tip. While the full length of a floater can be lifted cleanly from the surface, to try the same exercise with a submerged or partly submerged line would certainly strain the rod and might break it. It is also worth noting that a very short line is much more difficult to cast than is one of (say) 8–10 yds. A fly rod needs to be bent to realise its casting potential and the weight of 2–3 yds of line beyond the top ring is insufficient to get the rod working.

The simplest, and generally the most useful, cast is the 'overhead'. Upon it are based the 'double haul', used for distance casting, and the 'side cast' which helps to conceal the angler and his designs from trout at close quarters. Some modern writers on reservoir fishing seem to regard the traditional overhead cast as being old-fashioned and suggest that even the rankest beginner should start by learning to double haul with an extended rod arm. I am sure they are wrong. The overhead cast is disciplined and relatively easy to learn. With a little perseverance, anybody using it with typical reservoir tackle should be able to throw a line of between 15 and 20 yds accurately and without undue effort. When my casting begins to deteriorate at the end of a long day spent reaching for distance on some vast, grey reservoir, I can always redeem the situation, tighten my precision, and reduce or eliminate tangles or wind knots by reverting to the overhead cast.

Whatever cast is used, the rod should be held firmly. Whether you choose a grip with the thumb on top of the handle or one with the tight V between thumb and forefinger uppermost is a matter for personal preference. The former locks the rod more securely into its position as an extension of the forearm but the latter may be more naturally comfortable. I find that by holding the rod very close to the reel seating, well behind the point of balance, rather than in the middle of the handle, the rod does much of my work for me through its own impetus.

In all that follows, I assume the caster to be right-handed. Left-handers should easily be able to interpret the instructions for their own use.

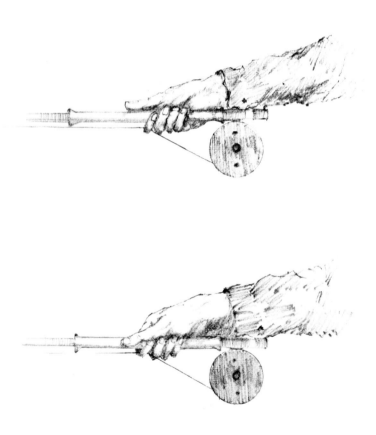

Fig. 23   Alternative Grips on a Fly Rod

Having set up your tackle with a short (say 3 yds), fairly steeply tapered leader and a reasonably bushy and visible fly with the point broken off (a Muddler Minnow is ideal), pull 2 or 3 yds of line from the reel and out through the rod rings. Having checked that you have a reasonable area of clear space both in front of and behind you, stand with your feet slightly apart, facing about 45° to the right of your planned casting direction (Fig. 24a). Hold the fly between the forefinger and thumb of the left hand. The rod should be held in the right hand, pointing along the axis of your forthcoming cast, with its tip low – no more than 8 in or so above the ground or water – and the right elbow tucked loosely into your side (Fig. 24b).

Keeping the right wrist straight, and with the right elbow still held against the side, lift your right hand swiftly up to your right shoulder, raising the rod to the 12 o'clock position and checking it there. As you do this a strong belly should form in the line and, if the fly is released when the rod is about two-thirds of the way up, the line will stream upwards and backwards (Fig. 24c). Pause briefly at the top of this back-cast to allow the line to unfurl behind you (Fig. 24d), and then move the rod smartly forwards and downwards, checking it at the 2 o'clock position (Fig. 24e) and 'following through' by allowing it to drift down to the 4 o'clock one (Fig. 24f). This action is not unlike that used when driving a nail into a wall with a hammer and, if it is correctly executed, the line should extend gently on to the water in front of you. If an insufficient pause is left between the upward movement (the back-cast) and the forward cast, the effect will be that of cracking a whip; the fly may break off and the line and leader will almost certainly topple into the water in an untidy heap. If too long a pause is left – or if insufficient force is put into the back-cast – the line will catch on the ground behind you.

Now, pull a further yard or so of line from the reel and, keeping the line between the left hand and the bottom rod ring tight, repeat the cast (Figs 24g, h and i). Half-way through the rod's forward travel, release the left hand's grip on the line which, drawn by the impetus of the line already extended beyond the rod tip, will 'shoot' through the rings.

The rod is a spring, tensioned by the weight of the line in the air. If that weight is removed by releasing the line too soon, the rod's power will be dissipated and the line will fall untidily around the angler's ears. It is essential, therefore, to perfect the timing of the left hand release.

This basic exercise should be repeated until back-cast and forward cast flow smoothly together, a further yard or so of line being extended from time to time as confidence grows. With more

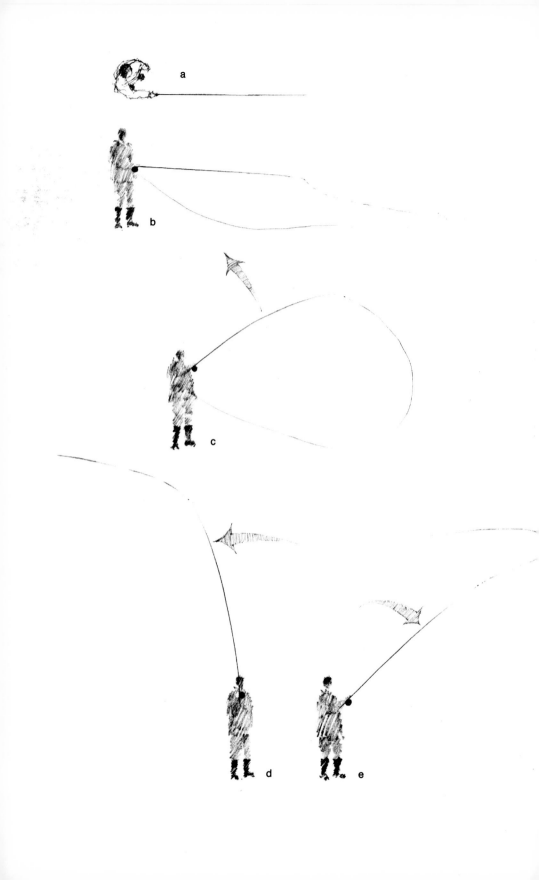

a

b

c

d

e

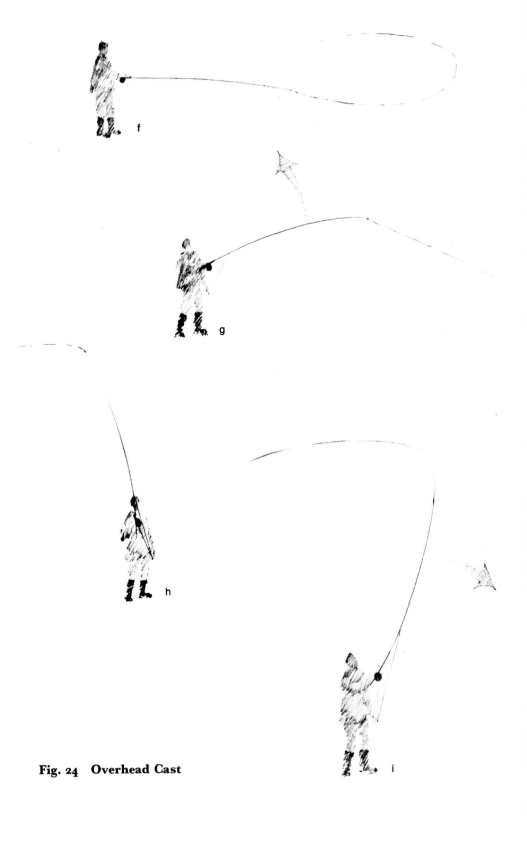

Fig. 24 Overhead Cast

line out, the 'check' at the top of the back-cast will prove almost impossible to achieve and can be replaced by a drifting of the rod back towards the 11 o'clock position. If it is allowed to drift further, the line will prescribe a wide arc rather than a tight loop (quite possibly catching on the ground behind you), and power for the subsequent forward cast will certainly be lost.

Once this simplest of all casts has been mastered, you should find that you can extend line on the forward stroke and go straight into the back-cast without actually allowing the line to come into contact with the water. This is accomplished by checking the forward cast in about the 2 o'clock position, rather than following through, and is termed 'false casting'. It is used to lengthen line without disturbing the fish, to change direction and to dry a floating fly by wafting it back and forth through the air. When fishing a sunk fly, false casting should be kept to a minimum; it wastes time, and no saying was ever truer than that the fly that catches fish is the one in the water.

Concentrate on accuracy rather than length, which will come with experience; never simply cast 'into the blue' but select a target (even if it is only a particular ripple on the surface) and seek to hit it. And do not practise for more than about an hour at a time, to start with anyway.

The commonest casting faults are easily cured.

If the rod fails to bend under the weight of the extended line after the back-cast, ensure that the line between the left hand and the bottom rod ring is remaining taut throughout the back-cast. If it is, the upward movement of the rod should be speeded up. The back-cast must be executed as positively, firmly and cleanly as the forward one. Indeed, it is impossible to achieve a good forward cast unless it has been preceded by an equally good back-cast.

If the line strikes the ground behind or the water in front of you during false casting, the rod itself must be moving too far back or too far forward, and it is a simple matter to check it a little earlier.

If the line or leader fall in a heap on the water, instead of unfurling on to the surface in a straight line, the probability is that you are pushing your forearm forward during the follow through, instead of keeping your elbow close to your side and your wrist straight.

If flies break off during the back-cast, or there is a whip-like cracking sound as the line turns over behind you, the pause between back and forward casts is too short.

If the fly strikes the rod during its travel, tilt both rod and forearm slightly to the right.

And, if the line splashes on to the water instead of arriving gently, aiming a foot or so above the surface should solve the problem.

When you can perform an overhead cast instinctively and without effort, you may reasonably consider starting to reach for distance. This is achieved by technique rather than by muscle power or brute strength, and by modifying the overhead cast in two ways.

Firstly, the overall length of the rod can effectively be increased by straightening the right arm instead of keeping the elbow to the side; a longer rod produces greater leverage, which provides greater line speed, which produces greater distance. However, control over the rod becomes markedly more difficult when the arm is moved away from the side, and greater concentration and physical discipline are required if mastery of the line in the air is to be maintained. In particular, although flexing of the wrist is undesirable during an ordinary overhead cast, it is likely to prove disastrous with the arm extended. The arm must become a rigid extension of the rod.

Secondly, line velocity can be increased on both back and forward casts by pulling sharply downwards with the left hand at the beginning of the backward movement, allowing the weight of the line straightening out behind you to pull the left hand up to the bottom ring as the 1 o'clock position is reached, pulling sharply downwards again as the forward cast is started and then releasing the line in the normal way (Figs 25a–d). Although this technique, known as 'double hauling', is especially effective when used with a shooting head, it can also be employed to advantage with full length weight forward lines. It is also useful for casting into or across the wind, or for shooting line when the back-cast area is obstructed by trees or bushes. Of paramount importance is the need to keep the line between the left hand and the bottom rod ring tight. If this tension is not maintained, the extra power gained by extending the arm and double hauling will be negated.

Such are the refractive properties of water that a rod waved to and fro' in a vertical plane is very much more apparent to fish than is one wielded horizontally. It therefore pays to keep the rod as low as possible, particularly when casting to fish close in to bank or boat, or when the water is very calm or clear. To this end, the 'side cast' has been developed from the overhead one.

With the rod being used in a horizontal plane, the line will inevitably be travelling low over the ground. Its irresistible sag at the end of each forward and back-cast will limit the angler's effective range to a maximum of about fifteen yards and, with line and leader turning through a horizontal arc rather than a vertical one, accuracy will be more difficult to achieve.

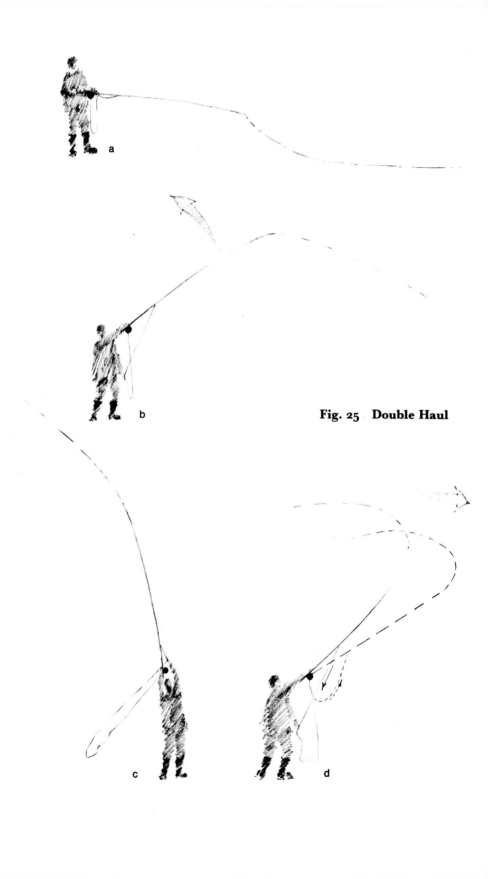

Fig. 25 Double Haul

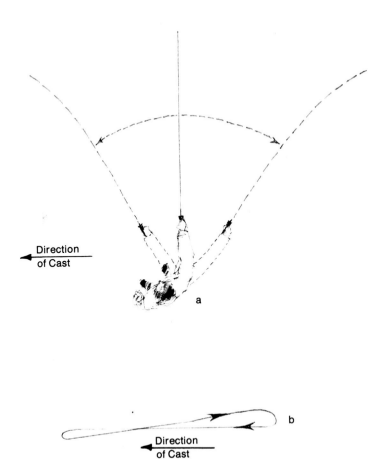

Direction
of Cast

a

Direction
of Cast

b

Fig. 26   Side Cast

With the body still at about 45° to the casting direction, the rod will be moved back and forth between 10 o'clock and 2 o'clock (Fig. 26a). The rod tip should be held slightly below the horizontal at the beginning of the back-cast, rising to just above it at the end. This will serve to lift the line a little as it extends to the rear and to help avoid snagging it unnecessarily on tall grass or other obstructions. The rod should be parallel with the ground during its forward travel, the point being dropped slightly again at the start of the next back-cast (Fig. 26b). Apart from these variations, the technique is identical to that used in the normal overhead cast.

To try to lift a sinking or a sink-tip line straight from the water and into an overhead back-cast is to court disaster. At best it will severely over-stress the rod and, at worst, it may break it. Such lines should be fully retrieved – or almost so – before the next cast is begun. However, if it is necessary to pick up 5 yds or so, a 'roll cast' should be used to lay the line on the surface before the overhead back-cast is begun. A roll cast can also be used to extend line over the water when trees or other hazards limit the back-cast area.

The starting position is exactly the same as that used for the overhead cast but with the rod and forearm perhaps tilted slightly to the right. However, in this case, the lifting of the rod from below the horizontal to the near vertical is a much slower process; we are not seeking to tension the rod during the backward movement, but simply to position the line so that the rod may work against it during the forward cast. Nevertheless, if the movement is too slow, or the pause in the vertical position is too long, the line will sag badly and the forward cast will lack power. The forward movement, which should be swift and positive, is just like that used in the overhead cast. If it is correctly executed, the line will lift from the water and roll over in a large loop, finally laying itself out neatly on the surface (Figs 27a–d).

Beyond these four casts, many others have been devised to meet specific circumstances – for throwing a slack line, for putting a left- or right-handed curve into the leader, for ensuring that the fly lands before the line does and so on. All of them are derivatives of either the overhead or roll cast and we do not need to confuse ourselves with them here. But one other fishing technique requires thought before we can count ourselves ready to set off in pursuit of trout.

In order to appear life-like, trout flies must be 'worked' through the water. Even with dry flies and those imitative patterns like midge pupae which are best left to hang static beneath the surface film, the angler must counteract drift and the wind's influence by manipulating his line. The objects of retrieving line in a particular manner are threefold – to control the behaviour of the flies in the water, to maintain contact with them so that a fish may be hooked as soon as it takes and to ensure that loose line already retrieved is free to slip back through the rod rings if a hooked fish makes a run.

We shall consider the various speeds at which flies can be retrieved, and the types of movement that can or should be imparted to them, in subsequent chapters on different styles of fishing. But consideration of the mechanics of retrieving line now will save repetition later.

Many fly-fishermen, several eminent writers amongst them, advocate the use of a 'figure-of-eight' technique in which the line is

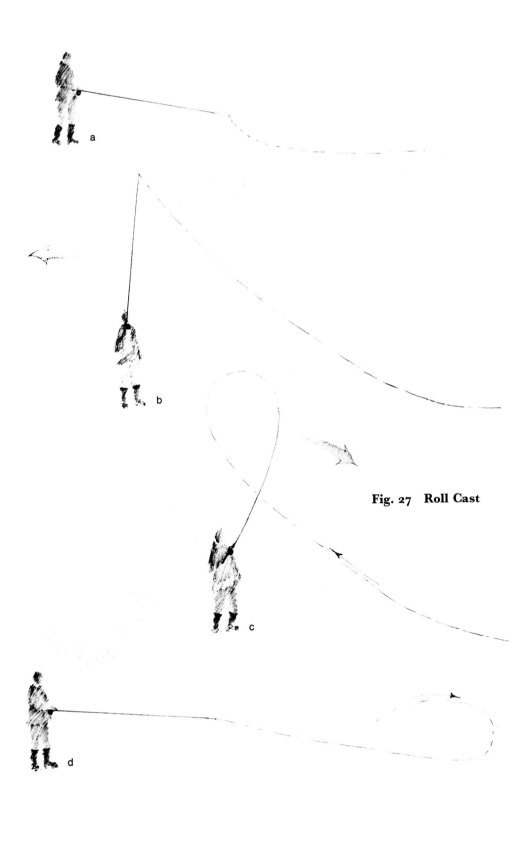

Fig. 27   Roll Cast

bunched up in the left hand as it is pulled in. Others suggest that it should be held in loose coils. Personally, I find that however carefully either of these methods is used, there is a tendency for the loose line to tangle as it is worked out for the next cast, and I prefer simply to let recovered line drop on to the ground or into the bottom of the boat. Some authorities might suggest that this puts the line at risk of being trampled underfoot and damaged, or of catching on roots, thistles or other obstructions when a fish runs it out. My answer would be that, while these problems certainly occur from time to time, they can almost always be avoided with a little care, and I am satisfied that this system is generally less troublesome than either of the other two. Whatever method is being used, the line should always pass from the bottom rod ring to the left hand via the index finger of the right hand so that it can be trapped against the rod's handle during striking.

When wading and fishing with a shooting head or a sinker, the inertia of submerged, retrieved line can cause difficulty with the next cast. This can easily be overcome by using a line-tray – a mesh-bottomed tray fastened to the fisherman's waist. Line recovered into it will be kept well above the water and will run out easily when false casting is begun.

In concluding this chapter, I would reiterate that trying to teach oneself from a book is undoubtedly the least satisfactory means of learning to cast. I have sought to explain the basic techniques involved and hope that those who cannot obtain expert, personal assistance may be able to use them to make a reasonably effective start. But the written word can never replace demonstration and critically analysed practice as a means of instruction. If you can find a qualified tutor at the beginning of your fly-fishing life, a few pounds invested in acquiring some of his expertise will be money well spent. And, if you are self-taught, never be too proud to accept or seek expert advice, however experienced you may be. There is little to be lost and much to be gained from so doing.

CHAPTER 8

Reservoir Bank Fishing

There can be few more daunting sights for the novice trout fisherman or the newcomer to a particular reservoir than a vast, bleak expanse of apparently featureless grey water stretching, unbroken by any sign of movement, towards a far horizon. But for the reassurances of other anglers and the fishery reports in the angling press, it would be easy to believe that we were confronted by an aquatic desert. Even when convinced that trout do actually live here, finding them may still seem a depressingly distant prospect.

Of course, had we been wise we would have watched the weather reports carefully for two or three days before setting out. By relating the prevailing wind to a map of the reservoir, we would have been able to eliminate shallow, straight, upwind stretches of shoreline from our list of possible fishing sites. We might also have consulted one of those books like *Stillwater Trout Fisheries** to see whether this particular water was amongst those upon which skilful and experienced fly fishers had offered their thoughts and suggestions. Forearmed with such background knowledge we should have been able to decide in advance the general areas in which we were most likely to find trout at this particular time of year and to have arrived at the waterside with a plan of campaign at least partially worked out. As it is, we shall have to rely on such advice as busy fishery staff may be able to provide. Other anglers may, quite naturally, be reluctant to guide strangers to their own favourite places; none of us likes to fish in more crowded surroundings than necessary. But no trout fisherman should ever be too proud or too shy to consult knowledgeable locals – or too trusting to leaven what they say with his own understanding of the implications of weather, fish behaviour and the reservoir's geography.

All those factors that we considered in the chapters on the fish, his food and his surroundings may be brought into play here and, while

* *Stillwater Trout Fisheries*, Edited by H. F. Wallis, Published by Ernest Benn Ltd, 1976.

we will not always be right, it should be possible with practice to achieve a very reasonable and consistent degree of accuracy in fish locating. Nothing builds confidence more surely than the knowledge that the choice of a particular fishing area is based on logical reasoning and that, should this one prove unproductive, another has already been selected by a similar deductive process.

While we are on the subject, there can be no doubt that confidence is of fundamental importance to success in angling; confidence not only in the fish-producing potential of a particular spot on the reservoir bank, but also in our chosen tackle, fly patterns, tactics and fishing techniques. It is certainly noticeable that if confidence is reduced by a poor day (and we all have them), an angler's casting deteriorates, his retrieve becomes automatic and mechanical, his choice of fly becomes irrational and his chances of catching fish are seriously reduced.

Blagdon has a well-earned reputation for good fishing early in the morning and late in the evening, and for often being quite remarkably difficult through the day. I go there as often as I can and greatly enjoy every second of every visit, but never arrive before about 4 o'clock in the afternoon. There would be little point in flogging away for eight or ten hours before sunset, only to be too tired, dispirited and lacking in confidence to make the most of that magical evening rise.

But I digress.

Having selected the area in which we plan to fish, we must now choose a precise spot within that area. (I presume that the banks are not so crowded as to severely limit the options available to us.) Of course, the visible movements of rising trout may sometimes take the decision out of our hands but, more often, we shall find ourselves confronted by an expanse of water seemingly no less lifeless than any other along the shoreline. Seek out a small promontory or headland where the ground slopes fairly steeply down into the water, and make use of any breeze there may be. Try to put the wind on to your left shoulder if you are right-handed or on to the right one if you are left-handed. By so doing, you should be able to ensure that the fly travels back and forth well away from your face during false casting.

Before actually starting to fish we will need some flies. Imitative patterns will be covered in the next chapter and I shall limit myself here to suggesting a modest collection of traditional patterns and lures which should serve as well for boat as for bank fishing. The traditional dressings have all established reputations for themselves on highland lochs as well as lowland stillwaters and smaller put-and-take fisheries. Many of the lures were largely, if not exclusively, designed with rainbow trout in mind and, while some of them may

ALEXANDRA

BLACK AND PEACOCK SPIDER

BLAE AND BLACK

BUTCHER

COACHMAN

DUNKELD

GREENWELL'S GLORY

MALLARD AND CLARET

PETER ROSS

SOLDIER PALMER

TEAL, BLUE AND SILVER

ZULU

(Flies tied by the author)

TRADITIONAL AND ATTRACTOR PATTERNS

MIDGE PUPAE

PLASTAZOTE CORIXA

SHRIMP

CORIXA

KILLER BUG

STICK FLY

SEDGE PUPAE

INVICTA

BRER RABBIT NYMPH

DAMSELFLY NYMPH

POLYSTICKLE

(Flies tied by the author)

IMITATIVE PATTERNS

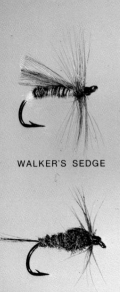

WALKER'S SEDGE

PALMERED SEDGE

LAST HOPE

SEPIA/CLARET NYMPH

GOLD-RIBBED HARE'S EAR NYMPH

PHEASANT TAIL

GREENWELL'S GLORY

MAYFLY

MAYFLY NYMPH

DADDY LONG-LEGS
(CRANE FLY)

(Flies tied by the author)

IMITATIVE PATTERNS

ACE OF SPADES

MUDDLER MINNOW

SWEENEY TODD

WHISKEY FLY

WHITE LURE

WORM FLY

(Flies tied by the author)

LURES

prove highly effective on almost any stillwater, the majority are best suited to use on heavily rainbow-stocked lakes and reservoirs.

The list of flies and lures for stillwater trout fishing is immense and new patterns appear almost every month. Most of the innovations represent passing fads and have been forgotten by everybody except their originators within a matter of weeks. A few withstand the test of time and find permanent places for themselves in the fly boxes of fishermen up and down the country.

Some fishermen weigh themselves down with huge cabinets containing thousands of flies of every shape, colour, size and design. Others, contending that it is not what you use but how you use it that matters, are happy to fish with no more than one or two patterns from the beginning of the season to the end. A sensible balance can be struck between these extremes. I carry two pocket-sized boxes. One, foam lined, contains artificial nymphs, pupae, corixae, shrimps and so on in one half, and an assortment of lures in the other. The second houses dry flies in spring-top compartments in the base and traditional wet flies in clips in the lid. The contents of both boxes can be adjusted as the season progresses and, no matter how attractive to the trout a particular dressing may prove to be, I rarely, if ever, need more than two or three copies of it for a single day's fishing.

Personally, I am more than happy to fish the season through armed only with the following collection of traditional flies and lures, and with the imitative artificials listed in the next chapter. For those who dress their own flies, the tyings may be found at Appendix 'A'.

Traditional and Attractor Patterns (sizes in brackets)

Alexandra (8–10)	Greenwell's Glory (12–14)
Black & Peacock Spider (10–12)	Mallard & Claret (10–12)
Blae & Black (12–14)	Peter Ross (10–12)
Butcher (8–12)	Soldier Palmer (10–12)
Coachman (10–14)	Teal, Blue & Silver (8–10)
Dunkeld (10–12)	Zulu (10–12)

Lures (all in sizes 8 to 10 long-shank or tandem)

Ace of Spades	Whiskey Fly
Muddler Minnow	White Lure
Sweeney Todd	Worm Fly

While lures are almost always fished singly on the point of the leader, many people use traditional patterns in teams of two or three with one fly on the point and the others on droppers. Droppers can complicate a fisherman's life by tangling with other flies both during casting and when a fish is being netted. The beginner would be wise to stick to a single fly or lure, and I shall refrain from suggesting positions within teams for traditional patterns until we reach the chapter on loch fishing.

Anybody who turns to a book hoping to find a fly, or a small collection of flies, guaranteed to catch trout on all waters at all times is doomed to disappointment. No such book exists. Indeed, one of our sport's greatest attractions is its uncertainty, and there would be little pleasure and less satisfaction to be had from it if we could be sure of taking trout whenever we went to the waterside. However, certain simple principles can be applied to fly selection and are useful for as long as they are recognised for the generalisations they are. In this field there will always be exceptions to prove the rules, and a quite outrageous choice of fly will sometimes produce re-sults when more conventionally selected patterns have failed.

Early in the season, when the water is cold, the fish are still sluggish and dour. They are likely to be quite deep down, especially if the winter has been severe, and their feeding will be spasmodic. Under such circumstances, an appeal to their curiosity is likely to be more effective than one made to their feeding instincts, so a lure or a reasonably flashy traditional pattern could well prove more appropriate than an imitative one, and a sinking line may be needed to carry it down to them. For some unexplained reason, black and white lures seem more attractive to trout during March and April than do those dressed in gaudier colours. But traditional patterns are smaller than lures and those with a little flash and sparkle in them probably catch the fishes' attention more readily than those exclusively and drably dressed in fur and feather. The Butcher and the Peter Ross are both reliable stand-bys early on, but – and this is one of those contradictions that make fly fishing so intriguing – an Invicta can also prove as killing at this time of year as it will later on when the sedges are hatching.

As the season progresses and the reservoirs warm up, the trout should move into shallower water to browse above and around the weed beds. The full range of lures and traditional patterns now comes into its own, and the bank fisherman will find floating and sink-tip lines to be more generally useful than sinkers. Rainbow trout often show a marked preference for dressings incorporating orange, gold and red – hence the efficiency of patterns like the Whiskey Fly and the Dunkeld. Black remains a useful stand-by throughout the year with the Black and Peacock Spider, the Blae and Black and the Zulu all being useful at any time. And the nymph-like silhouettes of such traditional dressings as the Peter Ross and the Mallard and Claret may well account for these flies' successes at any time from April onwards.

While there are strong and logical reasons for concentrating on imitative patterns when the water abounds with natural insects for the fish to eat, lures and flashy traditional patterns may frequently prove useful too. Daphnia-feeding trout, and those engaged in 'smutting' – taking tiny, often unidentifiable insects from the surface film – will rarely accept even the smallest imitative dressing, but a lure or, perhaps, a large Butcher or Teal, Blue and Silver can often divert them from their preoccupation if retrieved quickly.

The problem of fly selection is at its most difficult for the lure or traditional fisherman in high summer. So many patterns are likely to catch fish, and yet the trout can often be remarkably finicky. A lucky dip system may eventually produce the right answer but, at this time of year above all others, it is sensible to seek the advice of fishery staff and local anglers. And, if such advice is not available, it is probably wiser to resort to the old maxim of 'bright day, bright fly; dull day, dull fly' than simply to go on scrabbling around in the fly box hoping eventually to find a more or less satisfactory cure for mounting frustration.

Come September, lures which resemble small fish may well account for larger, fry-feeding trout provided that they are used intelligently rather than simply cast out and pulled back in a mechanical, automatic manner. And, with the brown trout feeding hard and moving towards the streams in preparation for spawning and for the winter ahead, predominantly black lures and drably coloured traditional patterns like the Mallard and Claret and the Black and Peacock Spider can produce dramatic results if fished sensibly.

So, having chosen ourselves a potentially fruitful point on the reservoir shore at which to start fishing and, by applying such logical reasoning as we may have been able to muster, chosen a suitable fly or lure, we can, at last, begin to think seriously about catching trout.

If the reservoir is a popular one, look around you but do not necessarily emulate your companions along the bank. I am prepared to bet that most of them will already be standing thigh deep, as far out as they can wade, double hauling into the distance. Most modern reservoir fishermen have developed a strange, lemming-like characteristic and seem quite unable to resist the temptation to plough into the water before even starting to work out line. The habit – for habit it is – is both counter-productive and harmful.

We saw in an earlier chapter that the vast majority of the trouts' food is to be found in the marginal shallows and that the fish may, therefore, be expected to do most of their feeding in such areas. But

trout are shy creatures and wading causes considerable disturbance
however quietly and cautiously it may be done. This being so, it is
hardly surprising that on some heavily fished reservoirs, where
wading is standard practice, few fish are to be found within 40 yds of
the bank in daytime; or that bank anglers find it necessary to use
shooting heads and distance casting techniques to reach fish driven
out beyond the range of lighter tackle and more delicate methods.
But more serious than this is the damage done to the habitats of
those creatures upon which trout live. A single wading angler can
destroy quite substantial quantities of weed and small-animal life
during the course of a day. Multiply his efforts by the number of
people fishing a particular reservoir in a season and it at once
becomes obvious that vast areas of underwater vegetation are likely
to be trampled out of existence each year, denying food and
sanctuary to nymphs, larvae, snails and crustacea, and removing
from trout any motive for coming close inshore. It is no coincidence
that in nature reserves and other areas where fishing is forbidden
trout can almost always be found browsing quietly within 5 or
10 yds of the bank, or that where the banks are too sheer and the
water too deep for wading, fish can often be taken right under the
rod-tip.

I would not deny that wading may be necessary on occasions – to
reach a specific fish feeding around a weed bed, for instance, when
the reservoir bed shelves steeply downwards 30 or 40 yds from the
bank with only a few inches of water in the intervening shallows, or
when an infertile band caused by summer draw-off of the water
separates the angler from his quarry – but it should be used
judiciously rather than gratuitously, and always with care.

Many reservoir beds are treacherously pitted with pot-holes,
ditches or areas of soft mud. So, when you must wade, a wading stick
or a long-handled landing net should always be used to probe ahead
for such hazards, particularly if the ground is unfamiliar.

Now, start well back from the water and, before beginning to
cast, watch the surface closely for a few minutes. The most
dedicated non-angler can spot the rise of a trout to a floating, adult
fly or to creatures trapped in the surface film, but it takes a practised
eye to identify the movement of a fish a foot or more down. If the
water is choppy, the most apparent sign of a fish's presence is likely
to be a calm, 'oiled' patch at the surface, caused by the displacement
of water as the fish turns. In smooth water, a slight humping of the
surface, or the appearance of a minute whirlpool may disclose his
whereabouts to you.

Obviously, if you can positively locate fish you should cast
directly to them – having first ascertained whether any of their

brethren, lurking between you and your quarry, are likely to be frightened by your activities and to spread alarm to other trout in the vicinity. If you cannot – and this will very often be the case on large reservoirs where much of the fish's feeding is done well below the surface – you will have to 'fish the water'. The techniques for doing this with floating and sinking lines are different but, whichever is used, a logical system should be adopted so that the largest possible area may be covered.

The wind will carry a floating line across the water's surface, particularly if it is blowing from the side, and this can and should be used to the angler's advantage.

Starting with a short line of (say) 5–10 yds, staying back from the waterside and keeping your silhouette low to avoid disturbing fish in the marginal shallows, cast to a point about 45° downwind of you. Do not retrieve the fly but, rather, allow the wind to catch the line and push it round until it is lying almost parallel with the bank. Lift off and cast again, directly across the wind this time, fish the cast out as before, move a pace or so closer to the water and repeat the whole process. Do not attempt to cast upwind or the breeze will put so deep a belly into the line that effective striking will become unacceptably difficult. When you reach the water's edge, lengthen line by a yard or so with each cast until the fly is falling 20 yds or so in front of you and being retrieved from a similar distance downwind.

Since feeding trout generally travel into the wind, there is no need to move along the bank except in calm weather. Theoretically, fish moving along parallel with the shore should come to you in the end. That this actually happens in practice can often be demonstrated when successive anglers, fishing at intervals over half a mile or so, have flurries of sport as a shoal of rainbows cruises along from one to the next. Should you wish to move as you fish, it is sound policy to progress slowly downwind, towards the fish, rather than upwind, away from them. If a shoal of rainbows is located and then seems to disappear, it can quite frequently be found again by quickly moving a hundred yards or so upwind.

But we are getting ahead of ourselves.

Since trout tend to swim into the wind, and since an artificial in profile is likely to be more visible – and therefore more attractive – to them than one seen from directly in front or behind, we should obviously seek to keep our fly or lure travelling as nearly directly towards the bank as possible. Providing that there is a reasonable breeze, the passage of a floating line over the water's surface should ensure that this 'crossing' presentation is achieved almost without assistance from the angler. Naturally, the fisherman must maintain contact with his fly and, in order to do so, he may have to recover line slowly, but an exclusively, or almost exclusively, wind-powered retrieve will often prove far more deadly than a faster, manual one.

With a floating line, the depth at which the fly is fished can be increased by casting a slack line and allowing the fly to sink for a while before the wind catches the line and starts to pull the fly round, or by 'mending' line – that is to say, flicking the line into an upwind curve once a cast has been made. However, neither of these techniques will compensate adequately for the effects of a really strong wind which may offer the angler no alternative but to use a sinking or sink-tip line. It should be remembered that, however far a fly may have been allowed to sink initially, retrieval with a floating line (and, to a lesser extent, with a sink-tip) will pull it back towards the surface and, the faster the retrieve, the faster the fly will rise through the water.

The wind has virtually no effect on a sinking line and cannot, therefore, be used to assist with presentation of the fly. The fisherman must do all the work himself, casting in a fan pattern to cover as much water as possible, allowing time for the line to sink to the required depth and retrieving his fly in such a way as to attract the trout.

It is all too easy to become mechanical in our speed and tempo of retrieve, and the only way to avoid this is to think constantly about how we want the fly to behave in the water. Some patterns are at their most effective when recovered very slowly, others seem to work best when moving fast; there are no hard and fast rules but, by and large, a steady, leisurely action generally proves more successful than does a rapid or jerky one. When in doubt, I have quite often found a satisfactory answer by visualising the speed at which a light wind would carry the fly round, and then emulating it.

Although a fisherman using a floating line can vary the depth of his fly a little, the man using a sinking one can do so to a much greater extent, and far more accurately. Indeed, the key to successful sunk line fishing lies in finding the depth at which the trout are feeding, being able to return the fly to that depth consistently and being able to predict – or, at least, to recognise – when the fish move up or down in the water. An interesting characteristic of trouts' feeding habits is that, however far they may be prepared to move laterally to collect an item of food, they will rarely move upwards or downwards more than a few inches to do so unless they are actually taking creatures on or in the surface film.* So, the depth at which the fly is presented is critical.

---

* Large, floating patterns, like artificial sedges and grasshoppers, will often provide exceptions to this rule, bringing deep-lying fish up to the surface.

Early in the season and in cold weather, when the fish are on or near the bottom, the most effective technique is to cast a fairly long line and then count slowly to (say) 30 before starting to retrieve. If the hook snags on the reservoir bed, or comes back with weed on it, reduce the count after the next cast to 25, and continue to adjust it until the fly is working just above the bottom.

Many anglers fail to realise how slowly even a dense sinking line drops down through the water. It is worth remembering that a Wet Cel 1 takes 7 seconds to sink 1 ft; that a Wet Cel 2 covers the same distance in 5 seconds; and that even a Hi-D line takes 3 seconds to drop those 12 in.

It is also worth noting that a sinking line 'sags' as it sinks through the water; the fly will still be above the lake bed when the belly of the line touches bottom, and will be pulled downwards as the line is retrieved (Fig. 28). So, a fine balance will have to be struck between recovering line early to keep the hook clear of snags and obstructions, and allowing it to sink deep enough to be attractive to the fish.

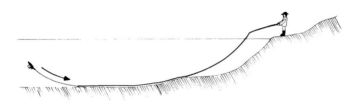

Fig. 28   A Sinking Line 'Sags' in the Water

Lastly, while we are on this subject, a fly sinking through the water at the end of a sinking line describes a (somewhat elliptical) arc about the rod tip. As an extreme example, a 20 yd cast in very deep water will simply result in the line hanging straight down from the rod tip if it is left for long enough. In order to counteract this, line should be fed out through the rod rings after the cast has been made when fishing over deep water.

The first indication that a trout has taken the stillwater fisherman's fly or lure may be either visual or tactile. When using a floating line or a sink-tip, the angler may see a swirl at the surface where his fly is or, if the wind has formed a belly in the line and is pushing it across the surface, he may see a slight straightening of the line or a checking of its progress. Generally speaking, far more fish will be hooked by the angler who has trained himself to spot these signs and concentrates on doing so than by the one who relies on his sense of touch alone or who loses concentration and allows his eyes (and probably his mind) to wander. Of course, with a sinking line a take will almost always be felt rather than seen, and it is probably true to say that as many fish are pricked or hooked and lost with sinking lines as are lost in similar fashion with floaters and with sink tips – but without the fisherman's knowledge.

However the take is sensed, the hook should be firmly set at once. Almost all writers on fly fishing have noted that 'striking' is a misnomer for the action in question, but the point bears repeating here. At the first sign of a take to a wet fly or lure, the rod should be swiftly but smoothly raised, just as if the angler was going into a back-cast, the line being held securely in the left hand and kept tight. The action should be firm rather than violent and can well be described as feeling for the fish and then tightening into it. If the trout appears to have hooked itself, as often happens when lures and traditional patterns are retrieved relatively quickly, the hook hold should not be trusted; the fisherman should take the first opportunity to set the hook firmly, driving the point in beyond the barb.

'Smash takes' occur far more often in stillwaters than in streams or rivers. At one moment the angler is quietly retrieving his line, watching the surface for signs of fish and pondering upon the wonders of nature, the next the rod is almost wrenched from his hand. Only if he is fortunate will he find himself with a firmly hooked fish on the other end.

Although there is no ready remedy for this particular problem, it is worth understanding the two possible causes. The first and, perhaps, the commonest is that the fly and the fish may both have been travelling reasonably fast and in different directions at the moment of impact. It would be easy to suggest that a slower retrieve might have prevented the damage, but it is just as possible that the lure would have failed to attract the trout altogether had it been moving less quickly. The second type of smash take occasionally occurs when a fly is being fished very slowly or even when it is hanging motionless in the water. I had a solid, size 10 hook straightened in one such incident, and was able to see precisely what happened. The fish approached and took the fly at a leisurely pace. Then, before I could set the hook, he bolted off at a tangent instead of spitting the unpalatable artefact out, tightening the line and almost pulling the rod from my grasp in the process. Presumably, he simply felt the hook's point and panicked. That there appears to be no answer to such an event is of little consequence; it happens very rarely indeed.

A trout in a river rarely travels far when hooked. The lie in which he waits for his food to be carried down to him on the current will never be far from the bolt-hole to which he retires when threatened or frightened, and for which he will make soon after being hooked. Stillwater trout, which have to cruise in search of food, cannot lay such contingency plans but, instead, usually run for deep water on finding themselves in difficulty. People newly come to lakes and reservoirs are often caught off guard by the ferocity displayed and the lengths of line run out by even quite small fish.

Some fishermen choose to play fish by winding in line until they have direct contact from the reel, and then reeling in or allowing their quarry to pull off line against the reel's drag. Broadly, I believe this to be a mistake.

The winding in of loose casting line in order to make contact with a fish can be a risky and time-consuming business, particularly early in the fight when the trout is fresh, energetic and unpredictable in its behaviour. Even with a multiplying reel, it may be difficult or even impossible to reel in fast enough to maintain contact when a trout runs straight towards you. And the inertia of a reel can sometimes be sufficient to snap a strong leader when a powerful fish makes a last dash for freedom.

Personally, I prefer to control my fish by hand lining, allowing loose line to fall on to the ground and trapping the line from the butt ring between the index and second fingers of my rod hand, unless a fish takes up all the slack, in which case I will play him from the reel thereafter. Although line trailing on the ground may catch in tree roots, thistles or other obstructions, or become trapped underfoot, such disasters rarely occur in practice.

Whatever happens, the line must be kept tight or there is a real possibility that the hook will fall from the fish's mouth. If a trout jumps, as rainbows often do, the point of the rod should be dropped towards it to put a little slack into the line and then lifted to regain contact the instant the fish is back in the water.

Although there are no guidelines as to how long it should take to play a trout of a particular weight, there is nothing to be said for spinning the process out unnecessarily. To do so increases the risk of the hook loosening its hold and pulling free, or of the fish finding an obstruction on the bottom around which he can – wittingly or unwittingly – snag the line. Breakages very rarely occur from putting too much pressure on a fish and it generally pays to hold a trout as hard as reasonably possible, shortening line whenever you can and only giving line when absolutely necessary.

If you can keep out of sight when playing a trout, by using such cover as may be available and by keeping your silhouette low, the fish will be less easily alarmed and there will be less danger of a last, furious and potentially leader-breaking run just as you are preparing the net or leading your quarry towards a suitable landing site.

The net – if you are using one – should be made ready in good time and allowed to stand with the mesh soaking in the water while you play the fish out. No attempt at netting should be made until the trout has rolled on to its side and its head is being held above the water. At this point, the net should be positioned with the whole of its rim beneath the surface. Never scoop at a fish, but draw it steadily over the rim and lift the net smoothly from the water. If the trout is a heavy one, lifting the net straight from the water is likely to buckle the arms or the handle. It is safer to lift the rim just above the surface without taking the fish's weight and then, by raising the handle to a near vertical position, thus enmeshing your quarry, to pull it on to the bank. If no net is available, wait until the fish is fully played out, draw it towards you, grasp it firmly across its back just behind the gill covers and lift it from the water.

There is one final job to be done before you admire your catch or start to tell others of your success – even before you remove the fish from the net or the hook from its mouth. Your catch must be killed quickly and humanely. Two or three firm taps on the top of the head, just behind the eyes, will achieve the purpose, providing that they are administered with a suitable instrument rather than a light and unwieldly landing net handle, a stone or some other makeshift and almost inevitably inadequate object.

On some fisheries, particularly syndicate ones, anglers are allowed to return fish to the water. This should always be done with extreme care as an incautiously handled trout may develop fungal disease which can then spread to other fish, or its internal organs may be damaged. There is much to be said for the use of barbless hooks where fish may be returned. Contrary to many peoples' expectations, trout do not throw them very much more easily than they do barbed ones. Even when given a slack line, the mere act of towing line and leader through the water is generally sufficient to hold the hook in place, and barbless hooks are very easy to remove.*
If an unwanted fish can be freed in the water by running a hand

* There is now a 'micro-barb' hook on the market which seems a most useful compromise between barbed and barbless hooks.

down the leader, grasping the hook shank firmly and easing the point out, then that is the ideal. Otherwise, it should be handled gently with wet hands, placed back in the water (*never* thrown into it), and held upright until it has regained its equilibrium sufficiently to swim off.

So far, we have really only considered the capture of a single trout from a reservoir with a lure or traditional pattern under near perfect conditions, but the weather will not always be so kind. A breeze and a ripple on the surface are assets in this style of fishing – they aid concealment and fish location, they mask occasionally indelicate casting, and they can be used to move the fly attractively through the water.

High winds can be very uncomfortable but rarely pose as many problems as complete calms do. Intelligent guesswork will usually lead the angler to a steadily sloping downwind shore where fish may be expected to be found feeding in, or at the edge of, the coloured water stirred up by the waves. Casting into the wind may be difficult – or even impossible – but there will almost always be some area of bank where the local wind is blowing from the side. Ideally, it will strike the fisherman's non-casting arm, carrying the line away from his face and body during casting. But even if it is blowing in the other direction it should still be possible to cast quite safely over reasonable distances, either by moving the rod back and forth very close to the side of the head so that the fly travels downwind of the angler, or by turning one's back on the water and dropping the fly on to it on the back-cast. The only real problem now is to prevent the line from tearing across the surface like a thing possessed. It may be necessary to use a slow sinker or a sink-tip, or to 'mend' the floating line repeatedly and pay out slack to compensate for the speed of the wind. The chief risk in this last technique is that so great a belly will form in the line on the water that effective striking will become almost impossible and the hooking of fish will be reduced to a matter of chance. Under these circumstances more than any other it is essential to watch the line carefully for any sign of a take, to strike firmly and instantaneously in an upwind direction (thus tightening against the natural tension of the line) and to get the line off the water's surface as quickly as possible by lifting the rod tip high and, perhaps, moving backwards to take up the slack.

A flat, glassy calm can make life much more difficult – particularly when it is accompanied by clear blue skies and bright sunshine – and demands a substantially greater degree of stealth and care. One of the greatest enemies faced by the angler here will be line-wake, those little furrows in the water's surface caused by the movement of line, leader and (especially) knots, which so surely warns the trout of our designs. It can be avoided, to some extent, by carefully de-greasing the leader with a mixture of fuller's earth and liquid detergent so that it sinks at once, and by retrieving very slowly, or by using a slow sinking line.

With no wind into which to swim, the fish are more likely to be facing and moving in any direction. And, with no ripple to distort or break up images seen through the surface film, they will have an uninterrupted view of the outside world. All of which means that the fisherman will have to take every precaution to avoid being seen by his quarry. It should be remembered that a dense weed bed in the water can offer cover just as effective as that provided by undergrowth or bushes on the bank.

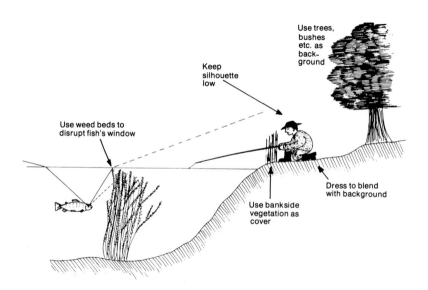

Fig. 29   The Use of Cover

Then, as there is no wind to carry the fly line round, towing the lure tantalisingly behind it, we shall have to give a good deal of thought to the way in which we will cover the water, and to how we can best impart 'life' to our lure.

If we consider all of these calm-water problems dispassionately, it may become apparent that an imitative pattern – the fishing of which generally involves delicate presentation and a very slow retrieve – is likely to be more effective than a traditional one or a lure. We shall be discussing imitative fishing in the next chapter.

Finally, there is the question of how often we should change flies, move or both if we are failing to catch trout. There can be no hard and fast rules here but, as we said earlier, confidence is essential to successful fishing. If your confidence in a particular pattern fades, change it; but always try to base your selection of the next dressing on logical reasoning. If you become bored with a particular spot, move; but work out where you are going to, and why, before doing so. And bear in mind that there is more to catching trout than simply putting the right fly into the right place at the right time. Fishing depth and speed of retrieve can both be critical. So, if others around you are catching fish while you are not, make sure that you know exactly how they are using their chosen patterns, as well as which patterns they have chosen.

CHAPTER 9

Imitative Fishing

Having suggested in the Introduction that it is wise to complement one's favourite fishing style with a sound working knowledge of the other techniques available, perhaps I should admit that my own personal preference is for imitative methods. That is not to say that I am in any way reluctant to use a lure or a traditional pattern on appropriate occasions but simply that, by and large, I find more interest in the pursuit of trout by imitative means than by any other. The reasons are simple.

It is rarely, if ever, possible when using a lure or a traditional pattern to say precisely why a fish has taken our fly. We may suspect that it mistook a Peter Ross or a Mallard and Claret for an ascending nymph, or a pure white Baby Doll for a minnow, but we cannot be sure; we may believe that its curiosity was aroused by a Dunkeld or a Whiskey Fly, but the thesis will never be proved. And if we cannot say why a fish has taken a particular pattern, how can we possibly apply any real logic to fly selection or to our style of retrieve?

In contrast, if we select an artificial dressed specifically to resemble, say, a midge pupa, and induce it to behave as a real midge pupa does in the water, and the trout which takes it is subsequently found to have been feeding on midge pupae of similar size and colour to our imitation, it might seem reasonable to assume that we have truly deceived our quarry by appealing to its most consistent and predictable instinct, that of feeding. And, by summoning such knowledge as we may have of the appearance, behaviour and seasons of the various creatures trout eat, we will have applied reason and logic to our choice of fly, so stacking the odds in our favour. All this being so, it is scarcely surprising that, on lowland waters, the competent imitative fisherman generally catches more fish during the course of a season than does a comparably able angler who habitually uses lures or traditional patterns.

There seems to be a fairly widespread myth that imitative fishing is a throwback from Halfordian days on the chalk-streams and that, even if it has a place in the stillwater angler's arsenal, it is only really suited to smaller stillwaters where long casting is unnecessary. I have never heard any rational argument put forward to support these theories. As we shall see, the various styles of imitative fishing which lend themselves to use on stillwaters bear little resemblance to those commonly employed on streams or rivers, and I have consistently found imitative artificials to be just as effective on fertile lochs and reservoirs as on smaller lakes.

It is, perhaps, worth making the point here that imitative fishing is essentially (although not exclusively) a bank fishing technique. Its success depends largely on slow retrieval of the artificial fly and on our ability to spot takes when they occur. Even when anchored from both ends, a boat is a relatively unstable platform and generally makes both these requirements more difficult to meet. In addition, an imitative technique is often most useful around weed beds in shallow water; and the imitative angler may well wish to move frequently, looking for likely fish-holding areas – both of which factors militate in favour of fishing from the bank rather than from a boat.

Incidentally, the term 'nymph fishing', widely used to describe the techniques discussed in this chapter, is, if taken literally, inadequate. The imitative fisherman may, on occasions, use a representation of a nymph, but he is likely just as often to fish with artificials designed to simulate larvae, pupae, snails, shrimps, corixae, minnows or any of the adult, winged insects that trout eat. This point is not simply an academic one; the term 'nymph fishing', used in the wider sense, certainly excludes the use of floating flies, and its constant repetition in books and in the angling press may well be partly responsible for the lack of thought accorded to dry fly fishing by so many stillwater trout anglers.

I suppose that it should be admitted that the word 'imitative' is by no means perfect either. To suggest that any concoction of fur, feather, silk and tinsel, built on to so rigid and unnatural an object as a fish hook, could ever truly imitate a natural creature would be the height of impertinence. But, accepting this, and for want of a better, the word will suit our purpose.

Artificial trout flies may be imitative in varying degrees. Some are carefully modelled on actual insects – water boatmen, midge pupae or whatever – and may be quite accurate likenesses of their living counterparts. Others are caricatures – dressings embodying the main recognition points of the natural creatures and in which, perhaps, exaggeration of certain features has been found either to elicit a feeding response from fish, or to induce selection of the angler's artificial from amongst a host of naturals on or in the water. Many imitations of sedge pupae come into this category as, indeed, does the Invicta which is often taken when the fish are feeding on hatching sedge pupae, even though its designer may have created the illusion accidentally. Then there are the general patterns – those dressed to represent a group of insects rather than a particular species. Sawyer's Pheasant Tail Nymph and my own Palmered Sedge are both examples of this type of fly. And finally we come to the 'food suggesting' patterns, those bearing no apparent similarity to any specific natural creature, or to any group of natural creatures, but which, when fished slowly, are generally taken by trout with all the quiet confidence normally reserved for more truly imitative artificials – or for natural food items.

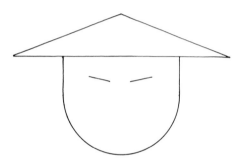

Fig. 30 'The Chinaman'

Richard Walker, possibly the most thoughtful and articulate of all modern fishing writers, has advanced a theory which bears heavily on the design and choice of imitative patterns. He contends that, however crude the drawing at Fig. 30 may be, everybody recognises it as representing a Chinaman simply because it includes a couple of basic identification features – narrow, slanting eyes and a flattened, conical hat. He further submits that a trout appears to identify items of food by the same process and that its feeding response can be triggered by a small number of instantly recognisable features – the bulbous thorax and the white breathing filaments of a midge pupa, for instance, or the silvery grey flanks and the large eyes of a minnow. And, just as we would still recognise the 'Chinaman' whether the sketch showed him in evening dress or athletic kit, so will a trout ignore gross points of difference if enough recognition points are present. If this is so – and Mr Walker's arguments seem not unreasonable – then the fly dresser and the fisherman may tie and use artificials which incorporate (and possibly exaggerate) likely recognition features with high expectations of success, and without having to worry greatly about precise imitation. It is also apparent that trout do not necessarily see underwater creatures as we do, and that some vagueness of outline – roughness even – often enhances an artificial's effectiveness.

The actual selection of an imitative pattern may thus be made in any one of three ways. If we are very lucky – and it happens far less often on stillwaters than on rivers – we may see trout feeding, be able to identify what they are eating, and pick an artificial to match the natural. Failing this, we should be able to make a very fair guess as to what the trout are likely to be eating in this particular water at this time of year, and choose an imitation of that food form. Finally, we may be able to examine the stomach contents of a captured trout and match our choice of fly to our findings – but, of course, the capture of the trout involved implies the use of one of the first two methods, or resort to a traditional pattern or a lure. The second method, the educated guess, generally proves more useful than either of the other two.

Although trout do eat a vast range of aquatic creatures and floating insects, and artificials have been designed to represent or suggest the vast majority of these species, only a relatively small proportion of the fish's potential larder will be in evidence at any particular stage of the season. As examples, Alder larvae are only readily available during late April, May and early June, sedges hatch most prolifically from mid-summer onwards, and crane-flies are generally associated with the back end of the brown trout season – August and September. Provided that the angler knows which food items are likely to be about at a specific time, he can concentrate on a fairly small range of artificials. A calendar showing the seasons of the creatures upon which trout most often feed is at Appendix 'B'.

The fisherman may be able to narrow his choice of flies even further if he knows that certain species tend to hatch at specific times of day. Midges, for example, appear spasmodically from dawn through to dusk, but they are most prolific in the early morning and the late evening and their pupae attract trout most readily at these times. Sedges often show a marked preference for hatching late in the day, but pond olives most frequently appear between mid-day and mid-afternoon.

Then, we can take into account the preferences shown by some aquatic animals for certain types of water. The claret nymph's predeliction for a relatively acidic environment contrasts sharply with the pond olive nymph's dislike of it, snails need plenty of dissolved, calcareous mineral salts, and freshwater shrimps will only thrive in well oxygenated water. It therefore follows that artificials representing snails and pond olives may reasonably be excluded from our list of 'possibles' when fishing acidic, highland lochs; claret nymph imitations are likely to be of little use on fertile, lowland stillwaters; and shrimp-like patterns should be reserved for areas where the water is consistently well aerated.

So, if the fisherman knows what the trout's main food items look like, and where and when they are most likely to be available to the fish – which study is an intriguing one in its own right – the number of patterns from which he will have to choose his fly for a specific water, on a specific day, perhaps even at a specific time of day, should really be quite small.

All that I have said so far suggests that the imitative stillwater angler needs a sound working knowledge of entomology, but those daunted by the prospect of launching into a degree course on the subject can take heart. We have already seen that by far the greater part of a trout's overall food intake consists of quite a small number of insect species. The beginner who limits himself to using artificial midge pupae in an assortment of sizes and colours, a couple of different sedge pupa imitations, a floating sedge and an olive nymph, and presents them to the fish intelligently, may expect rather more than modest success. And, as his experience grows, he can expand his armoury to keep pace with his knowledge.

The list of imitative flies on page 123 is fairly comprehensive and should meet the needs of all but the most demanding fisherman. As far as possible, the naturals and their matching artificials are listed in order of importance. In many cases, several artificials have been designed to represent a single species of trout food. One proven example of each type of dressing can be found at Appendix 'A' for those who tie their own flies.

There is a school of thought, supported by several experienced and skilful fishermen, which contends that it does not much matter what fly you use, provided that it is correctly presented to the fish. There can be no doubt that, on occasions, this is true, especially with dressings like leaded shrimps and sedge pupae. But the most ardent advocate of this argument must have known days when even relatively uneducated stock fish in small put-and-take fisheries became remarkably difficult to catch and refused absolutely to have anything to do with any artificial of the wrong size, shape or colour, regardless of how it was presented to them. Fish which have seen many anglers' flies, or which have become used to foraging amongst a wealth of natural food in a highly fertile fishery, can be

Natural	Artificial	Colours and sizes (in brackets)
Midge pupae	Midge Pupae	Red, black, brown and green (8–14)
Sedge larvae	Stick Fly	(10–12 long-shank)
Sedge pupae	Sedge Pupae	Amber, yellow and green (10–12)
Hatching sedge pupa	Invicta	(10–12)
Adult sedges	Palmered Sedge	(10–12)
	Walker's Sedge	(10–12)
Olive nymphs	Gold Ribbed Hare's Ear Nymph	(10–12)
Olive duns	Greenwell's Glory	(12–14)
Claret and sepia nymphs	Sepia Nymph	(12)
Claret and sepia duns	Pheasant Tail	(12–14)
Mayfly nymph	Mayfly Nymph	(8 long-shank)
Mayfly	Mayfly	(10 Mayfly hook)
Caenis	Last Hope	(17–18)
Minnows/fry	White Lure	(8–10 tandem)
	Polystickle	(8–12 long-shank)
Corixa	Corixa	(10–12)
Crane fly	Crane Fly	(10 long-shank)
Shrimp	Shrimp	(10)
Damselfly nymph	Damselfly Nymph	(8–10 long-shank)
Dragonfly nymph	Brer Rabbit Nymph	(4–8 long-shank)
Snail	Black and Peacock Spider	(10–12)
Alder larva	Brer Rabbit Nymph	(8–10 long-shank)
Freshwater louse	Killer Bug	(12–14)

infuriatingly (or intriguingly) selective, and it seems foolish to handicap oneself unnecessarily by concentrating on presentation without paying similar attention to fly selection. In order to achieve consistent success, the two disciplines must go hand in hand.

In imitative fishing, 'presentation' is the art of placing our chosen artificial unobtrusively in front of a fish, and then moving it in a manner and at a speed appropriate to the natural it is meant to represent. All the creatures trout eat have their own characteristic patterns of behaviour and, if the angler's artificial can be made to behave in the same way as its natural counterpart, the chances of fish mistaking it for the real thing must be greatly increased.

A few hours spent watching insects and small fish in an aquarium can provide the fisherman with a fund of understanding far greater than any he could ever hope to acquire from reading even the most authoritative tome on stillwater entomology. Take the corixa, for example. Most fishermen know what it looks like – a small beetle with powerful paddles and a marbled back. Some have heard that it surfaces from time to time to collect an air bubble (which gives its belly a silvery sheen) and that it can fly. But how many have actually seen this creature, so beloved of trout in so many lakes and reservoirs, going about its daily business? The corixa swims to the surface along an extraordinarily erratic, jerky, zig-zag path and traps quite a substantial air bubble around the hairs on its abdomen. So large is this bubble that the insect is now buoyant, and the return journey to the weed amongst which it lives is a noticeably laboured affair. Indeed, if it stops to rest, or grasps a small, detached piece of greenery instead of the main stem, it will start to float back towards the surface again. Only when it can hold on to a securely anchored piece of vegetation, or when its air bubble is depleted, can it hold its position in the water without effort. All of which suggests that the corixa is best represented by a buoyant imitation fished on a sinking line which will pull it down through the water, rather than by the more widely used sinking pattern fished on a floating line. Such a buoyant pattern exists, and the dressing for it is given amongst the other imitative dressings at Appendix 'A'.

However disparate the behavioural patterns of the various creatures eaten by trout may be, it is generally true to say that all of them move far more slowly than the average angler realises. While sticklebacks (say), or pond olive nymphs, may appear to flit through the water at great speed, in fact they rarely do so. The illusion is created by the animals' diminutive sizes. Time them over a distance of a foot or so and they will, in reality, be found to be quite sluggish. Sticklebacks idle along or even hang motionless in the water until disturbed, and then dart off for only 6 in or so before coming to rest again. Although some of them are capable swimmers, upwinged nymphs rarely move far from the weed beds which both protect and sustain them, and therefore need only to travel from one frond to another. However clearly anglers used to fishing with traditional patterns or lures may claim to understand this, it is remarkable how difficult they seem to find the transition from a relatively fast retrieve to a necessarily very slow one. As a broad rule of thumb, if the line or leader creates even the smallest wake on a flat calm surface when being used with an artificial nymph or pupa, the angler's retrieve is too fast and should be slowed down.

It should be said that the extent to which fish will accept an imitative pattern retrieved at an unrealistically high speed, or with a motion untypical of the natural species it purports to represent, varies from artificial to artificial. Natural midge pupae spend long periods hanging motionless immediately beneath the surface film, and a static artificial, fished just below the surface on a leader greased to within an inch of the fly, will deceive large numbers of trout. But just as many fish will fall to a similar pattern fished on a carefully degreased leader and retrieved just fast enough to prevent it from sinking more than an inch or so. On occasions, this latter technique can be markedly more effective than the other, more realistic one, presumably because greased nylon on the surface disturbs the fish or arouses their suspicions. It may be, too, that an element of exaggeration of movement can attract trout or induce them to single out our artificial from amongst a vast horde of naturals, just as exaggeration of the recognition points in the dressing of an artificial can.

The need for precise presentation might be thought to militate against the use of droppers when fishing with imitative patterns. If each artificial must be retrieved in its own particular way, it seems unlikely that more than one fly in any team of two or three could ever be induced to behave entirely naturally. Why should trout be interested in a midge pupa jerked through the water by an angler concerned with the realistic presentation of a corixa on the point? Or with an Invicta fished very slowly in mid-water in deference to an Alder larva being scraped along the bottom? But it is, in fact, quite possible to fish imitative patterns together provided that they are teamed up sensibly. Many experienced fishermen use a nymph or a spider pattern on the point with two, three or more midge pupae on the droppers. The nymph can be replaced by a floating sedge (which will help to support the pupae) if the fish are feeding right in the surface film. And a sedge pupa on the point with an Invicta as the first dropper and a floating sedge at the top can work wonders on a warm summer's evening. The important thing is to match together artificials which all do well when fished at the same speed – and to ensure that the fishery rules allow the use of more than one fly at a time.

A traditional pattern or lure is generally retrieved at a relatively high speed, either manually or by the action of the wind on a floating line. A trout taking it must, inevitably, be moving at least similarly fast, and will almost always turn away as soon as the fly is in his mouth. Thus, the angler is rarely left in any doubt as to what has happened; a tightening of the line and a more or less positive pull on the rod tip are unmistakable signals. As a bonus, the fish will often hook itself. The take to an imitative pattern fished on or near the surface should be almost as obvious to those with even moderately good eyesight; a swirl in the water or a humping of the surface where the fly should be are both likely to produce an instinctive strike from anybody with any fishing experience at all. The problem comes with an imitative pattern fished more than about a foot down. Because the fly is moving very slowly, and because fish are naturally reluctant to expend more energy than absolutely necessary in the acquisition of a single item of food, takes can be very gentle indeed. If the fly is taken 'on the drop', as it sinks through the water having just been cast, the signs may be almost imperceptible. A skilful imitative fisherman will often strike for no reason that he can specifically put his finger on and find that he has hooked a fish. And I am absolutely certain that many would-be nymph fishermen entirely fail to notice at least 50 percent of their takes, which discourages them and may even tempt them to return to traditional patterns or lures.

So, the spotting of takes when fishing imitative patterns is a visual exercise rather than a tactile one and, obviously, we should do what we can to ensure that our takes are made as visible as possible.

The first step is to examine the flies we mean to use. Those designed to be fished in or just beneath the surface film will be unweighted. If lead or copper wire is incorporated into their dressings, they will sink quickly and will require too fast a retrieve to keep them high in the water. But those intended for use a foot or more down should be weighted. Not only will this carry them down at a reasonable speed, they will also pull the leader with them, keeping it taut, rather than simply drifting down at the same speed as the leader and, perhaps, the tip of the fly line. If the leader is taut, the point at which it breaks through the surface film will be in direct contact with the fly, and takes will be easier to see.

This effect can be enhanced by partially greasing the leader, but this technique is so often misinterpreted and then criticised that a detailed explanation is called for. First of all, let us be clear that we are talking about leaded flies fished at least a foot beneath the surface, and often very much deeper. For flies manipulated within the upper foot or so of the water, a leader of between 9 to 12 ft should suffice, and it should be entirely degreased. But a leader of ordinary length cannot be used to fish a nymph (say) 6 ft beneath the surface without running the risk of bringing the fly line into the fish's window. So a longer leader is required, and the deeper the nymph is to be fished the longer the leader will need to be. As we may well wish to fish our artificials at a variety of depths throughout the course of a day, it is generally worth using a long (say 18 ft) leader the whole time. Such lengths of nylon are surprisingly easy to cast.

An unweighted fly sinks slowly, as does an ungreased leader (Fig. 31a) and, as there is only loose contact between the fly, the leader and the line on the surface, gentle takes may be very difficult to detect.

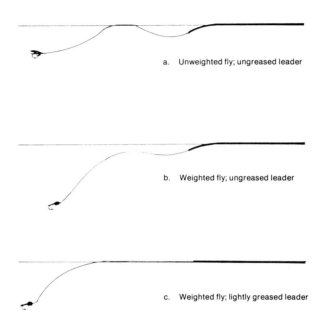

a. Unweighted fly; ungreased leader

b. Weighted fly; ungreased leader

c. Weighted fly; lightly greased leader

Fig. 31

A weighted fly sinks quickly but the leader to which it is attached will still sink in a haphazard manner if ungreased (Fig. 31b). Although contact between the fly and the visible part of the line and leader will now be more direct, takes will be only marginally easier to detect.

However, if the top two-thirds of the leader are lightly greased, the leader will sink progressively under the weight of the fly (Fig. 31c), contact between the leaded nymph and the point at which the leader cuts through the surface film will be direct and takes should be much easier to spot. It must be remembered that the greased portion of the leader floating on the surface has almost the same fish-frightening potential as the floating fly line of which it is an extension, so we can really only use the technique with a longer leader than normal, and must still leave a substantial length of the point ungreased. And it must be clearly understood that mucilin on a leader will not support the weight of even the lightest fly and cannot, therefore, be used to control the depth at which an artificial nymph or pupa is fished.

There are several other things we can do to improve our ability to notice gentle takes to deeply fished nymphs and pupae.

The lure or traditional pattern fisherman dislikes flat calm conditions which do nothing to conceal either indelicate casting or line wake. The nymph fisherman, remaining aware of these hazards, may actually welcome a mirror-like surface, or specifically seek out a sheltered corner of the fishery. Some writers on imitative fishing talk about watching the tip of the fly line, but the leader is a much better indicator of takes – especially where it cuts down into the surface film – and it is far more visible on smooth water than on a rippled or rough surface.

Then we should consider the reflected background against which we will be watching the leader. The worst I know is a cornfield which rises up behind a narrow lake at one particular fishery that I visit often. No matter what precautions I take in the preparation of my tackle, the leader blends perfectly into this background of mirrored corn, and spotting takes can be almost impossible. But, by moving a little, some large, dark trees on the far bank can generally be used to provide a solution, and lightly greased nylon stands out well against their reflections.

Although calm conditions generally favour the imitative fisherman, they are not essential. Provided that the wind is not so strong as to tow the fly round at breakneck speed, lifting it to the surface and making realistic presentation impossible, takes can still be detected by watching the curve of the line on the water. They may be difficult to spot but will usually be signalled by a slight checking of the line's progress or a straightening of its curve. Should this happen, do not stop to wonder whether the change in the line's behaviour has been caused by a fish or not – strike. You may be surprised to discover how often what seems like intuition pays off.

For those with less than perfect eyesight, a bushy, buoyant dry fly, tied on as a dropper half-way up the leader, can be used in much the same way as a coarse fisherman uses a float. But you should make sure that the fishery rules allow the use of droppers.

And, finally, when fishing in poor light conditions, at dusk for instance, holding the point of the rod a little higher than usual during the retrieve may prove helpful, the curve of the line from rod-tip to water providing a useful, if somewhat insensitive, take indicator.

From all that we have said so far, it must be apparent that the imitative fisherman needs to pay the greatest attention to stealth and concealment. Since the whole exercise is a visual one, there is little to be gained (and, possibly, much to be lost) by casting further than the range at which a leader can be clearly seen on the water's surface. This 'visual range' will vary with the light level, the amount of ripple on the surface, the reflected background and the quality of the angler's eyesight, but it is never likely to be more than about 20 yds and will very often be much less. I suppose that something like 75 percent of the fish that I take from stillwaters are hooked within 15 yds of where I am standing – or, rather, kneeling. Some irreverent friends have expressed amusement at the care I take to find cover and to avoid being silhouetted on the skyline, but I have not the slightest doubt that the effort involved is well repaid in numbers of fish caught.

So far, we have only considered the use of imitative patterns fished in or below the surface film. Throughout the 1950s and 1960s there was a general prejudice against the use of floating flies on stillwaters and, indeed, some people are still reluctant to accept that a dry fly can be highly effective on appropriate occasions. As a generalisation, it is certainly true that stillwater trout find something like 90 percent of their food beneath the surface and only about 10 percent on top of it and that, on some waters, this latter percentage may be even smaller. But this does not alter the fact that on most lochs, lakes and reservoirs, many trout spend some of their time taking adult, winged flies from the surface, or that catching fish thus engaged is a fascinating and exciting business.

The techniques for fishing dry flies vary considerably with the species of insect being imitated, and correct presentation is just as critical here as it is with sub-surface patterns.

On many waters, the floating flies most commonly eaten by trout are the sedges. They tend to hatch during the late afternoon or evening and an imitation fished at dusk, especially around reed beds and in other areas where vegetation grows out of the water, will often be taken with great enthusiasm by the fish. These representations of the newly hatched insects are most effective when pulled across the surface either in short twitches or in 2 to 3 ft streaks, both movements being suggestive of the naturals' struggling and flustered attempts to get airborne. But a floating pattern can also be effective during the daytime when the adults which hatched the previous evening may be found in large numbers in and around the marginal vegetation. At such times, a bushy, high floating dressing may prove useful if simply cast out, ideally into the path of a cruising fish, and left motionless on the water's surface. This technique can be particularly killing on a warm, still summer's day when the fly can remain undisturbed by any breeze for quite long periods of time. Although it may be necessary to lightly grease part of the leader to prevent it from sinking and becoming an impediment to efficient striking, the last foot or 18 in should always be carefully degreased. And, as in almost all dry fly fishing, a calculated pause must be left between the rise and the strike. The length of this pause is impossible to define but, if fish rising to a dry fly are consistently missed, lengthening it is a more likely cure than shortening it. Strangely, fish taken by this method are often larger than the average for the water.

Artificial crane-flies (Daddy-long-legs) should be fished entirely without movement, just as daytime sedges usually are. Always select, or tie, patterns with the legs and wings angled backwards as this is how the natural appears after a forced landing on the water, and trout can be more selective with this species than with almost any other. Unlike some sedge dressings and many sub-surface imitative patterns, artificial crane-flies very rarely catch fish out of the natural's season – chiefly during August and September – and they are generally most effective when fished in places where trout are taking real crane-flies from the surface. In late summer, when the insects are about in substantial numbers, it may well pay to seek out a spot where the wind blows gently on to the water from the land and may be expected to be carrying large numbers of these hopelessly inept fliers with it. Like Mayflies, grasshoppers and blue-bottles, crane-flies, both real and artificial, can also be used for dapping, a delightful technique which we shall consider when we come to the chapter on loch fishing.

Many other imitative artificial dry flies can be used to tempt trout in their appropriate seasons – representations of Pond and Lake olives, of the Broadwings (Caenis – the aptly named 'Angler's Curse'), of adult midges, Damselflies, beetles and moths. It would not be practicable to catalogue each one here, describing in detail the areas in which it should be used and the methods of presentation. Suffice it to say that they should all be fished on standard 9- to 12-ft leaders, at least the last 12 in of which should be left ungreased, that they should be cast into the paths of rising fish whenever possible and that, beyond these general guidelines, the angler should take note of the seasons, habitats and behavioural patterns of the natural insects he seeks to represent.

At the beginning of this chapter I confessed to preferring imitative fishing to other methods, explained some of my reasons and intentionally omitted one.

For me, imitative stillwater trouting's greatest attraction lies in the breadth and depth, the sheer magnitude, of the subject, and in the scope for study and experiment that it offers. Half the joy of the sport is derived from observing nature at work and drawing upon the knowledge thus gleaned to bring about the downfall of a trout by calculated deception. If this chapter is thought to be less than a step-by-step guide to imitative fishing, then that is as it should be. I have attempted to set out the basic principles involved in the hope that they may provide other fishermen with sound foundations upon which to build. But I would not wish to deprive newcomers to this branch of the sport of the fun to be had from learning at the waterside.

CHAPTER 10

Stillwater Stalking

During the past twenty years or so, several extremely skilful fishermen have spent a good deal of time perfecting techniques for selectively removing very large trout from certain stillwaters.

Barrie Welham was probably the real pioneer in this field and the list of big fish that he has taken from Alex Behrendt's Two Lakes is an impressive one. But Two Lakes, being a membership-only fishery, is not readily accessible to the general public, and it was not until Sam Holland opened his trout farm at Avington, near Winchester, and then turned three adjacent lakes into a day-ticket water, stocking them with enormous rainbows, that the fly fishing public began to take any serious interest in what, for want of a better term, may be called specimen trout hunting.

The possibilities offered by this new type of fishing were well illustrated by the capture of a succession of vast fish from Avington by Richard Walker, Alan Pearson and a small number of other anglers. Equally, the fact that specialised tackle and tactics were needed for it was clearly shown by a stream of fishermen who failed to catch Mr Holland's larger fish, many of them being repeatedly broken in the attempt.

Mr Holland's breeding and stocking policies drew a spate of adverse comment in the angling press, chiefly from people who disbelieved his ability to farm-rear big, bright, active young fish – of a size and quality that had only ever hitherto been seen in large, prolific stillwaters like Blagdon – and who had never actually tried to take a double-figure rainbow from a small, gin-clear lake. In spite of this, several other fishery managers started to stock with heavy Avington rainbows during the late 1970s, and many owners bought in smaller fish of the same pedigree. Nevertheless, even today, the number of waters holding substantial numbers of trout weighing more than 10 lb is still limited, tickets on them are, naturally, fairly costly, and the pursuit of such fish is generally regarded as being a somewhat esoteric exercise.

The important point about this whole saga is not that a few people have caught a few huge trout but that, in doing so, they have evolved a style of fishing which can be used to take sporting fish of above average weight from any stillwater with sufficient clarity and underwater light to allow the angler to study his quarry, and then place a mid-water lure precisely in the path of a cruising trout. Such waters must, besides being clear, be fairly shallow and sheltered.

In the heading to this chapter I have used the word 'stalking'. It conveys very properly the stealth and caution needed for the capture of seen, feeding trout, often within no more than 2 or 3 yds of the rod tip. But the overall fishing method could, perhaps, be described more accurately as 'ambushing' trout.

The tackle needed is not very different to that used for more conventional nymph fishing. The rod should be powerful and reasonably stiff and, because most of our casting will be at very short range, it is helpful to load it with a floating line (or, better still, a shooting head) at least one size, and possibly two sizes, heavier than normal. As ever, the leader should be matched to the weight of the heaviest fish you expect to catch, and this is one area of the sport in which droppers quite definitely have no place, a single fly always being used. Imagine the dismay if, when playing the fish of a lifetime, some 'fiddling, insignificant' 2-pounder were to sieze the bob fly or the dropper, causing a breakage in the process. The length of the leader must be something of a compromise, and will be dictated by the depth of the water being fished. It should be short enough to make short casting as simple and precise as possible and yet long enough to allow the chosen artificial to sink right to the bottom when necessary. And, in spite of what I said about landing nets in the chapter on tackle, if there is any possibility of catching really big trout, then a large, strong net must be regarded as an essential.

The actual shape and colour of the fly used seem to be of relatively little consequence for these tactics. The important thing is that it should be dressed on a large hook and well leaded so as to sink quickly to the required depth or to the bottom. Mr Sawyer's rather grimly named Killer Bug is a useful pattern for the purpose, as are weighted damselfly nymphs, dragonfly nymphs, corixae and so on. Alternatively, patterns like the Orange Partridge, dressed very short on very big hooks in the fashion of low-water salmon flies, can be made to sink quite quickly, too.

The success of this particular fishing style is entirely dependent upon our ability to spot fish in the water and to plan our tactics around their movements. Although the ability to see fish is not a gift given to all anglers in equal measure, it can – and should – be

developed, particularly by those who would go in search of
exceptional trout. Polarised glasses and an eye-shade or a broad
brimmed hat are a great help, but the real art lies in being able to
look *into* the water, rather than at it, and in being able to interpret
what we see there. Occasionally a fish will come trundling past, 2
or 3 ft beneath the surface, in perfectly clear water, entirely visible
to even the most determined duffer. Far more often it will be deep
down, partly – perhaps almost completely – concealed by weeds,
the opacity of the water and glare from the surface. All the angler
may see is a vague, partial outline, possibly a head or a tail, which
somehow stands out from the surrounding greenery, or a faint
movement suggesting the presence of a fish. Once we know where to
look and what to look for, the trout should begin to take shape, and
we may start to consider how to catch him.

It should be apparent by now that the key to this kind of fishing is
patience. Careful, unhurried observation is essential to the consistent capture of unusually large fish. While there will always be
exceptions to prove rules, the man who turns up at the waterside
and cannot wait to start casting will rarely catch anything other
than trout of average weight.

Having identified our quarry, we must estabish the precise path it
follows. Trout in stillwaters, especially big trout, tend to patrol very
clearly defined routes as they cruise in search of food. The size of the
circuit varies with the size of the water, its depth and the amount of
weed present. In shallow, weedy water the path taken is generally
very much shorter than it is in deep, open water, and the whole of it
may fall within the angler's field of view. But where fish follow
enormous circuits which may take 15 minutes or more to complete,
they may be visible for no more than a few seconds or, at best, a
minute or so in every quarter or half an hour.

The point chosen for the 'ambush' should be somewhere along
that part of the circuit closest to the angler and, ideally, one to
which he can cast from a well concealed position to an open, weed-
free patch on the lake bed. Bankside vegetation undoubtedly
provides the best cover from view and full use should be made of it,
but an intervening weed bed between the angler and the fish can
serve almost as well if the bank is lacking in rushes, bushes, trees or
whatever. And it is worth bearing in mind that if you can place
yourself between the fish and a tall, broken background such as a
wood, that too can provide useful concealment provided that you
are wearing suitably drab or camouflaged clothing.

Even when we have confirmed the route taken by the fish and
found ourselves a concealed position from which we can throw to it,
we should still resist the temptation to start casting. Whatever may

have been said about 'tame and gullible stew fed fish', big trout are cautious creatures. Wait until he has gone past you and only then cast, with as little fuss as possible, aiming to land your fly right on the patch of sand or silt that you identified earlier. Here it should be able to lie, undisturbed and without collecting weed, until our quarry returns. The greatest hazard during this waiting period is that some smaller fish may come along and pick up the artificial from the bottom before the fish we were after reaches us. It happens remarkably often.

When our target fish does come round again, the fly should be left, static, until the trout is level with it or has just passed it. If it is moved while he is approaching he may have time to spot the deception. But by raising the rod tip fairly smartly or, better still, pulling on the line with the left hand to avoid potentially fish-frightening rod movement, when he is level with or just beyond the fly, lifting it from the bottom and, perhaps, creating a small but eye-catching puff of silt or sand in the process, his response should be instinctive. I say 'should', rather than 'will', because the trick will not work every time. It may only do so half the time, or a quarter of the time, or less. But this induced take technique is certainly the surest way of tempting big and often very wary trout where an area of lake bed clear enough to allow the fly to lie undisturbed can be found.

Where no bare patch exists on the bottom, where a solid carpet of weed stretches unbroken from bank to bank, our tactics must obviously be different. We will require very much more accuracy in judging the depth at which the fish is swimming and, even when we can achieve this, we shall still be confronted with a four-dimensional problem. Not only will we need to be able to position the fly accurately in terms of direction, distance and depth, but we will also have to learn to time our cast correctly if the artificial is to have reached the trout's level before the fish arrives, without sinking into an entangling mass of vegetation.

All of which suggests that this exercise is far less sure than the one previously described. And, indeed, it is. Nevertheless, trout will often take a fly as it sinks, or when it is moving slowly in a horizontal plane, so all is not lost.

Assessing the distance of a fish beneath the surface can be very difficult. The size of the trout is an unknown quantity and, if the water is clear, a 4-pounder 3 ft down and a 10-pounder 7 ft down may look very similar. The only answer to this problem is experience, and yet even the most practised specimen trout hunter can still be fooled from time to time.

Casting to your chosen trout as it approaches over its weedy background is a delicate business. He will probably be facing us, and extreme care must be taken not to alarm him. Concealment is as essential as ever here, and accurate side casting is infinitely preferable to waving rods about above our heads. But the real problem lies in getting the fly to the fish's feeding level at the right time. We have already noted that sub-surface feeding trout are generally reluctant to move up or down more than a few inches in order to take an item of food, and the characteristic is even commoner in large fish than in smaller ones. In fact, unless the depth of the fish is known exactly, the most skilful and experienced angler will still find such a combination of space and time almost impossible to achieve. And, even if he does manage it once in a while, there is no certainty that a big fish will take a quietly sinking artificial, however realistic the fly may look to us. So, we come back to the principle of the induced take.

It is far better to cast a little early and, having allowed the fly to sink to beneath the trout's level, to pull it upwards past his nose than to watch with mounting frustration as our quarry cruises by 3 ft below our descending artificial. This induced take in mid-water often seems to be just as attractive to trout as does that which starts from the bottom – indeed, the two techniques vary little in essence. But the one is obviously easier to set up than the other, and is therefore likely to be the most useful.

When quick, accurate recasting becomes necessary, as it often does with this type of fishing, the key to success is to be found in pointing the rod directly at the target *before* lifting the line from the water.

For those hell-bent on the capture of exceptional fish, the list of refinements that can be introduced to these two basic tactics is almost limitless. Weed beds can be used to conceal line and leader as can the broken silhouettes of over-hanging trees. Nylon and fly lines can be dyed to merge with their backgrounds and rods can be rubbed down with a mild abrasive to eliminate flash. But whatever method is used, and however many precautions are taken, the fisherman will always be confronted with the problem of playing and landing his trout once he has hooked it.

I am not a salmon fisherman but understand that the average salmon caught on rod and line in the British Isles weighs about 6 lb. A 6-lb trout is by no means an uncommon fish on many stillwaters. Some of the public day-ticket reservoirs occasionally produce fish of 8 or 10 lb or more, and a few smaller put-and-take waters like Avington and Church Hill Farm are stocked with substantial numbers of rainbows in the 10- to 20-lb class. And yet we expect to bring these fish to the net with quite ordinary tackle, the sort of equipment more commonly used for the taking of trout from fisheries where a 4-pounder causes comment.

Because the waters from which big trout may be caught by stalking tactics are unlikely to be large, and because the fish will almost always be hooked close to the bank on strong tackle, the difficulties of playing and landing them will be less than those associated with taking trout of similar weights from sizeable lakes or reservoirs on tackle intended for smaller fish. Nevertheless, large trout in small stillwaters can run for considerable distances, and they can present other problems, too, chief amongst them being the fisherman's almost constant proximity to the fish and the consequent risk that he will alarm it into suddenly bolting. Once again, the solution lies in concealment. When a trout has been hooked, there is a temptation for the angler to stand up so that he can see what is going on. But it is remarkable how this action seems to focus the fish's mind on the source of its troubles, and how much more violently a trout fights when played by a standing and visible angler than when his adversary is kneeling and concealed. Indeed, if a fish is unable to see the fisherman on the bank it will often express little more than mild annoyance at having its freedom of movement restricted, and may well settle down to almost casual cruising after an initial run or two. While it can take some time to wear down a fish behaving thus, at least the risk of breakage should be minimised, and strength-sapping side-strain can be judiciously applied to a point just short of that at which the creature may become alarmed and bolt off again. With care, by keeping out of sight and offering the net as a refuge, it may even be possible to trick the fish into netting itself – as Richard Walker did when landing his one-time record rainbow.

The actual landing of a large trout needs particular thought and care and the point at which the fish is to be brought ashore will require some consideration. Heavy waterside vegetation or a steep, cliff-like bank may turn the operation into a nightmare; clear, sloping margins should render it relatively straightforward. And the net should be both big enough and strong enough for the job in hand. The whole operation is already fraught enough with difficulty, and there is little to be said for exacerbating our problems by trying to use a net into which the fish will not fit, or which is likely to collapse under any substantial weight.

If the fishery rules permit it, help from an experienced colleague may allow a particularly heavy fish to be landed quickly, before it loses its equilibrium and becomes an ungainly dead-weight on the end of the leader. If offered, such assistance should always be accepted, especially if one's net is believed to be inadequate for the task in hand. The only proviso here is that the volunteer really must know what he is doing. Heaven forbid that an enthusiastic and excitable novice should ever lose us the fish of a lifetime.*

Finally, if all this talk of enormous trout sounds a little daunting, I would only reiterate what I said earlier. The techniques we have considered in this chapter need not be reserved exclusively for the capture of very large fish. Provided that the water is clear enough for us to see our quarry, they can be used in the pursuit of selected trout in any lake or reservoir. And, for many people, the deceiving of a particular, seen, feeding fish provides a far greater sense of satisfaction than does any amount of time spent blindly flogging the water.

---

* Incidentally, assistance in landing fish is currently prohibited at Avington.

CHAPTER 11

Going Afloat

To most anglers a boat is no more than a means to an end, and many people go afloat each season blindly accepting what they find when they reach the waterside, with little or no thought for the extra equipment they may need in order to fish successfully, or even for their own safety. To an extent, this is understandable. Few fishermen have their own boats for stillwater trouting. The vast majority simply hire those that are available where they fish, purchase and maintenance being undertaken by the owners or managements of those waters. But, with a little thought, it is almost always possible to improve upon what is provided in terms both of comfort and of suitability for fly fishing. Of course, some people do buy boats of their own for stillwater trouting so, in this chapter, we shall consider their overall needs as well as such minor modifications as can be made to improve hired vessels.

The main requirements for a boat for lake or reservoir trouting are that it should be big enough to comfortably accommodate two anglers and their tackle, that it should be stable, that it should be as uncluttered as possible with a minimum of snags for lines to get caught on, and that the seating should allow both occupants to fish for long periods without tiring.

When considering length, it is not enough simply to work out the space taken up by two seated people and their personal effects. Thought must also be given to the risk at which each puts the other when casting; a hook and a fly line can constitute a considerably offensive weapon when propelled by a powerful reservoir rod, and the enthusiastic individual fisherman cannot always be relied upon to see that his back-cast area is clear when a great trout rolls on the surface to one side of him or the other. So, a boat's length must be sufficient to ensure that two casting anglers can be seated far enough apart for safety. While it is quite often done, I believe that for three people to try to fish from any boat is inadvisable. Flying hooks aside, such crowding cannot be conducive to any real degree of concentration. Personally, I prefer to fish on my own, but some water authorities forbid this on safety grounds. With these thoughts in mind, 14 ft should be regarded as a minimum on lochs and reservoirs where the angler may wish to take all his tackle, food and spare clothing with him when he sets off in the morning. On smaller lakes, where fishermen may be expected to fish from a boat for only part of the day, or to return to shore from time to time – and where unpleasant weather is of less consequence – 12 ft may suffice.

Stability is required both for angling efficiency and for comfort as well as for safety. A great deal of frustration can accrue when a fisherman, afloat on a flat calm lake and casting as gently as he is able, can do nothing to stop a boat from rocking back and forth with every movement of his arm, sending warning ripples out across the surface like radio waves. But of much more concern is the boat which, comfortable as it may be in settled conditions, rolls disconcertingly as soon as a slight chop builds up, and which must be held head to wind or pulled for home when the weather becomes a little rough. Fortunately, such abominations are rare. The British have been building boats for thousands of years. A traditional hull shape, well suited to use on large inland waters, has been evolved over many generations and varies but little from one part of our islands to another. The warning is really issued to those who might be tempted to use flimsy, trailable or car-portable craft on lakes or lochs for which they were never designed, and upon which a sea-like swell can develop with surprising rapidity.

On smaller stillwaters, those of up to 50 acres or so, which can never become really rough, a flat-bottomed punt or rowing boat may serve, especially if there is a good deal of shallow water. But such craft are unwieldly in any sort of a wind and should never be used on a large lake or loch. It should be said, too, that the use of boats on small lakes can have a disastrous effect on the fishing, particularly when the water is calm and clear. Time and again I have seen people go afloat on a flat, glassy lake, and then watched an immediate decline in the sport for 100 yds or more around the anchored or drifting boat, while bank fishermen further away have continued to catch trout.

Most fishermen retrieve line on to a thwart or directly into the bottom of a boat. To repeatedly find the line caught up round a loose board or jammed in some diabolically placed crevice is annoying. To find it similarly jammed as an angry trout runs off at speed across the lake is very much more so. And the discovery that the mesh of a landing net has become apparently inextricably entwined around some hitherto unnoticed screw or nail head just as that same fish begins its final, dogged struggle around the anchor rope is enough to move even the mildest of country parsons to immoderate language.

The number of line and net snagging protruberances that a boat has will depend on the material from which it is built, its detailed design and, in some instances, its age. Wooden boats, built as they usually are by laying boards on to a fairly complex frame, tend to have far more than their smoothly moulded fibreglass counterparts, and old wooden boats often have more than new ones, particularly if they have not been meticulously maintained.

Whatever the state of his boat, the angler can easily take a few basic precautions to ensure that the sort of traumas described above will not intrude into his day or, at least, that they will be kept to a minimum. A polythene sheet laid on the bottom boards for a yard or so around the seat from which he means to fish, and tucked behind or pinned to the vessel's internal framework should completely mask such hazards as nail heads, splinters of woodwork and loose boarding. Fishing tackle and other bits and pieces should be carefully stowed before pushing off so as to be both accessible and unobtrusive. The buckles on fishing bags are amongst the most consistent catchers of lines, and the best place for the bag is beneath the thwart upon which the angler will be sitting, with the buckles on the same side as the casting arm. Since line is retrieved with the non-casting arm, to the angler's non-casting side, it cannot then catch on the bag. The landing net should be prepared for use and stowed ready to hand and clear of snags before fishing begins. And oars and rowlocks should be properly stowed, out of the way, when starting a drift or when the boat is at anchor.

It is difficult to place too much emphasis on the need for tidiness in boats. There can be nothing more certain to destroy concentration or the pleasure of a relaxed day afloat than the need to find a particular spool of monofilament from amongst an assortment of more or less useful gear, soggily washed by ebbing and flowing bilge water, and jumbled up amongst the bottom boards.

One thing we may almost always be sure of is that the seating arrangements in a hired boat will be unsatisfactory, but this, too, is something which can easily be put right with a little forethought and effort.

The ideal position for boat fishing is seated astride a high thwart, preferably on some sort of easily dried padding. This obviates any need for the angler to sit with his legs tucked up against his chest, and elevates him high enough to make consistently long casting reasonably easy while keeping his silhouette low enough to avoid scaring every fish for miles around. However, it is neither the best position for rowing nor even for sitting as a passenger during the possibly choppy journeys to and from the fishing area. The thwarts in most boats are designed for these two latter purposes and are supported at their ends between 6 and 12 in below the gunwales. In order to raise himself to a suitable level for fishing, it is well worth the angler's while to build a portable seat which can be laid across the boat from one side to the other, resting on the gunwales. The different boats used for lake and reservoir fishing vary but little in the beam. A plank 5 ft 10 in long, 8 in wide and 1 in thick, with a length of 1-in square timber screwed to the under side of each end as a stop, will be found to fit the vast majority of angling boats available for hire in Britain. Such improvised seats do no damage to the gunwales, but thin sheets of foam rubber stuck on to the bottom of the seat, inboard from the stops, will provide peace of mind for even the most fastidious owner, and will prevent any minor slipping that might otherwise have occurred.

The seat can be further improved by sticking a fairly thick – say 2 in – sheet of foam rubber on to the top so that it overhangs the

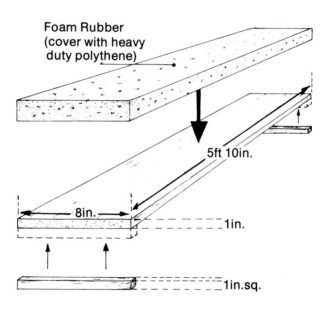

Fig. 32   Gunwale Seat

edges slightly, and then covering the foam with imitation leather or some other robust plastic material. Rumps tire quickly on bare boards and such a seat, cheap and easy to make, can provide a very much higher degree of comfort than a hard, low, narrow and sharp-edged wooden thwart. Inflatable boat cushions are available from some tackle shops, and may provide partial answers for those who would prefer not to be cluttered with a full-sized portable seat. And, if a lightly inflated 18 in by 4 in inner tube can be obtained, that will make a very satisfactory alternative, too.

Incidentally, I know of one particular fishery where the boats – flat bottomed, fibreglass craft – have been fitted with moulded plastic chairs, mounted so that they will revolve on pylons at bow and stern, in addition to the central rowing thwarts. Apart from the fact that they are a little too high even for my long legs, they are very comfortable, but I cannot believe that these particular boats, or their seating arrangement, would be suitable for use on larger waters where they would have to be pulled over considerable distances and where wind and waves would constitute regular hazards.

Motors of various types, both inboard and outboard, are valuable for running out to and back from fishing areas, but their in-discriminate use can have a noticeably adverse effect on the fishing. Where they are allowed, they should be employed judiciously, and the fact that power is available should not blind the angler to the presence of oars as an alternative means of propulsion, particularly when moving from the end of one drift to the start of another. And, of course, oars must always be available, no matter how supposedly reliable the engine may be.

Some water authorities forbid petrol engines of any sort, either inboard or outboard, on their reservoirs. Where this is the case, an electric outboard, run from an accumulator, can provide a useful alternative. Indeed, with its non-polluting, silent and vibration-free running, an electric motor may very often be more satisfactory than a petrol one or even than oars, causing less disturbance both to fish and to other fishermen. The great disadvantage of electric motors at present is that the accumulators have strictly limited lives before they need re-charging. It is to be hoped that the current search for alternative power sources to oil-based fuels may produce longer lived batteries.

I have already said that a boat may be used as a static casting platform or allowed to drift with the wind. In either event, some simple but essential equipment will be needed to ensure that it behaves as the angler wants it to.

The anchors supplied with hire boats on lakes, lochs and

reservoirs are often highly unsatisfactory. In some cases no anchor of any sort is provided, in others simple concrete blocks, secured by lengths of rope barely long enough to reach the bottom in any reasonable depth of water, are expected to suffice. An anchor must meet three basic requirements if it is to be truly efficient. It must be designed to take a secure grip on any type of bottom (apart from hard, flat rock), it must be fitted to a rope – or, better still, a chain – at least twice as long as the depth of the deepest water in which an angler may wish to anchor, and it must be easily tripped for retrieval.

For efficient nymph fishing afloat, the boat needs to be held completely still and, to this end, it should be anchored from both ends – which, of course, means that the fisherman will need two anchors.

Probably the most generally useful anchor for the stillwater fisherman is the well proven Danforth pattern. It is available from virtually any chandlers in an assortment of weights but need not be particularly heavy for inland waters. A 2 kg (roughly $4\frac{1}{2}$ lb) Danforth should be quite adequate for use as a sole or primary anchor, and a secondary one need only be about half that weight. The Danforth's particular advantages over other types are that, having large, flat flukes, it holds as well in mud as on any other bottom, that it is markedly lighter than those of other patterns with similar holding properties and that it folds flat and is therefore easy to stow away when not in use.

A 'spring' – a weight of about 14 lb mounted on the cable about 10 ft from the anchor – will often help an anchor to grip on a bottom upon which it might otherwise have dragged.

All sorts of gadgets and gimmicks have been invented or pressed into service to control direction and speed of drift, from chains hung over the side to leeboards clamped to the gunwales, and from simple drogues to sophisticated 'drift control rudders'. Each has its advantages and disadvantages, and each has its adherents and denigrators. Drogues aside, all of them seem to have been dreamed up, tested and developed by the same imaginative and inventive school of Midlands reservoir fishermen that pioneered the techniques for deep lure fishing at Grafham and its neighbouring waters. Some of the devices are banned on some waters, partly because they can be unsafe under certain conditions, partly because they can cause damage to boats and partly because the managements of a few fisheries consider their use to be unsporting.

Like many other anglers, I prefer not to arrive at the waterside weighed down by a mass of ironmongery and I have, therefore, never used either a drift control rudder or chains. The former is simply a rudder which can be clamped to the transom of the boat and the blade of which, once adjusted, can be locked into position. Since a boat blown by the wind drifts across the lake's surface faster than the upper layers of water, the rudder will influence its angle and direction of drift, and may be used to steer a course following the shoreline or a particular underwater feature.

A leeboard, which must be clamped to the downwind gunwale, will slow down the drift and can be used to steer a fairly oblique diagonal course across the wind. It should be emphasised, however, that even if leeboards are permitted by the fishery's rules, and anglers elect to use them, they should only be deployed in fairly light airs. A 5-ft plank dug into the water on one side of a boat propelled laterally across a lake by anything more than a moderate breeze can produce serious instability, and the twisting on timbers or fibreglass never designed to take such stresses can cause considerable weakening of or damage to the boat's structure.

A chain lowered over the side, hanging either straight down or in a loop from bow to stern, is said to slow and control a boat's drift in much the same way as a drogue does, and to provide the angler with limited information on the depth of water over which he is fishing; if you know that you have 15 ft of chain out, there should be no difficulty in establishing whether you are in water more or less than 15 ft deep, or in locating the 15 ft contour during the course of a drift. But, apart from the performance involved in lugging such a weight down to the water, my own feeling is that a chain is likely to rattle alarmingly when being deployed, and I have therefore never used one. Instead, I have, on occasions, used the boat's anchor and spring hung overboard amidships to stabilise a slow drift when there was insufficient breeze to justify the use of a drogue. This system has the particular merit that the boat can be made to come to a gentle standstill in a predetermined depth of water at the end of the drift, allowing the angler then to fish the downwind, offshore shallows which often seem so attractive to feeding trout.

Drogues have been used to slow drifting boats and to control their angles of drift for many years. Essentially, they are no more than 'underwater parachutes' made of canvas. Several designs are available and they differ widely in price, but I have never been able to convince myself that the expensive ones are really very much more efficient than their cheaper counterparts except, perhaps, in that they may be more durable. The great advantage of a drogue over other devices is that it is light in weight and can easily be folded for storage in the bottom of a fishing bag when not in use.

A drogue will serve no useful purpose in a light breeze as it is necessary for the boat to be drifting across the surface at a reasonable pace before it can deploy properly and start to exert an influence. But in a moderate breeze or a light wind, a drogue secured amidships can slow and steady a boat to a remarkable extent. If the wind is fresh or strong, there may be considerable advantage in putting the drogue out through some form of fairlead near the bow, or in attaching it to the anchor chain's strong point. A boat drifting head to wind rides the waves much better and provides far less freeboard for the wind to act against than does one drifting broadside on; and, as a bonus, drifting in this way allows two anglers to fish out sideways from the boat, casting at right-angles to the line of drift and fishing their flies 'around the corner' – a technique (called 'fishing the fall' in Scotland in the nineteenth century) which often proves particularly attractive to trout as we shall see when we come to consider boat fishing in detail.

Of course, a boat cannot be drifted bows-on in light or moderate breezes as the surface area available to the wind for its propulsion will provide insufficient impetus to deploy the drogue properly.

One warning note. A drogue should always be fastened to a really secure strong point within the boat, rather than to a rowlock or any other piece of ancillary equipment. If it is not, there is a real risk that it will pull its anchorage away and disappear into the depths, possibly causing structural damage to the boat itself. If purpose-made strong points are not provided, the drogue's rope should be made fast either to a firmly secured thwart, to the anchor rope's own strong point, or to the mooring ring. If the user has any control or influence over the maintenance of boats used for fishing, he should seek to have proper fairleads fitted to the gunwales at points which will produce acceptable angles of drift when the drogue rope is run through them; the most useful one will be located approximately at the centre point of the gunwale and alternatives might be provided a couple of feet either side of it to cater for changes in drift angle caused by an increase or reduction in the number of people using the boat.

Before we leave the whole subject of aids to boat angling, some mention should perhaps be made of echo-sounders. Personally, I have never used one, but a number of experienced anglers, particularly those who fish the great limestone loughs of western Ireland, tell me that they find such electronic equipment an invaluable aid to reading the beds of those lakes, and that echo sounders have real safety value. In addition, some modern instruments are said to be able to pick out shoals of fish, although whether using them thus reduces the element of mystery which is – for me, at any rate – one of angling's greatest appeals is a matter for the individual to decide.

So far, we have only looked at boats and their equipment from the point of view of their capabilities and limitations as fishing aids. But safety afloat is of (literally) vital importance and it might be as well to consider here the basic equipment and precautions necessary to minimise the dangers – they can never be entirely eliminated.

Just as most drivers consider themselves to be experts on the roads, most anglers consider themselves to be skilful boatmen. It is, therefore, surprising to see just how many people are quite happy to push off for a day's fishing without giving a moment's thought to the serviceability of their craft and its equipment, or to the weather. There seems to be a general feeling amongst stillwater anglers that lakes, lochs and loughs present none of the hazards of the open sea, and that to show any concern for personal safety afloat is somehow a bit old-maidish. Nothing could be further from the truth. While some inland waters are, indeed, sufficiently small and sheltered to be spared the worst excesses of our fickle weather, many are extremely large and can become very rough quite quickly. Hills and mountains around upland waters can make the wind flukey and unpredictable, and lowland reservoirs can be subject to sudden, long lasting and dense fog blanketing. I well recall being out on Lough Corrib when two of us, both young and fit, were almost entirely unable to make any headway at all rowing against what had seemed from the shore to be no more than a fresh breeze. We were not, in fact, carried over to the far side six miles away, but were very tired indeed when we eventually succeeded in beaching the boat not too far from our point of departure. Corrib's near neighbour, Lough Mask, is notorious for its roughness and for the shoals of jagged rocks, some of which break the surface while others lie treacherously just beneath it. And, of course, since fish are often found around such underwater features, the temptations for fishermen to approach close to them are strong, which increases the risks.

The managements of commercially run fisheries generally en-force basic safety regulations and are careful not to allow boats out if dangerous conditions are expected. But many stillwaters, especially in Scotland and Ireland, are not commercially run, and here it is entirely up to the individual angler to decide whether to go out or not, and what safety measures to adopt.

Nobody should contemplate going afloat on a large stillwater unless they can swim at least sufficiently competently to avoid being an immediate liability to their companions in the event of an accident. And whatever the swimming competence of the oc-cupants, and however optimistic the weather forecasters may be, there should always be one serviceable life jacket available for every person in a boat, and each person should know exactly where his or her life jacket is, even if it is not worn while fishing.

Similarly, some form of buoyancy for the boat itself should be regarded as essential on any large water where rough weather is a possibility or submerged rocks are known to exist. Many modern boats have buoyancy built into them, but older ones rarely do. The inflatable buoyancy bags used by dinghy sailors are light, portable and can be secured out of the way beneath the thwarts. Or, for more permanent installation, sacks filled with table tennis balls or other small, light, airtight objects can be used.

However you plan to fish, whether from the bank or from a boat, it is always sound policy to obtain a weather forecast before setting out. If you know the wind speed and direction you are half-way to being able to work out where the fish should be. If you are taking a boat out on a large stillwater a weather forecast will be doubly important, and you should always be prepared to alter your plans – staying ashore if necessary – in the light of impending bad weather. If you have any doubts as to the significance of a forecast for a particular water you plan to fish, seek local advice.

Whatever the weather, it is sensible to leave a note of your name, address, car number and planned time of return with a responsible person at the fishery before setting out. If this is not practicable, some form of identification and the telephone number of someone who knows your plans should be left visible within your car for anybody suspecting that you may be in trouble.

Before leaving the shore, you should check that drainage bungs are in position and that the rowlocks and a baler have been secured to the boat by lengths of cord. Small clips of the kind used on dog leads are ideal for this if ring eyes are screwed to the boat in appropriate positions.

Broken shear pins are by far the commonest cause of outboard motor failure. If an outboard is being used, you should know how to replace a shear pin and have a spare one and an elementary tool kit with you. If the owner of a hire boat, or a fishery management, do not provide a spare automatically (and few do), ask for one. Shear pin breakages most frequently result from running outboards among rocks and other obstructions in shallow water, and great care must be taken when manoeuvring in areas where such hazards are evident; by far the best plan is to row out into deep water and only then to start the motor.

We discussed clothing in the last chapter, but it should be noted here that shoes are infinitely preferable to Wellington boots or waders in a boat. Contrary to an often perpetuated old wives' tale, boots and waders do not fill with water and drag a man under in the event of a capsize, but they can make swimming both difficult and tiring.

Once afloat on any large water, the angler should always know his position and the location of the nearest acceptable landing site. This may sound simplistic, but fishermen concentrating on their fishing in a drifting boat can become very preoccupied, and bad weather can close in with remarkable rapidity, drastically reducing visibility. Under such circumstances it is not always enough just to head for the shore; many highland lochs and Irish loughs are riddled with sharp, sub-surface rocks around their margins. On very large waters – like Loughs Mask and Corrib, for instance – it would not be over-cautious to take a compass with you and to make sure that you know how to use it, especially if bad weather is forecast and you are not employing the services of a ghillie.

Should the weather become rough while you are out on a large lake or loch, bring the boat's head to the wind before there is any risk of her starting to ship water; a boat drifting broadside on in choppy conditions is liable to take in water over the gunwales and is both unstable and uncomfortable, and if you try to row downwind (i.e. stern to wind) in a gale, there will be a strong tendency for the

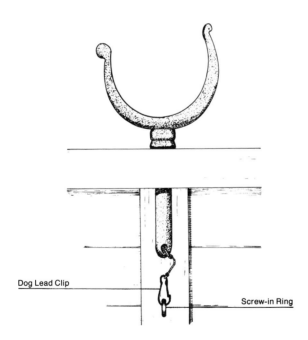

Dog Lead Clip

Screw-in Ring

Fig. 33 Rowlock Fastening

vessel to broach and swing broadside on. If you cannot row into the wind, or if your hoped for landfall is downwind of you, put a drogue out over the bows to keep them facing into the oncoming waves. If no purpose-made drogue is available, almost anything will do – a bucket secured by a rope through a hole punched just below the rim (rather than by the handle which would be likely to pull away), a bundle of clothing, or a couple of boards roped together into a

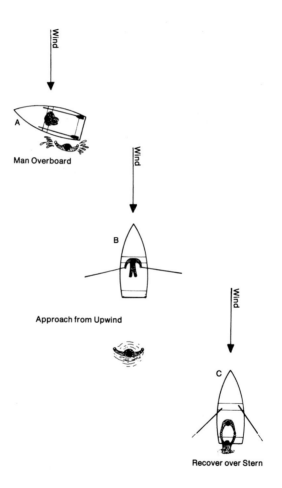

Fig. 34   Recovering a Swimmer

cruciform. Although it will continue to drift, almost any soundly built boat will ride the roughest seas provided that it is held head to wind. Do not stand up or try to walk about in rough weather, but keep the centre of gravity as low as possible.

Should an occupant of a boat have the misfortune to fall overboard, he should be approached from downwind at low speed. Having passed close to him, the engine (if one is being used) should be stopped and the oars manned to ensure that the vessel drifts slowly down on to the person in the water stern first. A swimmer should always be recovered over the stern of a boat – to try to bring a person in over the gunwales can cause a dangerous list, particularly if willing and well intentioned hands lean over the side to offer help.

Having waded through so depressing a catalogue of potential disasters, boat angling for trout may seem to be a more hazardous business than it really is. Many, perhaps most, of the lakes, lochs and reservoirs in Britain are small or sheltered enough to be virtually immune from the worst excesses of the weather and, where larger or more exposed waters are properly administered, the inexperienced or impetuous are protected by rules laid down and enforced by the managements. Providing that it is used intelligently and with forethought, a boat can add a delightful and challenging new dimension to stillwater fly fishing. Nevertheless, it is as well to be aware of such risks as may exist on large, windswept or ill-administered waters, and of the equipment and techniques that may be used to guard against them.

CHAPTER 12

To Drift the Loch

Techniques for taking trout from Scottish lochs and Irish loughs were already well established by the end of the nineteenth century. That they have changed little since then and, indeed, that the style is now widely used to great effect on lowland lakes and reservoirs (and provides the basis for the rules governing international fly fishing matches) is a tribute to the skill and understanding of those who evolved the methods a hundred years and more ago.

Early loch fishers drew heavily upon rods, reels and lines previously used for river fishing and they pressed trout, sea trout and scaled down salmon flies into service to meet the new conditions. By far the greater part of their fishing was from boats rather than from the bank, and they learnt to drift on the wind, casting a short line ahead of them, dribbling their flies back just beneath the surface and re-casting frequently.

This type of boat fishing has a special charm of its own. In calm weather it is a gentle, leisurely pursuit. Occasional sounds carrying across the water to the boat fisherman seem to emphasise his remoteness from the hustle and bustle ashore. It is sociable, too. Most bank anglers do what they can to avoid fishing cheek-by-jowl with others, but two people can happily spend a day side by side in a boat, interfering with each other's fishing not at all and comparing notes or talking between themselves when the mood takes them.

Generally speaking, the boat angler will catch more fish during the course of a season than will his companion on the shore, simply because he covers more water. But, inevitably, he will pay more for his days out and he will not as easily be able to move from one precise spot to another.

Most of the lochs and loughs for which this traditional fishing style was developed contain only wild brown trout. If we are coming to them from rainbow-stocked lowland lakes and reservoirs, it is worth remembering that their effective season is a fairly short one and that it is clearly divided into two halves. The fishing often starts quite early – perhaps in March – and improves steadily until the middle of June. But there is then a dull, dour period through July and August during which even the most practised loch fishers may experience very considerable difficulties, and it is not really until September that the fish come back on to the feed again. If we are planning a loch fishing holiday – the very remoteness of most waters of this type generally militates against simply taking occasional days on them – it is worth bearing these points in mind and making our booking either for the spring or for the late summer.

The tackle used for bank fishing on lowland reservoirs should serve as well for loch fishing from a boat although if a rod of 10 ft or so is available it may offer some slight advantage over a shorter one. Fairly light – say, AFTM 5 or 6 – floating, sink-tip and slow sinking lines will be required, the floating one almost certainly being used more often than the others.

While some traditional fishermen use leaders up to 18 or 20 ft long, a standard leader of 9 or 12 ft, knotted to a 2-ft butt length, should suffice for most purposes.

We shall, of course, need some flies. The traditional patterns suggested in the chapter on bank fishing are all suitable, but the accepted style of loch fishing calls for their use in teams of three, four or even five. One fly, attached to the loose end of the leader, is referred to as the 'point fly'. The others, tied to short lengths of nylon protruding laterally from the main leader, are the 'droppers', the top one being known as the 'bob fly'.

Anybody who can recall the first few times that he fished a team of wet flies will confirm the ease with which tangles can occur both during casting and while netting a fish. The more flies in the team the more often will these horrendous birds' nests develop and the more inextricable is the knitting likely to be. Droppers also create a possibility that the leader will be broken if a fish drags it through a weed bed or if a second fish takes while the first is being played. Neither of these events is at all uncommon. So, newcomers to this style of fishing would be well advised to start with no more than three flies on the leader – two will often do – and to have a number of spare leaders ready made up and wound on to 'cast carriers' so that loss of valuable fishing time may be avoided when inevitable tangles occur. It is also sound policy to make up one's own leaders from nylon monofilament, rather than to use expensive, knotless, tapered ones. Then, when a tangle does occur there will be little reluctance to cut the leader off and start again. The one stern warning I would issue here is that discarded nylon must always be taken home and burnt. Left lying around it would constitute a very real and totally unacceptable hazard to birds and animals.

It has been suggested – and it is probably true – that while the bob fly actually catches relatively few fish it serves to attract trout towards the surface and to the other flies on the leader. To achieve this purpose, a reasonably bright, flashy pattern is normally used or, alternatively, a bushy, palmered dressing which can be made to create a wake not unlike that caused by an adult sedge. In either case, it is as well to grease the leader down to the bob fly to help prevent the latter from becoming waterlogged. And when a palmered pattern is used, that too should be soaked in proprietary floatant to the same purpose.

It is normally sound policy to put a nymph on to the point – or one of those patterns which anglers often believe to be taken for nymphs by trout – and, in cold weather early in the year, there is something to be said for using a lightly weighted pattern here.

While certain patterns have traditional (and most effective) places as point or bob flies, few if any hard and fast rules govern the angler's choice of droppers. As ever, the views of skilful local anglers should be sought wherever possible.

So many traditional patterns are available, and choice is so heavily influenced by personal and local preference, that any short list of potentially useful teams of flies must inevitably be very arbitrary. It should be appreciated that the following selection is intended to provide no more than general guidance for newcomers to loch fishing. The dressings for all the flies can be found at Appendix 'A':

	Point	Dropper	Bob
March/April	Peter Ross or Butcher	Mallard and Claret or Blae and Black	Zulu or Coachman
May	Peter Ross	Mallard and Claret	Butcher
June/July	Greenwell's Glory or Dunkeld	Teal and Blue or Mallard and Claret	Soldier Palmer or Butcher
August/ September	Alexandra or Mallard and Claret	Teal and Blue or Blae and Black	Soldier Palmer or Zulu

In addition to traditional wet flies, it would be as well for the early season angler to arm himself with a small collection of black or dark coloured lures, and for spring and summer fishermen to have with them a floating sedge pattern or two, some midge and sedge pupae and, perhaps, a few imitative nymphs.

Before actually going afloat we should cast our minds back to the chapter on boat fishing. A day on the water can be made or marred by good or bad personal organisation. Firstly, we must check that the boat itself is fit and ready for use – that the bungs are in position (if they are fitted), that the rowlocks, anchor, mooring chain and baler are properly secured, and that buoyancy aids for the boat and its occupants are in good order. If an outboard motor is to be used, there should be a small tool kit including at least one spare shear pin. Before installing our tackle and other effects, the boards should be lifted and such water as may have accumulated in the bottom of the vessel baled out. There is little less pleasant than fishing with several inches of water slopping about around one's feet. Secondly, rods should be set up before leaving the shore and all fishing tackle, bags, picnic boxes and spare clothing should be properly stowed. Particular care must be taken with the rods themselves. If they are not positioned carefully, there is a risk of their being trodden upon or of protruding tips being broken.

The area in which we plan to start fishing should be chosen before pushing off from the shore. The deductive process involved is precisely the same as that used to select a promising spot on the bank but, of course, the options open to us will be much wider.

On any steep-sided, acidic highland loch or upland reservoir, it is sound policy to limit our choice to the shallow margins, to such offshore shoals as we may be able to identify and to the areas around the mouths of feeder streams. Detailed charts of these often remote waters are not always easy to obtain, and local advice should always be sought and listened to. Where ghillies are available their services are generally invaluable, but an unknown ghillie's knowledge and fishing ability should not be taken for granted. Many are very good indeed but, in common with so many other areas of craftsmanship in these 'get-rich-quick' days, true experts are becoming increasingly rare. Some modern ghillies are boatmen rather than fishermen and a few are scarcely even that.

Where mixed woodland runs right down to the water's margins, stretches of the shoreline edged by deciduous trees will almost always be more productive than those bounded by conifers. Fir trees and their like are inhospitable to insects, create highly efficient wind breaks and rarely overhang the water to any great extent. In contrast, eared willows, rowans, silver birches and so on provide rich grazing for a wealth of insect life, their lacy foliage offers relatively little resistance to the wind and their spreading branches often hang out far beyond the bank. Trout take full advantage of this, particularly in waters where aquatic food forms are sparse, and will lurk in the shade afforded by the trees' canopies, waiting to snap up the terrestrial insects which inevitably fall or are blown on to the water. It usually pays to concentrate one's efforts on the upwind side of an infertile lake or reservoir where suitable bankside vegetation may be expected to serve as a larder for the trout.

If the choosing of likely fishing areas is a reasonably straightforward exercise on highland lochs and upland reservoirs – even for those unfamiliar with the waters in question – it is far less so on the great limestone loughs of Ireland. By some quirk of nature, few if any Irish loughs experience temperature layering. This may be because their surface areas are so large, and they are surrounded by such relatively unsheltered, low-lying land, exposed to every Atlantic gale, that the water circulates too fast ever to allow a warm layer to develop. Whatever the cause, the effect is that well-oxygenated water is available from the surface to the bottom across the entire extent of each lough, that trout food abounds almost everywhere and that the fish are effectively free to cruise wherever they like in search of sustenance. Such circumstances clearly call for the assistance of an expert ghillie, for only by tapping local knowledge of these waters can we expect to find fish-holding areas with any real consistency. Treacherous, rocky shorelines and reefs, and the ferocious weather which is all too commonplace here, merely serve to underline the need for guidance from somebody who understands both the geography of the lough and its moods.

If I have painted too gloomy and forbidding a picture of Irish waters, it should be said that they produce some of the finest fishing in Europe and that, given good weather and good fortune, the anglers' rewards in terms of big, clean, beautifully marked, wild brown trout should repay the effort and planning involved in their capture many times over. And it is still possible to read the water, using the principles suggested in earlier chapters on the fish, their food and their surroundings. Wind or food lanes, more commonly in evidence on fertile lakes than on more acidic ones, will frequently provide guidance as to the areas in which trout are most likely to be found, and a knowledge and understanding of the creatures trout eat, their seasons and their life styles can all help to put us on the right track.

Having selected our fishing area, we must decide how we will fish it. The ideal on an upland loch is to choose a starting point from which we can drift along a continuous line, close into the bank, directly over a shallow shoal or across the mouth of a feeder stream without having to change direction or realign ourselves more than absolutely necessary.

The old and most traditional style of drifting calls for the boat to be laid broadside on to the wind with its occupants casting ahead of it (Fig. 35). In a light breeze this can be accomplished without the use of a drogue, but it is a good idea to lower an anchor or a heavy weight overboard amidships on the upwind side, allowing it to hang perhaps 4 or 5 ft below keel level, as this will help to stabilise the drift. It will also provide an early warning system so that the boat can be worked close into the shore without the occupants constantly having to worry about going aground. Or, if suitably secure rowlocks are fitted, an oar left hanging overboard from the upwind gunwale will help with the first stabilising requirement but not, of course, with the second one.

With a little practice two people should easily be able to keep a boat drifting straight and true, broadside on. One person alone will

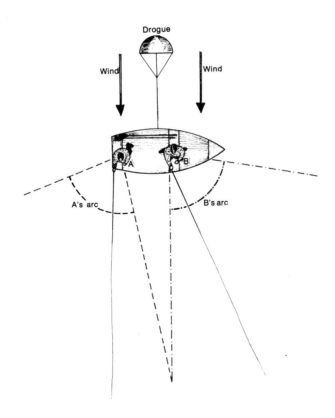

Fig. 35 Traditional Loch Drift

find it more difficult. Even when seated amidships, the positioning of his weight and the resistance he offers to the wind will tend to set the boat swinging slightly and an occasional pull on an oar may be necessary to prevent it from doing so to an unacceptable extent.

In any sort of a wind, a drogue will serve both to slow the drift and to stabilise the boat. It should be deployed on a fairly short rope and secured to a proper strong point within the boat.

Although I said earlier that the fishing technique on the drift was to cast downwind, there is a good deal more to it than that. The traditional style of loch fishing is a delicate business and one has only to watch a true expert to see just how much artistry is involved.

There is no 'ideal' casting range for this fishing style, but 15 yds is generally regarded as a realistic maximum and most practised anglers limit themselves to about 10 yds. The most effective tactic is to cast with and slightly across the wind, to allow the point fly and the dropper – or droppers – to sink a little, and then to retrieve the team very slightly faster than the boat is travelling. When only 3 yds or so of line are left between the tip ring and the point of the fly line, the rod should be raised slowly to an angle of $50°$ or $60°$, tripping the bob fly over the ripple and creating a minute wake with it. This action frequently seems irresistible to fish which, even if they do not take the bob fly, will often make a grab for a dropper or for the point fly having followed them for some distance; it should, therefore, be drawn out for as long as possible. It is important to keep the left hand, holding the loose line, quite close to the reel during the lift. If it is allowed to fall away and a fish takes as the rod is moving upwards – by no means an uncommon occurrence – there is a risk that the angler will 'run out of arm', that he will have stretched his arms so far apart that he will have no reserve of movement available with which to hook the trout and handle its initial struggle.

It goes almost without saying that any indication of a fish should produce an instinctive reaction from the fisherman. A rise, a swirl in the water, a calm patch in a ripple, a fish seen in the front of a wave – any of these should cause the angler to draw the fly if it is near the disturbance, tightening if any resistance is felt, or to lift off and re-cast quickly if the movement is more than a yard or so from his flies.

Once the cast has been fished out, the rod should be flicked upwards through the remaining $30°$, pushing the line into a back-cast in preparation for the next throw. Unnecessary false casting is a fruitless and counter-productive exercise at any time. From a boat drifting at any speed, it is also wasteful of good fishing water. No more than two false casts should ever be needed to extend line downwind, and one should normally suffice.

For two people to fish from a boat successfully requires a certain amount of co-operation and teamwork. Each must stick rigidly to his own casting arc to avoid interfering with his colleague. A casting range must be mutually agreed to ensure that neither throws a longer line than the other, putting down fish that might otherwise have been risen. The pair should make a habit of casting alternately so that their lines do not foul each other on the back-cast. And both of the boat's occupants should remain seated at all times. There are few things more certain to evoke justifiable irritation in the angler afloat than a partner constantly striving for distance, perhaps even standing up in order to throw a slightly longer line.

So far, we have only considered the traditional, broadside-on style of drifting, but there is much to be said for a system developed on the highland lochs in the nineteenth century and now widely used on all types of large stillwater. It relies upon there being a slightly stronger breeze than we might normally wish for when fishing from a boat, and entails putting the drogue out over the stern of the boat and drifting downwind bows first, or, in rough conditions, reversing the process and drifting bows to wind.

Not only does this method make for a very much more comfortable drift – a boat broadside on in a strong wind can be positively dangerous – but it also enables fishermen to present their flies more attractively to the fish. We saw in an earlier chapter that trout generally move upwind as they feed. A fly cast directly downwind is therefore likely to be seen tail on, or almost so, affording the fish a relatively uninspiring view of it. Worse still, if the fly is retrieved directly upwind, only very few fish are ever likely to see it. But a team of flies cast and retrieved across the wind should be seen by the maximum possible number of trout and, just as important, it will most often be travelling across the fishes' field of vision, rather than directly or almost directly away from it. The bows or stern-on drift offers another advantage, too. As we saw in the chapter on bank fishing, and as we shall see in a different context in the one on reservoir boat tactics, a fly accelerating slightly and turning at the same time often seems almost irresistible to trout. With a cast made almost directly across the wind from a boat drifting head- or stern-on, the line can be allowed to belly and swing round in just such an arc (Fig. 36). It is remarkable how often a trout will take a fly turning this corner, or just having done so.

Trout rising to wet flies fished on the drift frequently hook themselves, but it is as well to be on the safe side. As soon as a tug is felt, or a swirl or flash is seen in the vicinity of the leader, the hook should be set with a quick lift of the rod.

When a fish is hooked from a drifting boat it should, if possible, be brought round to the upwind side to be played out and netted. If it is large or unruly, or if for any other reason there is any likelihood of its charging about downwind of the boat, the second rod should retrieve his flies and stop casting until the trout has been brought safely aboard. In any event, and particularly if the drift is close to rocks or to the shore, it is the second rod's reponsibility to control the boat while a fish is being played.

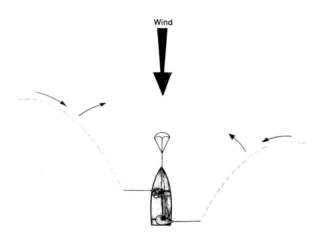

Fig. 36   Bows-on Drift or 'Fishing the Fall'

Those who, like myself, enjoy fishing on their own in a boat must be particularly careful when fishing near hazards or obstructions. It may take only a few seconds to bring the flies inboard, take up the oars and pull away when one has nothing else to concentrate on, but it is very much more difficult to trip and retrieve a drogue and then row clear of danger when a lively fish is churning about at the end of the line. And we should never forget that a drogue is intended to act as a form of sea anchor. Trying to row with one deployed is a singularly frustrating and unproductive exercise.

Repeated success on a particular drift always tempts one to row or motor back and try it again immediately, but it is generally unwise to do so. Even if the trout are cruising fairly steadily, the passage of the boat over the water, the actions of its occupants and the commotion caused by hooked fish are all likely to have disturbed a substantial proportion of the area's piscine population. It is much sounder policy to move on, returning when the water has been rested for a while. In any event, an upwind journey to the head of a drift should always take the form of a wide detour, rather than a direct pull over water we mean to fish in a few minutes' time, and it is undoubtedly better to row than to motor.

A fair breeze is, of course, essential to successful traditional, loch-style boat fishing. It moves the boat across the water and it sets up a ripple which helps to conceal both the boat's approach and the angler's activities from the fish. A flat, glassy calm spells disaster. Water is an extremely efficient carrier of sound and, however careful we may be, any noise caused by boots or other objects knocking or rasping against the boat's hull will be transmitted to every fish in the vicinity. For this reason, rubber-soled boots or shoes are essential, pipes should never be knocked out on the gunwales, and fish should not be killed on the botttom boards or even on the knee with the foot resting on or against the thwarts. In addition, the mere act of casting from a static boat on calm water will send warning ripples out across the surface. So, in the absence of a wind, the wise boat fisherman will head for the shore, put up an imitative pattern – a nymph, perhaps, or a floating sedge – and present it to the trout as delicately as he can. Better still, he might use the opportunity to explore one or more of the small hill lochs or lochans that are usually to be found above the main valley. They often provide delightful and exciting bank fishing as well as an enjoyable walk and pleasant scenery.

Wind is as essential to dapping as it is to traditional drifting techniques.

Dapping is a most charming style of boat fishing, extensively used on limestone loughs in Ireland but rarely practised elsewhere. In essence, it consists of allowing the line to billow out on the wind, tripping a natural or artificial fly over the surface of the water. The reasons for the technique's lack of general popularity are probably three-fold. Firstly, it is widely believed that highly specialised tackle is essential to success. Secondly, the Mayfly hatches in Ireland represent a major and dramatic facet of the overall dapping scene there; Mayfly hatches are rare on stillwaters in Britain, and almost unheard of on large ones. Thirdly, and quite wrongly in my view, some authors have suggested that, as a technique, it is both tedious and undemanding of skill.

It is certainly true that a purpose-built dapping rod – some 12 ft long or more – furnished with 6 to 8 ft of synthetic dapping floss, knotted to ordinary monofilament backing, will provide its owner with some considerable advantage over a companion equipped with more *ad hoc* tackle, particularly if the breeze is light, but it is not essential. As long as there is a moderate ripple on the water, a standard reservoir rod of about 10 ft – or, better still, a 14- or 15-ft carbon fibre coarse fishing rod – fitted with a nylon monofilament line of, perhaps, 5- to 7-lb breaking strain, either on a fixed spool reel or on an ordinary fly one, should serve quite adequately. A tapered fly line will not work; it is too dense.

Flies for dapping take a variety of forms. Broadly speaking, any large and bushy natural or artificial may produce results in its appropriate season. Mayflies, grasshoppers, Daddy-long-legs and sedges are the most commonly used in Ireland, but there is room for much experiment with damselflies, moths and even bluebottles or beetles. Whether a natural fly or an artificial is used is a matter for personal preference. It is possible that naturals attract more fish – although I have my doubts about this – but artificials are markedly more robust, and the angler using them is not faced with the problems of capture and storage which accompany the use of living insects. If artificials are used, they should generally be bushily dressed so that they will carry on the breeze.

A monofilament leader used for dapping should be short – between 3 and 5 ft – and, of course, only a single hook can be used.

The selection of a drift for dapping is made in exactly the same way as is one for traditional wet fly fishing. Because the anglers' lines will be blowing directly downwind, a broadside-on drift is essential if two people are fishing from the boat, but a single person can use a head- or stern-on drift and, indeed, should do so if the wind is at all fresh. It must be appreciated that the essential element for successful dapping is a reasonable wind blowing across the boat. In a flat calm, the fisherman's line will hang sullenly from the rod tip and, if the boat is drifting at almost the same speed as the wind, the effect will be much the same. So, our purpose should be to slow the boat as much as possible. To this end, a drogue will almost always be used. If the breeze is light and a suitable spot can be found where trout may be expected to be moving upwind in numbers – along a food lane, perhaps, or through a channel between two islands – it may well be worth halting the boat's movement across the water altogether by anchoring.

The artistry in dapping lies in being able to keep the fly just tripping over the surface. It takes a little practice. If the fly is allowed to drown or become waterlogged it will lose much of its liveliness and is likely to prove markedly less attractive to the fish. And if it is kept hovering above the surface, the trout will generally be unable to see or take it. In a steady, moderate breeze it should be possible to skip it from wavelet to wavelet, never allowing it to leave the surface for more than a moment or to become soaked. The line and leader will billow out in a curve from the rod tip to the fly and neither should ever touch the water.

A trout's rise to a dapped fly will generally take one of three forms. Most often, it will be a gentle affair, the fish seeming to suck the insect down. Sometimes, particularly in blustery conditions when the fly is dancing from wavetop to wavetop, it may be a fast and furious slash, not unlike the attack on a floating sedge being skimmed across the water. And, occasionally, the fish may try to drown the fly, flapping at it with his tail. However the take occurs, the angler's chief concern should be to allow the trout to turn down and get the fly well into its mouth. It is difficult to emphasise too strongly the need for self restraint at this time. Dry fly river fishermen will be familiar with the old rules of saying, 'God Save the Queen', or counting to three before striking. Indeed, the same guidelines hold true for conventional dry fly fishing on lakes and reservoirs. But, when dapping, one might almost sing a whole verse of the National Anthem, or recite the alphabet before 'feeling for the fish'. The wait, while nerve-racking, can hardly be too long.

If we are being honest, and excepting the great limestone loughs of Ireland, we will recognise dapping as a relatively minor stillwater tactic but, before we leave it, two more points seem worthy of mention.

Firstly, for those with enquiring minds, it offers considerable scope for experiment on British waters, particularly on our southern reservoirs. For instance, the trout in many of our large stillwaters are susceptible to a floating Daddy-long-legs in August and September, and there is no reason to believe that they would be any less easily tempted by a dapped one. I must confess that I have been as reticent as other fishermen in this respect, but there would certainly seem to be room here for a little innovative thinking. Secondly, it is worth bearing in mind that dapping is the ideal technique through which to introduce hitherto disinterested spouses to fly fishing! It does not demand great expertise in casting, so they are not frustrated by early ineptitude; the realism of, say, an artificial Daddy-long-legs seems to give them confidence in the fly's ability to catch fish; the whole exercise is intensely visual; and the take, when it comes, is often dramatic.

Although it does not fall strictly within the scope of this book, one last facet of boat fishing on natural waters deserves our consideration. Many Scottish lochs and Irish loughs hold substantial numbers of sea trout from midsummer through until the autumn, and these fish can provide spectacular and exhilarating sport on perfectly ordinary stillwater trout tackle.

As we saw in Chapter 2, the sea trout is simply a migratory brown trout, being born in running water, moving into the sea to feed – often growing very large in the process – and returning to the river of its youth to spawn. It is no coincidence that rivers holding few brown trout, or only very small ones, on account of their infertility, often produce good runs of salmon and sea trout. Indeed, it seems certain that these great sporting fish result directly from the water's barrenness, their forebears having been forced to abandon their native streams in their search for sustenance.

Sea trout do not breed in stillwaters but, where a lake or loch interrupts the seaward progress of a river, they will obviously pass through it on their way to the spawning grounds, and they will often remain there for a while, resting before the exertions of their run on up to the redds.

Nor do sea trout habitually feed in freshwater, although some may be found to have a few small food items in their stomachs after capture and it is quite often possible to re-awaken old feeding urges with a strategically placed nymph or dry fly, particularly in a river or stream. This fact is important to the stillwater fisherman for two reasons. Firstly, because sea trout are obeying a migratory call rather than the demands of hunger, their behaviour will not necessarily be affected as that of non-migratory trout will by the wind, temperature layering, weed beds, overhanging trees or any of the other things that govern food distribution. In short, we cannot always expect to find sea trout in the same places as we would expect to find brown trout. Secondly, a sea trout will be less ready to take a slowly fished imitative artificial than will a resident brown trout, which sets a premium on the use of traditional or attractor patterns.

The distribution of sea trout in lochs is largely influenced by the lengths of time they have been there. In general terms, sea trout rest in low water conditions and run on upstream when rain produces a rise in the height of the river. We may therefore expect to find newly arrived fish in a lake immediately after a spate, and many of them will remain close to the outflow of the river for a short time before moving on.

Sea trout show a clear preference for fairly shallow water and, having moved away from the outflow, will take up lies around the margins, over offshore shoals and close to islands. Because they plan to move on up to the redds, many fish will move quite quickly to the mouths of inflowing feeder streams, waiting there for rain to raise the water level so that they can continue their journeys.

Most of the characteristics associated with sea trout in rivers are still evident when the fish move into stillwaters. The small fish of between $\frac{1}{2}$ lb and $1\frac{1}{2}$ lb – the herling, finnock or peal – tend to shoal, although they will often separate and spread out when they have been in the lake for some time. And the longer the fish have been in freshwater, particularly in one place, the more difficult it will be to persuade them to take a fly.

The tackle used for taking sea trout in stillwater is very similar to that used for the rest of our loch fishing. Because the quarry may be bigger, leaders of, perhaps, 7 lb breaking strain are needed. And flies should be very much larger, sizes 6 and even 4 are by no means too big. But, these two components aside, the rods, lines, reels, landing nets and so on that we use in pursuit of resident brown trout will serve as well for our attempts to catch their migratory cousins.

Similarly, the loch fishing tactics described earlier in this chapter – both the traditional drifting style and dapping – can be employed just as effectively against sea trout. Although teams of three or four artificials are sometimes used, more normal practice is to fish only two flies on a leader, the point fly being an attractor – the Teal and Silver, the Dunkeld and the Alexandra are all useful here – and the bob serving as a wake fly, a Zulu, perhaps, a Soldier Palmer or a Butcher.

Those who fish for sea trout in rivers by night tend to be more successful than those who venture out only in the daytime, but the reverse is generally true on stillwaters. Although the reasons for this are unclear, we may be sure of one thing – sea trout lose none of their notorious shyness just because they have left the river. They are extraordinarily easily alarmed and, if stealth and concealment are prerequisites to success in any form of trout fishing, they are especially so here. Banging and stamping about in the boat will frighten every fish around, and standing up will put paid to any remaining possibility of sport.

Before closing this chapter, it should be said that the techniques described can be used just as effectively on fertile, lowland waters as on the lochs and loughs for which they were evolved. Interestingly though, methods developed for use at places like Grafham, Rutland Water and Chew do not seem to produce consistent results when applied to natural waters containing only wild brown trout. Whatever the reasons for this, the fact remains that recently developed reservoir fishing tactics work well on the lowland reservoirs for which they have been devised, and we shall consider them in the next chapter.

CHAPTER 13

Reservoir Boat Tactics

The opening of large, deep, fertile, mainly rainbow-stocked, man-made waters like Grafham, Rutland and the Queen Mother Reservoir at Datchet has presented boat fishermen with problems quite unknown on highland lochs, Irish loughs or shallow, lowland lakes like Blagdon or Loch Leven.

The traditional loch fishing style was specifically evolved to catch trout, particularly brown trout, feeding at or near the surface. Rainbows in deep, zooplankton-rich waters may feed at almost any level, and their capture calls for tackle and tactics which will enable them to be located, and a fly to be presented to them, wherever they may be. And, since most planktonic animals are far too small to be effectively represented on any reasonable fish hook, a formula other than a strictly imitative or food-suggesting one has to be used in order to tempt the trout.

When these problems first became apparent in the mid-1960s, the anglers who sought to resolve them included an imaginative and intelligent group of Midlanders. Some of them were relatively new to trout fishing and, unfettered by the lore surrounding established stillwater boat tactics, they developed revolutionary equipment and techniques to meet the new conditions.

Later, during the mid-1970s, these and other reservoir anglers turned their minds to very large brown trout which, having evaded capture for several years, were living out their lives on the bottom in very deep water. In some cases these fish seemed rarely if ever to feed in daylight or to move into the shallows, but those who went in pursuit of them found that an exaggerated version of the techniques hitherto used to take plankton-feeding rainbows in mid-water could occasionally bring about the downfall of a specimen-sized brown.

As we saw when we considered the history of stillwater trouting, some of the methods evolved by the Midlands school and others over the past fifteen years or so have caused a certain amount of indignation amongst more traditionally minded fishermen.

Whether the use of lee-boards, drift controllers, echo sounders, lead-cored shooting heads or multi-hued 6-in lures is acceptable or not seems to me to be a matter for personal preference, provided that their use is allowed for in the fishery rules and that it does nothing to impair the sport of others.

Before we consider reservoir boat tactics, perhaps I should explain that I am not greatly attracted to huge and generally rather featureless stillwaters like Grafham, Chew Valley and Datchet, so my personal experience of the new methods is somewhat limited. Nevertheless, when I have used the techniques evolved by the Midlands school, I have found them to be a highly efficient means of catching fish.

By the late spring, free-floating phytoplankton abounds throughout the lengths and breadths of most fertile, lowland lakes and reservoirs. Zooplankton, thriving upon this feast, is similarly widely distributed and the rainbows swim back and forth, mouths agape, growing fat on the soup of minute animal life. With so much water at the fishes' disposal, finding them can be a problem, but even plankton-feeding rainbows still show a marked preference for water no more than about 20 ft deep – which at least helps us to decide upon the areas in which we should concentrate our fishing efforts. The chief problems lie in the fact that the fish may be cruising at any level between the surface and the bottom, depending upon the time of day – and the depth at which the greatest concentrations of plankton will therefore be found – and in the selection of a fly with which to attract trout feeding on such tiny creatures.

Three separate requirements must be met if we are to identify consistently the precise level at which the trout are moving and then, equally consistently, present a fly to them at that level. Firstly, we must have a reasonable understanding of the vertical migratory habits of planktonic animals and of the factors that influence the migrations. Secondly, we must have the right tackle for the job. And, thirdly, we must know how to handle the boat to best advantage.

Let us consider each of these problems separately.

When discussing the fishes' food, we noted that plankton migrate vertically. During the night, dense clouds of plankton will often be at, or quite close to, the surface. As the sun rises, they start to sink through the water until at mid-day, or shortly thereafter, they may be as much as 60 or 70 ft down. These minute creatures have very limited locomotive ability and are, effectively, only moved by the currents in the water. So, in water less than 70 ft deep, they spend many of the daylight hours lurking close to the lake or reservoir bed. Obviously, in high summer they will start their downward migrations earlier and begin to move upwards later than they will during the shorter days of early and late summer. All this being so, it follows that we may expect to find plankton – and, therefore, plankton-feeding fish – quite close to the surface during the hours immediately after dawn and prior to dusk. Of course, it should be appreciated that, like most of the factors affecting trouts' movements, planktonic migration is an imprecise business. It seems to be influenced by temperature, light and the currents in the water. Similarly, we cannot always be sure that the fish will be feeding on plankton on any particular day or at any particular time; they can easily be diverted by a sudden rise of snails or a hatch of midges or caenis, or they may be put off their food altogether by a chill north-east wind. But, as a generalisation, the knowledge that rainbow trout do consume enormous quantities of plankton in lowland reservoirs throughout the summer, and an understanding of the plankton's behaviour, can be of great assistance when we find ourselves confronted by a vast and apparently lifeless expanse of water.

If we are to be able to present a lure to these fish temptingly, at any depth and from a drifting boat, we shall obviously need a fairly comprehensive collection of fly lines. The least we can get away with is probably a quick-sinking shooting head and a medium sinking one, a weight-forward slow sinker, a sink tip and a weight-forward or double tapered floater.

Reasonably stiff and powerful rods will be needed to handle this range of lines, to cast respectable distances over windswept expanses of water and to control the large and athletic fish we may expect to find in such reservoirs. While neither is by any means a 'broom pole', I find that the stiffer of my two 9 ft 3 in fibreglass rods is well suited to use with the various sinking lines and that its slightly softer actioned companion is ideal for floating line and sink-tip work.

For the type of lure fishing we shall be considering, a standard 9 ft leader, knotted to a 2 or 3 ft monofilament butt length, will serve for use at or near the surface, and a shorter one of no more than about 5 ft should be perfectly adequate for sub-surface fishing with the sinking lines. A breaking strain of 7 lb should be regarded as an absolute minimum leader strength at any of our larger reservoirs.

The lures we shall need for boat fishing in rainbow-stocked reservoirs are few in number and are all to be found amongst those listed in the bank fishing chapter. Early in the season – indeed, perhaps until the middle of June – black seems to be the most consistently successful colour. The Ace of Spades and the Sweeney Todd are both excellent, but it is as well to have a White Lure in reserve. By mid- to late-June, the rainbows should have begun their assault on a rapidly growing plankton population. As we said earlier, it would be quite impossible to represent daphnia or any other planktonic animal (apart, perhaps, from the phantom larva) on a hook, and even if we could there would still be little chance of persuading the fish to select our artificial from amongst the vast host of naturals in the water. But, by some extraordinary stroke of good fortune, plankton-feeding rainbows are remarkably susceptible to bright, flashy lures. Gold, orange, yellow and red seem almost always to be the most effective colours, and a Whiskey Fly or a Dunkeld fished at the right depth and retrieved quickly will frequently provide the answer to an otherwise almost insoluble problem.

As the season wears on and the clouds of plankton begin to fade, black lures come back into their own but at this time – in August and September – a Muddler Minnow can also be useful, either fished deep and slowly or fast at the surface, depending upon the behaviour of the trout. Nor should it be forgotten that trout in many reservoirs will be feeding on fry at this time of year. A White Lure or a Polystickle worked slowly around features like valve and filtration towers, or cast into areas where marauders are seen to be savaging shoals of small fish and allowed simply to sink slowly through the water, may well produce excellent results.

It will be appreciated that a boat must be anchored if a lure is to be fished at any great depth. If it is not, its movement across the surface will prevent the fly from sinking properly even if a quick-sinking shooting head is used. It should be remembered that even a Hi-D line only sinks about 1 ft in three seconds and that it therefore takes a minute and a half to go down 30 ft. In that time, a boat can drift as much as 20 ft, even in a flat calm. This, too, is one of the instances in which long casting is likely to be needed. As an approximate guide, it is necessary to cast a yard for each foot of depth to be fished. A boat can be allowed to drift when the fish are within 10 or 15 ft of the surface, provided that the breeze is no more than moderate and that the drift can be properly controlled. It was this need for boat control that caused Bob Church and his colleagues to design the lee-boards and drift control rudder discussed in Chapter 11, and to evolve new techniques for boat handling on large reservoirs. Those who would experiment with them should remember that these devices are only suited to use in relatively calm conditions. There is no doubt that lee-boards can damage boats, or that they may even prove dangerous if deployed in anything more than a moderate breeze or secured to the wrong (upwind) gunwale.

Rather than load themselves down with a great deal of bulky equipment, most anglers prefer to use only a drogue. If a lure is to be fished on a sinking line, the traditional broadside-on drift will be found to be worse than useless, even in the lightest airs. Not only will the boat almost always be moving too fast, but it will also be very difficult to keep in touch with the line, which can only comfortably be cast downwind and which the moving boat will tend to 'run over'. It was to resolve these problems that anglers on the Midlands reservoirs adopted the ancient and now widely used stern or bows-to-wind drift. It has several advantages – offering little air resistance, the boat will travel slowly over the water, even in a fresh breeze; the rods can fish out from opposite sides without interfering with each other; by casting a longish line across and slightly downwind, the lure can be sunk to a considerable depth; and, as the boat moves on, the fly will swim round that curve which we have discussed before and which causes the downfall of so many trout. The only disadvantage is that when fishing close in to the marginal shallows – as may often be necessary at fry time – only one rod can cast towards the shore. But this problem applies equally to the other methods of drifting and the only real solution to it is to land and fish from the bank.

Where the fish are already feeding deep down or in one particular spot, it may well be better to anchor and use the boat as a casting platform than to try to drift over the area again and again.

We can, of course, fish at almost any depth from an anchored boat, but one particular problem will quickly become apparent if we try to work a fly or lure more than about 10 ft down. When a sinking line is cast, its point will drop through the water in an arc until it is hanging vertically from the rod tip and we are retrieving upwards rather than horizontally. The solution is to cast as long a line as possible, to let out line after the cast until we are sure that the lure is at the right depth and only then to start our retrieve. This may sound a minor point but it is not. The number of fishermen who have no idea how their lines are behaving beneath the surface or even of the level at which their chosen lure is working is quite astonishing. It is well worth while to establish the rate of descent of any sinking line and then to count or time it as it goes down through the water. By doing this we should always know where our lure is, and we should be able to return it to the same depth again and again with subsequent casts.

When fishing close to the bottom in deep water, takes tend to come at two separate and clearly identifiable points on the retrieve. The first pull or two after the line has sunk are often deadly, and large numbers of fish may also be taken as the lure turns upwards to start its ascent to the surface. This latter instance is directly comparable with the take to a fly or lure curving round when fished from a drifting boat on a floating or sink-tip line. There may be some who would argue that a horizontally travelling lure which suddenly turns upwards appears to the fish to be escaping, and triggers an aggressive hunting instinct. Whatever the trout's cerebral processes, there is no doubt that turning artificials are very much more attractive to them than are those moving in straight lines.

The methods we have considered so far were specifically developed for the capture of rainbow trout, especially plankton-feeding ones, but techniques for fishing from anchored boats also seem to be fundamental to the taking of the large brown trout which live in some of our deep public water supply reservoirs. When Datchet was first stocked, the browns virtually disappeared for a couple of seasons and it was feared that they had perished. But then, one or two anglers, working large lures along the bottom in very deep water, began to catch them. They had grown to great sizes, but where they fed, and what on, remains something of a mystery. When spooned, their stomach contents rarely show anything other than the obvious remains of picnic bits and pieces, presumably dropped overboard by anglers. It seems reasonable to assume that these fish could not have put on the weight they have except at the expense of smaller, stocked rainbows. For this reason, if for no other, their removal from the water would seem desirable. They certainly contribute nothing to the fishery and could not conceivably be caught by more traditional methods.

The problems posed by these huge browns are by no means unique to Datchet. Regular visitors to Grafham have known for some years that similar fish lurk in the depths there and are occasionally taken with large, deep-fished lures in the trolling area. It seems probable that similar situations exist on other deep, fertile lakes and reservoirs. Wherever anglers are confronted with a challenge of this sort, it will almost certainly be most successfully met by the use of a static or very slow moving boat and the ability to get a lure down to the fish.

Speaking personally, I must admit that laying out a lead-cored line along the bottom in 60 ft or more of water and then inching back a big, shaggy lure is not a technique that I could much enjoy using myself, but I admire rather than criticise those with the single-mindedness to dedicate their fishing time to the attempted capture of these enormous fish.

It is a far cry from the great, grey expanses of Grafham, Chew or Datchet to the more intimate put-and-take fisheries which have recently sprung up around the country, particularly in the Home Counties. But boats are available on some of these small waters too, and their use deserves some comment.

I have not the slightest doubt that a boat on a lake of less than about 10 or 15 acres is generally a liability rather than an asset. This is especially so where the lake is long and narrow, enabling bank fishermen to cover most of the water, or where it is intensively fished – as so many commercial fisheries are. In such surroundings the trout already have little enough refuge from flailing fly lines without access to their last remaining sanctuaries being made available to the fisherman by giving him the freedom of the water. Where trout are unable to find a safe retreat of any sort they show increasing signs of stress as the season wears on and sport at the fishery deteriorates steadily.

There may be a valid case for keeping a small number of boats on any lake for the use of infirm or disabled anglers, but they should be used with the greatest possible caution and always at anchor. Drifting on small stillwaters simply multiplies the area disturbed by a static boat many times over. And, as I explained when we were considering loch fishing, under no circumstances should the boat fisherman ever stand up to cast.

Whether the lake upon which he is fishing is large or small, the boat angler should always be aware of the annoyance and inconvenience he can cause to others. When concentrating on one's fishing, it is only too easy to row or drift in the path of another drifting boat or along a shoreline in front of bank anglers without even noticing that one is doing so. The boat fisherman has a particular responsibility to remain alert to the activities and interests of other water users and to keep well clear of them.

Finally, whether the boat angler is fishing a large reservoir or a small lake, it is worth bearing in mind that flexibility will always provide the key to consistent success. Although we have only considered lure fishing in this chapter, and a fairly narrow aspect of lure fishing at that, the other stillwater techniques can be just as effective if used in the right place, at the right time and in the right way. Boats on reservoirs can add a great deal to the interest of fishing these vast and often rather featureless places, provided that they are used intelligently.

CHAPTER 14

Waterside Ways

Sportsmanship in trout fishing was once defined for me as 'observing the fishery rules in the spirit as well as in the letter, and doing nothing to impair the pleasure of others'. Although there are still some peaceful and uncrowded waters in these islands, they tend either to be in remote places or to be reserved for a small élite wealthy enough to pay for the privilege of using them. Economic and geographical necessities dictate that most of us will have to share lowland reservoirs close to major towns and cities or small put-and-take fisheries where the owners, seeking to make reasonable livings, must either allow as many rods on to the water as possible or charge very high prices in order to keep the numbers down. In short, the average stillwater trout fisherman today has to fish in more crowded surroundings than he would like. This is particularly so before mid-June and the opening of the coarse fishing season.

Where anglers find themselves cheek-by-jowl with others who may be using different and, perhaps, less delicate tackle and tactics, there is a risk that somebody's sport will be adversely affected. However, the risk can be greatly reduced by the application of a little common sense and a few basic guidelines.

By far the most frequent cause for complaint is the man who comes pounding along the bank and immediately starts casting within yards or even feet of a fellow angler. In the worst instance, he will plough into the water pushing a great bow-wave ahead of him and only start double hauling towards the far bank when the ripple is lapping at his wader tops. If the unfortunate soul who was already there when our villain arrived is trying to fish an imitative pattern delicately in the margins, he might as well move on. Even if he is using similar methods to those being employed by his new neighbour, his sport will not have been improved by the intrusion and it may well have been spoiled.

A familiar variation on this theme often occurs when only one angler is catching fish. Those on either side start creeping gradually along the bank towards him. I have actually had another fisherman appear from nowhere and start casting directly over my head while I was unhooking a trout. Such behaviour is of benefit to neither party. The reason for one person's consistent success against another's failure is far more likely to lie in his choice of tackle, his style of fishing and – above all – his skill than in his precise position on the bank. And those who sidle up to him in the hope of sharing his success are as likely to disrupt his sport as to improve their own.

To some extent, responsibility for solving these problems lies with both parties. It is difficult to lay down precise rules as to how far apart stillwater trout fishermen should be in order to avoid interfering with each other's sport; so much depends on the nature of the water. But the separations should certainly be substantially greater than those needed for coarse fishing and, as a generalisation, it is courteous to leave at least one and a half times the average fly-fisherman's best comfortable casting range – a total of (say) 45 yds – between oneself and the next person, unless you know him well and you have both agreed to fish close together. Incidentally, asking another angler whether he minds our fishing close to him does not absolve us from the basic principles set out above. Very few people would be so outspoken as to express an objection, even if our arrival was likely to spoil their sport.

If we have a responsibility to keep our distance from other fishermen, we should also recognise that some places on a fishery will provide markedly better prospects for success than others. Naturally, we hope to identify and take advantage of them. But, on a crowded water, it is selfish in the extreme to hog a particular spot all day if other people who have caught little or nothing are obviously waiting to fish there. This problem arises most often on small, heavily fished waters where there may be one or two obvious fish-holding areas, but it can cause friction on larger fisheries, too.

A particularly unattractive practice has developed on some reservoirs where fishermen actually 'stake themselves a claim' for the day by planting their landing nets in the shallows and setting up camp on the bank nearby. They may spend relatively little of their time actually fishing, or they may wander off for quite some distance, but should anybody else start to fish where they have 'hoisted their colours' he will be assured of a hostile reception. Such intensely territorial behaviour is both selfish and unnecessary. An occasional change of scenery almost always improves our concentration and our chances of success, and there is a good deal to be said for moving on every couple of hours or so regardless of whether anybody else has designs on our chosen fishing spot or not.

Hooks travelling through the air at the end of a fly line are dangerous. Nobody wants to be caught by one and nobody wants to hook a fellow angler. When walking along the bank, we should always aim to pass far enough behind other fishermen to be beyond the range of their back-casts and, at the same time, we should be at pains to avoid showing ourselves on the skyline or otherwise disturbing trout in the areas to which they are casting. If we have no alternative but to walk close behind them, we should wait until we are fairly sure that they are not just about to re-cast, ask whether we may pass, and then do so as quickly and unobtrusively as possible. This procedure is not simply a matter of courtesy. An angler concentrating on his retrieve and watching his line on the water does not have eyes in the back of his head and cannot be expected to look behind him every time he casts.

Because of his mobility, the boat fisherman is even more likely to cause annoyance to others or to interfere with their sport than is his colleague on the bank, and he must, therefore, remain constantly alert to what is going on around him. Under no circumstances should a boat ever be allowed to drift, or be anchored, within 50 yds of a bank angler. This tenet is actually written into the rules at many fisheries but, even where it is not, it should always be observed. And those who count themselves indifferent judges of distance should always err on the side of caution. Similarly, a drift should never be started directly downwind of another drifting boat and we should try to avoid rowing or motoring across another's line of drift. We saw in the chapter on loch fishing that a boat has enormous trout-frightening potential and that it is wise to rest even the most productive drift for a while after fishing it. So, it follows that we should never force another boat already on the water to choose between fishing over recently disturbed water or packing up and moving on.

The fisherman afloat must also be alert to the interests of other water users. Many stillwaters today – particularly large southern reservoirs – afford facilities for dinghy sailing, rowing and even skin diving. Their rules usually make clear who must give way to whom and, of course, they must be obeyed. But where no formal guidance exists, we should use our common sense and seek to avoid conflict, remembering that they have as much right to be on the water as we have.

Before leaving this somewhat forbidding list of things we should not do, two further points need to be made.

Firstly, there is the question of litter, all of which is unsightly and some of which is positively dangerous. No matter how artificial a reservoir's banks may be, its appearance can never be improved by cans and bottles, paper and plastic bags, cigarette packets or nylon 'birds nests'. In addition, bottles and rusty cans can puncture waders and cut feet, and nylon can and does entangle birds and kill them. There is no excuse for leaving such items at the waterside; they must be put into pockets or fishing bags and taken home to be disposed of properly. And before waste nylon is put into even so apparently safe a receptacle as a dustbin, it should be coiled up and cut into 1-in lengths.

Secondly, many stillwater anglers carry two rods or more, set up with different lines. One is left on the bank while the other is in use. Strangely, many people seem perfectly happy to leave their second rods lying on the ground, often in quite long grass, and are apparently totally oblivious to the risks involved. In the old days, good rods were provided with butt spikes which enabled them to be planted upright in the earth. The spikes were unwieldy and added unwanted weight, but the principle was sound. If laid flat, a rod is liable to be trodden on. It should always be propped up on a fishing bag, against a fence, in the forked branch of a tree or bush or even simply on a tussock, the aim being to make it as visible as possible.

First amongst the 'do's' comes an unashamed reiteration of a point made in an earlier chapter. It is deeply disturbing to see the lack of respect shown by some anglers for their quarry. People bludgeoning fish with lightweight, tubular aluminium landing net handles, or trying to hold the slippery creatures while beating them against fence posts or boat gunwales are quite common sights. Worse still are stories of wading anglers throwing fish ashore alive, rather than take the trouble to despatch them quickly and cleanly. Not only is such behaviour obscene, it could also provide useful ammunition for those who would take any opportunity to attack field sports.

With a little ingenuity and inventiveness, a priest need cost nothing. An 8-in length of $\frac{1}{2}$-in metal pipe, or a similarly sized piece of bamboo cane, weighted with lead sheeting or with a coach bolt, should prove perfectly adequate. It is as well to drill a hole through the handle so that the implement may be attached to the fishing jacket with a nylon cord – priests are easy to leave lying on the bank.

Most important of all, the priest must be administered promptly and efficiently while the fish is still in the net and before the hook is removed.

Finally, there is the question of advice.

At some time or other we must all have been in a position where those around us were taking fish consistently while we had not had so much as a tug on the line to show for hours of dedicated casting. The temptation to ask a neighbour what is he using is a strong one, and there is no good reason for resisting it; most anglers are friendly, helpful people, only too willing to talk to others. Nevertheless, two simple rules should be applied, one for his benefit, the other for yours.

The first goes almost without saying, and it is that we should choose our moment with some care. Obviously, we would not make ourselves popular if we were to tramp up to our would-be mentor while he is trying to cover a fish moving close in or concentrating on slowly fishing out a cast. But when he has just unhooked a fish, is taking a break, moving on or packing up, a courteous approach should be equally courteously received.

The second point is less obvious. The question most frequently asked is 'what fly are you using?', and it is amazing how often, having been told about, shown or even given a copy of the successful artificial, the inquisitor potters off happily expecting to fill his bag within minutes. A far more relevant, but rarely asked, question would be, 'how are you fishing it?' There can be little doubt that correct presentation in terms of fishing depth and style of retrieve is just as essential to effective fishing as is the correct choice of fly, probably more so. So, before we seek advice we should have worked out what we want to know. It is quite often possible to improve our chances dramatically simply by watching the other angler and noting the length of time he leaves between casting and starting his retrieve, and the speed and pattern of his recovery.

This short section has, of course, been written chiefly for newcomers to our sport. It is to be hoped that many of those who read this book will regularly find themselves catching trout, perhaps while others around them are doing less well. If we ourselves are approached for advice, we should always give it, and give it as fully and unambiguously as possible. One occasionally hears strange stories of so-called experts who are reluctant to help others or, even less comprehensibly, actually seem to revel in having misled or misinformed somebody less skilful than themselves. Ours is not a competitive pastime, and if we feel an urge to score points off each other by totting up and comparing numbers of fish caught, perhaps we should look elsewhere for our recreational pleasures.

CHAPTER 15

First Catch Your Trout

As our fishing expertise grows so, inevitably, will the number of trout we catch, and then we shall have to start thinking about the most effective ways of keeping, cleaning and cooking them.

Our rod-caught trout should differ from the sad, grey, limp corpses that litter fishmongers' slabs up and down the country in several ways. Firstly, they will be fresh; but freshness is a transient quality, and a conscious effort is required if it is to be maintained. Secondly, because of the growth rates of trout in fertile, lowland lakes and reservoirs, and because of the sizes at which fish are stocked in many waters today, our fish are often likely to be very much larger than the 'portion-sized' rainbows commonly supplied by fish farmers to the catering and retail industries; so, the recipes suggested in most cookery books, evolved with fish of $\frac{1}{2}$ or $\frac{3}{4}$ lb in mind, may be difficult to apply to the trout we catch.

Two further differences are of no great material consequence but deserve mention in a chapter on the culinary properties of trout.

Brown trout, being more difficult and less economical than rainbows to rear artificially, are rarely if ever available in restaurants or in the shops. But most fisheries are stocked with at least a proportion of browns, and rainbows are almost unheard of in natural, unstocked British waters. The brown trout's indigenous status is generally well known even to non-anglers, and a myth has grown up that it is noticeably better to eat than the rainbow. In fact, a trout's table qualities are entirely dependent upon its diet and the type of water in which it has been living. There can be no doubt that wild brown trout from Loch Leven, for instance, or from Lough Mask are particularly delicious, but so too are rainbows from Grafham Water and Datchet Reservoir. Which brings us to the fourth and final difference. Apart from newly stocked fish taken from small put-and-take waters, and unlike stew-reared commercial fish, most of the trout we catch will have lived for much or all of their lives on varied, natural diets. Gourmets place value on the salmon-like pinkness of some trouts' flesh. Such pinkness results solely from a high carotene intake and is most common amongst trout which have lived in waters rich in snails and shrimps. Although such pink-fleshed fish are almost invariably good to eat, so too may lighter-fleshed ones be. Indeed, some of the best fish I have eaten have been hardy, wild brown trout with pure white flesh which have had to work hard for their livings in fairly acid, upland waters.

But, to return to my original thesis, the first problem confronting the angler who has just landed and despatched a trout is how to keep it cool and thus fresh.

Until quite recently, a creel formed part of a trout fisherman's uniform. Made of wickerwork which allowed the air to circulate around the catch, it was reasonably efficient. Many people who fish rivers and unstocked, natural stillwaters still carry creels, but reservoir fishermen who expect to land bigger trout now generally prefer to use basses – woven fish baskets.

The Arabs have long known that water in a porous earthenware pot around which a breeze blows can become remarkably cold, almost freezing on occasions. Armies fighting in the desert have used the same principle with canvas *chaguls* hung in the wind or from moving vehicles. The effect is caused by evaporation from the vessel's outer skin, and if a bass is dipped into the water from time to time, or if a trout is wrapped in several layers of damp cloth, the cooling influence will be similar provided that the air is allowed to move freely around them. This is quite different from the pointless and sometimes damaging practice of hanging a fish-filled bass in water which may be quite warm in summer and which is sure to be alive with myriad minute creatures only too anxious to turn the tables on trout that have hitherto preyed on them.

An even more satisfactory solution is a lightweight, insulated cooler bag containing two or three of the liquid-filled plastic sachets which, having been frozen, remain very cold for long periods. Although rather bulky and, perhaps, better suited to boat fishing than to being carted about the bank, these boxes do keep trout very fresh. A good alternative is an insulating blanket and a one-gallon plastic container two-thirds filled with water and then frozen hard.

Incidentally, the worst possible container for fish of any sort is a polythene bag. It acts almost like a greenhouse and causes serious discoloration of the fish's skin.

Having caught our trout and taken them home in as fresh a condition as possible, they should be cleaned at once if they are not to be frozen. This is a simple exercise and, with a little practice, will take no more than a few moments.

Turn the trout on its back and, with a very sharp, pointed knife, cut forwards along the ventral centreline, between the pelvic and pectoral fins and right up into the 'V' formed by the gill covers. (If you try to cut backwards the knife is likely to stick on the bones and ligaments of the pelvic fins). Then reverse the knife and extend the cut backwards to the vent (Fig. 37a). The internal organs are loose within the body cavity. Cut the intestine close to the vent and again as far up between the gill covers as you can. Remove all the internal organs including the heart which will be found tucked up in the forward end of the body cavity. A dark red strip up to $\frac{1}{4}$ in wide (the kidney) will be found running down the full length of the body cavity immediately beneath the spinal column (Fig. 37b). Slit it with a knife and then scrape it out with a teaspoon – the point of the knife will have to be used to ease the remnants out of the cavities in the spinal column. Finally, clip out the gill filaments, wash the fish inside and out and dry it with kitchen paper or a cloth.

Although trout are at their best when eaten fresh, they do freeze well and can be kept for quite long periods in a frozen state without significant deterioration provided that they are frozen whole after extruding their excreta, washing in cold water and placing in polythene tubing or freezer bags. Cleaned trout keep only half as long as whole ones when frozen. As some waters produce fish with better table qualities than others, it is as well to mark each bag with the place and date of capture of its contents.

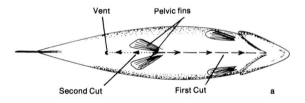

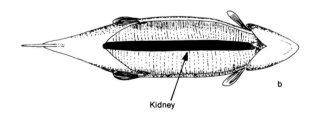

Fig. 37   Cleaning a Trout

Frozen trout *must* be completely defrosted before cooking, and it is worth bearing in mind that a fish of 2 or 3 lb may take the best part of a day to thaw out.

Non-anglers very often regard trout as a luxury but even only moderately competent fishermen are liable to become blasé about their fish, particularly if they frequent commercially run waters where the rules insist that every one caught must be killed. For them, the problem of how to put their catch to best use may demand thought and imagination. Some people sell trout in order to help defray their fishing expenses. While I would not criticise them for doing so, I fear that this must turn an essentially peaceful and non-competitive sport into a rather intense and mercenary operation. Most of us give trout away – they are greatly appreciated by those who see them but rarely – or exchange them for eggs or garden produce. But these are methods for disposing of a surplus and most fishermen – or fishermen's wives – will still be concerned to find varied ways of presenting those fish that are destined for their tables.

Large trout, over about 4 lb, can be very effectively cold smoked. The result is almost indistinguishable from smoked salmon. Although one or two techniques for cold smoking at home have been published, they are complicated and very time-consuming, and the results are rarely entirely satisfactory. A much surer solution is to hand the fish over to a professional who will charge for his services by the lb. When contemplating this, it is worth bearing in mind that however carefully a fish of poor quality is smoked, it will still be a poor quality fish. Some of the very large trout stocked into small put-and-take waters today are, in fact, tired, dark, old brood fish, barely fit for human consumption. Do not be tempted to have them cold smoked in the hope that they will provide an exotic starter at a dinner party – they will not.

While cold smoking is best left to a professional, hot smoking – an entirely different process, better suited for fish up to about $2\frac{1}{2}$ lb – can easily be done at home. The only similarity between the two processes is that the fish are steeped in wood smoke. In cold smoking this is achieved at a low temperature over a long period of time. In hot smoking it is carried out quickly and at a high temperature.

Several hot smoking kits are available on the market and all of them use the same simple principle. A quantity of fine wood dust is sprinkled into the base of a mess-tin-like container. The trout, wiped dry and salted, are placed on a wire tray to keep them clear of the wood dust and to allow the fumes to circulate around them. The container is then sealed, or almost so, with a tightly fitting lid and placed over a spirit or solid fuel stove. A $\frac{1}{2}$-lb fish needs about 10 minutes over the burner; larger ones may have to be cut into pieces and smoked for up to half an hour, depending on their size and thickness. The result is a most excellently smoked trout, probably better eaten cold than hot, which makes either a first-rate starter at luncheon or dinner when simply served with brown bread and butter and wedges of lemon, or a very pleasant focal point for a summer salad.

As an extension of this hot smoking exercise, the following simple recipe for smoked trout pâté is a firm favourite in our family and is a useful starter at any dinner party:

Smoked Trout Pâté   *(Serves 6 to 8)*

Four 8-oz or one 2-lb trout
Six tablespoons of double cream
The juice of half a lemon
Salt and pepper

Hot smoke the trout, remove the skin and strip away the flesh from the bones – this is very much more easily done while the fish is still warm than when it has cooled. Allow the flesh to cool and then pound it into a smoothish paste. Mix in the cream, add the lemon juice and season to taste. Place either in a single large dish or in individual ones and decorate with thin slices of lemon, cucumber and radish.

Slightly surprisingly, this pâté freezes well and can be kept in the freezer for up to three months.

There are, of course, many ways of cooking trout, ranging from the magnificently simple – fried in butter over an open fire at the waterside – to the complex and sophisticated. The recipes that follow have been chosen because each of them meets three criteria. Firstly, they are all easy; while some need more ingredients than others, none calls for any real culinary expertise. Secondly, as a collection, they cover the whole range of common trout sizes – from the wild $\frac{1}{2}$ lb brown of a highland loch to the brilliant 4 or 5 lb Grafham rainbow. Thirdly, and perhaps most important of all, they have all been well tried and tested. It goes almost without saying that they are all suitable for both fresh trout and for fish from the freezer.

To Grill Trout
Grilling is one of the simplest and most delicious ways to cook trout, and is best suited to fish of between $\frac{1}{2}$ lb and 1 lb in weight.

Turn the grill on (medium to hot) a good 10 minutes before putting the trout under it. Dot the trout with butter, place them under the grill, turn only once and brush from time to time with melted butter. A ½-lb fish will need about 5 minutes a side and a bigger one slightly more.

Serve a grilled trout on its own for breakfast, or with new potatoes and a mixed salad at lunch or dinner.

To Fry Trout

Melt 2 oz of butter in a frying-pan over a medium heat. When the pan is hot, place the trout in the butter and turn several times during cooking. A ½-lb fish will take about 10 minutes to fry; larger ones or thick trout steaks may need between 15 and 20 minutes.

Trout with Almonds   (*Serves 2*)

2 small trout or 2 trout steaks
4 oz butter
The juice of half a lemon
2 oz chopped, blanched almonds
Salt

Fry two trout or trout steaks as above. Simultaneously, melt 2 oz butter in a small pan, add 2 oz of peeled almonds, a little salt and the lemon juice, and cook gently for a few minutes until the almonds start to brown. To serve, pour the butter and almonds over the fish.

Trout with Orange, Almonds and Capers   (*Serves 4*)

Four 8-oz trout
Flour
Vegetable oil
4 oz butter
Two oranges, peeled and sliced
2 oz flaked almonds
1 tablespoon capers
Salt and pepper

Season the flour with salt and pepper, dredge the fish in the flour and fry in an oil and butter mixture until cooked (see 'To Fry Trout'). Remove the fish to a warm serving dish.

Lightly brown the almonds in 2 oz butter over a gentle heat and add a little orange juice as soon as they start to brown. Add the capers and the peeled and sliced oranges, and warm thoroughly. Pour over the fish and serve with sauté potatoes and broccoli, with watercress or with a green salad.

Baking is probably the most effective way of cooking large fish – those of about 2 lb or more in weight.

Simple Baked Trout *(Serves 4)*

Preheat the oven to 375°F (gas mark 5; 190°C). Liberally rub a piece of baking foil with butter and place the trout in the centre of it. Pull the edges up and join them at the top to prevent the juices from running out while the fish is cooking. A 2½- to 3-lb fish will take about an hour to bake.

Baked trout may be served straight from the oven with wedges of lemon. Alternatively, the skin and bones can be removed once it has cooled slightly and it can then be served cold with a salad, making a very pleasant summer luncheon dish. Or, small portions can be placed in individual dishes, covered with aspic jelly, garnished with thin slices of cucumber or with parsley and served as a starter with melba toast.

The left-overs from a large, baked trout can be made into:

Trout Fishcakes

Take equal amounts of cold, baked trout and cold, mashed potato, mix them together thoroughly and season to taste with salt, pepper, finely grated lemon rind and chopped parsley. Shape the mixture into balls, brush with egg yolk and roll in breadcrumbs. Flatten the fishcakes slightly and then fry them.

Baked Trout with Fennel

Four 8-oz trout or one 2-lb one
Fennel leaves – finely chopped
¼ pint white wine
1 oz butter

Preheat the oven to 350°F (gas mark 4; 175°C). Season the trout with salt and pepper and place them in a well buttered oven-proof dish. Sprinkle generously with fennel leaves and moisten with white wine. Cover the dish with baking foil and bake; 8-oz fish will need to be cooked for 25 minutes, a 2-lb one will need about 1 hour. When cooking a large fish by this method it is often necessary to top up the wine from time to time.

Remove the trout to a warm serving-dish and put the juice into a small pan. Boil the juice to reduce its volume and thicken it by adding the butter. Pour the juice over the trout and serve at once.

For a slightly more sophisticated method of baking trout, you may wish to try the following:

Truite en Papillote *(Serves 4)*

Four 8-oz trout
2 tablespoons finely chopped onion
½ lb finely chopped mushrooms
2 tablespoons finely chopped parsley
Butter
Salt and freshly ground black pepper
4 slices of lemon
8 tablespoons dry white wine

Clean, rinse and dry the trout. Sauté the finely chopped onion, mushrooms and parsley in 4 tablespoons of butter until the onion is transparent. Season to taste with salt and pepper, and stuff the fish with this mixture when cool.

Cut four rectangles of foil large enough to enfold the fish completely. Brush the foil with olive oil or melted butter and place a fish in the centre of each piece of foil. Sprinkle each trout with salt and freshly ground black pepper, top with a slice of lemon and pour 2 tablespoonfuls of melted butter and 2 tablespoonsfuls of dry white wine over each fish. Bring the foil up over the trout and double fold the top ends to make a tight packet from which the juices cannot escape.

Place on a baking-sheet and bake for 15 to 20 minutes in a pre-heated oven at 375°F (gas mark 4).

Finally, as a *pièce de résistance*, we greatly enjoy the *Cordon Bleu*:

Trout Grenobloise *(Serves 4)*

4 even-sized trout
½ pint water
2 lemons
6 peppercorns
1 slice of onion
1 dessertspoon grated horseradish
2–3 tablespoons dry sherry
Salt, pepper and sugar
4 tablespoons single cream
Chopped parsley

2

Set the oven at 350°F (gas mark 4). Clean and trim the trout, place them in a covered dish with the water, a squeeze of lemon juice, the peppercorns and the onion, and poach in the pre-set oven for about 15 minutes. Allow them to cool in the liquid, then skin carefully and arrange in the serving-dish.

Pare off a little lemon peel, cut into fine strips and blanch. Remove the white pith from the lemon and cut the fruit into segments. Put the horseradish, sherry, salt, pepper and sugar into a bowl, mix in the cream carefully and add the lemon. Spoon this over the trout and sprinkle with lemon rind and chopped parsley.

Serve with brown bread and butter.

Appendix A
Fly Dressings

It is a sad fact of life that the majority of trout flies available in the shops today are of very indifferent quality. This is particularly so where they have been mass produced by people overseas who have never even seen a trout or a fly rod. Rarely are stillwater nymphs or pupae available in leaded form, and even when they are it is impossible to tell how heavily they have been weighted. Traditional wet flies are almost invariably over-hackled and, in the worst instances, the dressings are liable to unravel and disintegrate after very little use. But, with a little practice, even those with only moderate eyesight or who previously thought themselves to be 'all fingers and thumbs' can tie trout flies every bit as effective as the commercial articles. In addition, there is a great deal of satisfaction to be had from catching trout on a pattern of one's own tying – perhaps even of one's own design – and fly-tying offers a pleasant means of extending enjoyment of our sport into the long evenings of the closed season.

So, to those who have yet to venture into this new craft, I suggest that the purchase of a simple fly-tying kit would represent a first-class investment. And, for those who are already converted, the dressings that follow cover all the artificials listed in the text of this book.

Traditional Wet Flies

Alexandra (? W. G. Turle)

Hook	10–12
Silk	Black
Tail	Red ibis substitute
Body	Silver lurex
Hackle	Black hen's
Wing	Peacock sword fibres
Cheeks	Red ibis substitute

Black and Peacock Spider (T. C. Ivens)
(Not a true traditional pattern but so popular since first widely publicised in T. C. Ivens' *Still Water Fly Fishing* in 1952, and so useful in a team of wet flies, that I include it as one here.)

Hook	10–14
Silk	Black
Body	Bronze peacock herl
Hackle	Black hen's – very sparse

Blae and Black (Modified) (Traditional)

Hook	12–14
Silk	Black
Tail	Golden pheasant tippet fibres
Body	Black floss silk ribbed with medium silver wire
Hackle	Black hen's
Wing	Grey duck quill slips

Butcher (Jewhurst)

Hook	10–14
Silk	Black
Tail	Red ibis substitute
Body	Silver lurex ribbed with fine silver wire
Hackle	Black cock's
Wing	Blue mallard quill slips

Coachman (? Bosworth)

Hook	10–14
Silk	Black
Body	Bronze peacock herl
Hackle	Red cock's
Wing	White swan's quill slips

Dunkeld (Traditional)

Hook	10–12
Silk	Brown or orange
Tail	Golden pheasant topping
Body	Gold lurex ribbed with fine gold wire
Body hackle	Hot orange cock's (or none)
Hackle	Hot orange cock's
Wing	Rolled bronze mallard

Greenwell's Glory (Wet) (? after James Wright)

Hook	12–14
Silk	Primrose
Body	Primrose tying silk, well waxed and ribbed with fine gold wire
Hackle	Furnace cock's
Wing	Starling quill slips

Mallard and Claret (? Murdoch)

Hook	10–14
Silk	Brown
Tail	Golden pheasant tippet fibres
Body	Claret seal's fur ribbed with fine gold tinsel
Hackle	Red cock's
Wing	Rolled bronze mallard

Peter Ross (Peter Ross)

Hook	10–14
Silk	Black
Tail	Golden pheasant tippet fibres
Body	Rear two-thirds; silver lurex. Front third; red seal's fur. The whole ribbed with fine oval tinsel.
Hackle	Black hen's
Wing	Rolled teal

Soldier Palmer (Traditional)

Hook	10–12
Silk	Black
Body	Scarlet seal's fur ribbed with fine gold tinsel
Hackle	Red cock's, dressed palmer and ribbed with fine gold wire

Teal, Blue and Silver (Traditional)

Hook	8–12
Silk	Black
Tail	Golden pheasant tippet fibres
Body	Silver lurex ribbed with fine silver wire
Hackle	Blue hen's
Wing	Rolled teal

Zulu (Traditional)

Hook	10–12
Silk	Black
Tail	Scarlet wool
Body	Black seal's fur
Hackle	Black cock's, palmered and ribbed with fine silver tinsel

Lures

Ace of Spades (David Collyer)

Hook	6–12 long-shank
Silk	Black
Body	Black chenille
Wing	Black hen hackle, tied Matuka style
Overwing	Bronze mallard
Hackle	Guinea fowl

Muddler Minnow (Don Gapen)

Hook	6–12 long-shank
Silk	Brown
Tail	Oak turkey quill slips
Body	Gold lurex ribbed with fine gold wire
Wing	Oak turkey quill slips
Head and Ruff	Spun deer hair, trimmed

Sweeney Todd (Richard Walker)

Hook	6–10 long-shank
Silk	Black
Body	Black floss silk ribbed with oval silver tinsel
Collar	Magenta fluorescent floss
Hackle	Crimson cock's
Wing	Dyed black squirrel hair

Whiskey Fly (Albert Whillock)

Hook	6–8 long-shank
Body	Gold or silver Sellotape, ribbed with DRF scarlet nylon floss and varnished overall
Tag	DRF scarlet floss
Hackle	Hot orange cock's
Wing	Hot orange calf's tail

White Lure (Traditional)

Hooks	6–10, two or more tied in tandem
Silk	White
Bodies	White floss ribbed with oval silver tinsel
Wing	Four white cock's hackles tied back to back

Worm Fly (William Black)

Hooks	8–10, two or more tied tandem
Tag	Red floss silk or wool
Bodies	Bronze peacock herl
Hackles	Red cock's

Imitative Patterns

Midge Pupae (now 'traditional')

Hook	8–14 down-eyed
Silk	Black
Tail	Three or four ostrich herl fibres, cut to $\frac{1}{8}$ in
Abdomen	Black floss silk ribbed with fine oval silver tinsel or; red floss silk ribbed with medium silver tinsel or; brown floss silk ribbed with fine gold wire or; pale green rayon floss silk ribbed with stripped peacock herl and varnished
Thorax	Bronze peacock herl for the red and black versions; brown seal's fur for the brown and green ones
Breathing filaments	White wool cut to $\frac{1}{8}$ in

Plastazote Corixa (David Collyer)

Hook	10–12 down-eyed
Silk	Brown or olive
Body	Plastazote, cut to shape
Back	Olive or brown quill slip
Paddles	Two fibres from back quill slip
Head	Built up from tying silk

Corixa (Lapsley)

Hook	10–12 down-eyed
Silk	Brown
Underbody	Fine lead wire, flattened horizontally, then white floss silk, covered overall with medium silver lurex
Overbody	Heat-stretched clear Swannundaze
Back	Speckled quill slip, well varnished
Paddles	Cock pheasant tail fibres

Shrimp (Lapsley)

Hook	8–12 down-eyed
Silk	Brown
Underbody	Fine lead wire
Body	Mixed brown, amber and scarlet seal's fur (brown predominating)
Back	Latex strip, lapped back and forth and then varnished
Overall rib	Fine gold wire

NOTE: Once the fly has been tied, strands of seal's fur should be picked out with a dubbing needle and trimmed to form legs.

Killer Bug (Frank Sawyer)

Hook	8–12 down-eyed
Silk	Buff
Underbody	Fine lead wire
Body	Wool – Chadwicks No. 477

Stick Fly (Traditional)

Hook	10–14 long-shank
Silk	Brown, black or yellow
Underbody	Fine lead wire
Body	One strand of peacock herl and three of pheasant tail spun together and ribbed with fine gold wire
Collar	Light buff floss silk
Legs	One turn of furnace cock's hackle

Sedge Pupae (Lapsley)

Hook	10–12 down-eyed
Silk	Black
Underbody	Fine lead wire (optional) wound over with white floss silk
Abdomen	Amber, yellow, sea green or brown seal's fur ribbed with medium gold tinsel
Thorax	Bronze peacock herl
Legs	One turn of grey partridge hackle tied as a beard

Invicta (James Ogden)

Hook	10–14 down-eyed
Silk	Brown
Tail	Golden pheasant topping
Body	Yellow seal's fur
Body hackle	Red cock's, wound palmer and ribbed with fine gold oval tinsel
Hackle	Red cock's with a few blue jay fibres
Wing	Hen pheasant tail fibres

Brer Rabbit Nymph (origin unknown)

Hook	8–12 long-shank (4–8 for high summer)
Silk	Brown
Underbody	6–10 turns of fine lead wire under thorax (optional)
Tail	Three or four pheasant tail fibres
Abdomen	Brown wool ribbed with fine gold wire
Thorax	Rabbit's guard hairs
Wing case	Pheasant tail fibres
Legs	One turn of grey partridge hackle trimmed off above and below

Damselfly Nymph (Lapsley)

Hook	8–10 long-shank
Silk	Green or yellow
Tail	Three medium olive cock's hackle points about $\frac{1}{8}$ in long
Abdomen	Olive or green seal's fur ribbed with fine gold oval tinsel
Thorax	As abdomen (unribbed) with eight strands of cock pheasant tail fibre over the top
Wing cases	The butts of the pheasant tail fibres turned back and divided so that they project for about $\frac{1}{8}$ in on either side of the abdomen
Legs	One turn of grey partridge hackle tied as a beard

Polystickle (Richard Walker)

Hook	6–8 long-shank (silvered)
Silk	Black or brown
Underbody	Front third, red floss silk; rear two-thirds, brown or olive floss silk ribbed with broad silver tinsel
Body covering	Stretched PVC strip built up into a fish shape
Back and tail	Darkish raffene moistened and tied in before the body is built, brought down over the body and tied in at the head: cut and shaped at the tail
Throat	Scarlet cock's hackle fibres tied in as a false hackle
Head	Built up with tying silk and well varnished

Large Red Sedge (Dry) (Richard Walker)

Hook	10–12 up-eyed
Silk	Brown
Tag	Fluorescent orange wool
Body	Cock pheasant centre tail fibres
Wings	A bunch of cock's hackles (red) square at the tips, or a bunch of pheasant tail fibres
Hackle	Two red cock's hackles

Palmered Sedge (Dry) (Lapsley)

Hook	10–12 up-eyed
Silk	Brown
Body	Medium/large furnace cock's hackles closely palmered and trimmed to a wedge shape
Shoulder hackle	Small furnace cock's hackle
Antennae	The stalks of the last two hackles used (optional)

Last Hope (Dry) (John Goddard)

Hook	17–18 up-eyed
Silk	Pale yellow
Whisks	6–8 fibres from a honey dun cock's hackle
Body	Two or three Norwegian goose or condor herls – grey buff
Hackle	Dark honey; very short in the fibre

Sepia or Claret Nymph (Lapsley)

Hook	10–14 down-eyed
Silk	Black
Tail	4–6 black cock's hackle fibres
Abdomen	Dark brown seal's fur ribbed with fine silver tinsel
Thorax	Dark brown seal's fur
Wing case	Any black quill slip
Hackle	One turn of black hen's hackle

Gold Ribbed Hare's Ear Nymph (David Collyer)

Hook	10–14 down-eyed
Silk	Brown or black
Tail	Hare's body guard hairs
Abdomen	Hare's body fur trimmed and ribbed with gold oval tinsel
Thorax	Hare's body guard hairs (some picked out and trimmed as legs)
Wing case	Dyed black turkey tail

Pheasant Tail (Dry) (G. E. M. Skues)

Hook	14 up-eyed
Silk	Orange
Whisks	3–4 strands of honey dun cock's hackle
Body	2–3 strands of cock pheasant centre tail feather fibres
Hackle	Brilliant rusty dun cock's hackle

Hackled Greenwell's Glory (Dry) (after James Wright)

Hook	12–14 up-eyed
Silk	Yellow, well waxed to take on an olive tint
Whisks	A small bunch of furnace cock's hackle fibres
Body	Tying silk ribbed with fine gold wire
Hackle	Two bright furnace cock's hackles

Mayfly Nymph (Lapsley)

Hook	8 long-shank
Silk	Black
Tail	Three cock pheasant tail fibres
Body	Rear third, pale buff condor herl ribbed with black nylon monocord; front two-thirds, yellow seal's fur
Wing case	Cock pheasant tail fibres
Legs	Grey partridge hackle tied as a beard

Mayfly (Dry) (Traditional)

Hook	10 Mayfly
Silk	Black
Tail	Three cock pheasant tail fibres
Body	White raffene ribbed with black nylon monocord
Hackle	Two badger cock's hackles with one medium blue dun cock's hackle wound through them

Daddy-long-legs (Dry) (origin unknown)

Hook	10 long-shank
Silk	Brown
Body	Cock pheasant tail fibres ribbed with fine copper wire
Legs	Cock pheasant tail fibres, knotted
Wings	Medium blue dun cock's hackle points
Hackle	Red cock's

Appendix B
The Stillwater Fisherman's Calendars

Imitative Patterns

	MAR	APR	MAY	JUN	JUL	AUG	SEP	OCT
Alder Larvae								
Caenis								
Claret Duns								
Corixae								
Daddy-Long-Legs								
Damselfly Nymphs								
Freshwater Lice								
Freshwater Shrimps								
Lake Olives								
Mayflies								
Midges (Black)								
(Large Red)								
(Green)			(Small)				(Large)	
(Small Brown)								
Minnows and Fry								
Sedges		(Larvae)						
Sepia Duns								
Snails								

Primary choice: ——————
Secondary choice: — — — — —
Nymph only: ••••••••••••

Lures, Traditional and Attractor Patterns

The table that follows should only be regarded as a guide. Any of the flies shown may produce good results in months far removed from those shown in the calendar, but the seasons given below are those in which the patterns have generally been found to be most effective.

	MAR	APR	MAY	JUN	JUL	AUG	SEP	OCT
Alexandra			- - -	━━━	━━━	━━━	━━━	
Black and Peacock Spider	━━━	━━━	- - -	- - -	- - -	━━━	━━━	
Blae and Black	- - -	━━━	━━━	━━━	━━━	━━━	━━━	
Butcher	━━━	━━━	━━━	━━━	━━━	- - -	- - -	- - -
Coachman	━━━	━━━		- - -	- - -			
Dunkeld	━━━	━━━	- - -			━━━	- - -	
Greenwell's Glory (wet)	━━━	━━━	- - -					
Mallard and Claret	━━━	━━━	━━━	━━━	━━━	━━━	━━━	
Peter Ross	━━━	━━━	━━━	- - -	- - -	- - -	- - -	- - -
Soldier Palmer	━━━	━━━	━━━	━━━	━━━	━━━	━━━	
Teal, Blue and Silver	━━━	━━━	━━━	- - -				
Zulu	━━━	━━━	━━━	━━━	━━━	━━━	━━━	
Ace of Spades	━━━	━━━	- - -	- - -	- - -	- - -	━━━	
Muddler Minnow				- - -	- - -			
Sweeney Todd	━━━	━━━	- - -	- - -	- - -	- - -	━━━	
Whiskey Fly				━━━	━━━	━━━		
White Lure	- - -	- - -				━━━	━━━	- - -
Worm Fly				━━━	━━━	━━━	- - -	- - -

Primary choice: ━━━━━━━

Secondary choice: - - - - - - -

Bibliography

'Black Palmer', *Scotch Loch Fishing*, Blackwood, 1882.
Church, Bob, *Reservoir Trout Fishing*, Cassell and Company Ltd, 1977.
Clarke, Brian, *The Pursuit of Stillwater Trout*, A & C Black Ltd, 1975.
Collyer, David J., *Fly-Dressing*, David and Charles (Holdings) Ltd, 1975.
Falkus and Buller, *Freshwater Fishing*, Macdonald and Jane's, 1975.
Frost and Brown, *The Trout*, Collins, 1967.
Goddard, John, *Trout Flies of Stillwater*, A & C Black Ltd, 1969.
Harris, J. R., *An Angler's Entomology*, Collins, 1952.
Henzell, H. P., *The Art and Craft of Loch Fishing*, Phillip Allan, 1937.
Ivens, T. C., *Still Water Fly Fishing*, Andre Deutsch Ltd, 1952.
Jacques, David, *The Development of Modern Stillwater Fishing*, A & C Black Ltd, 1974.
Lapsley, Peter, *The Bankside Book of Stillwater Trout Flies*, A & C Black Ltd, 1978.
Macan and Worthington, *Life in Lakes and Rivers*, Collins, 1951.
Mottram, Dr James, *Fly Fishing; Some New Arts and Mysteries*, The Field and Queen (Horace Cox) Ltd, 1915.
Phillips, Ernest, *Trout in Lakes and Reservoirs*, Longmans, Green and Co., 1914.
Plunkett Greene, Harry, *Where The Bright Waters Meet*, Phillip Allan, 1924.
Sawyer, Frank, *Nymphs and the Trout*, A & C Black Ltd, 1958.
Spencer, Sidney, *The Art of Lake Fishing*, H. F. & G. Witherby Ltd, 1934.
Walker, Commander C. F., *Lake Flies and Their Imitation*, Herbert Jenkins, 1959.
Walker and Petterson, *The Rainbow Trout*, Lawrence and Bullen Ltd, 1898.
Wallis, H. F. (editor), *Stillwater Trout Fisheries*, Ernest Benn Ltd, 1976.
Westropp, Victor, *Fishing on Lake Vyrnwy*, Lake Vyrnwy Hotel, 1973.
Williams, A. Courtney, *A Dictionary of Trout Flies*, A & C Black Ltd, 1973.

Index

Artificial flies printed in bold type are illustrated in colour between pages 104 and 105.